A Brief History of the Descendants of Arthur McCann

Also by Michael J. McCann

Forgotten Loyalties
The Disappearances
The Ferguson Family Psalm Book
In These Disconsolate Woods
Twilight Road
Project Changeling
The Long Road Into Darkness
A Death in Winter
No Sadness of Farewell
Persistent Guilt
Burn Country
Sorrow Lake
The Rainy Day Killer
The Fregoli Delusion
Marcie's Murder
Blood Passage
The Ghost Man

Fig. 1 Warrenpoint, Newry, Ireland

A Brief History of the Descendants of Arthur McCann

Michael J. McCann

The Plaid Raccoon Press
2024

A BRIEF HISTORY OF THE DESCENDANTS OF ARTHUR McCANN
Copyright © 2024 by Michael J. McCann

The Plaid Raccoon Press supports copyright, which protects creativity and the right of authors to profit from the fruits of their considerable labour. Thank you for buying an authorized edition of this book and for complying with copyright laws by not reproducing any part of this book, paperback and/or e-book, without permission from the publisher.

This book is entirely the product of the author's hard work and creativity. No artificial intelligence applications or similar tools were used to write it, nor will they ever be. Organically grown books are always the best!

ISBN: 978-1-927884-32-4 (paperback)
978-1-927884-33-1 (e-book)

Front cover image: © Michael J. McCann
Back cover image: "St. Edward's Cemetery" © Timothy D. McCann.
Author photo: Michael J. McCann

Visit the author's website at www.mjmccann.com

In loving memory of my father,
Hugh McCann;
to my cousins;
and to my son.
This is who we are, Tim.

Table of Contents

1. The Mist of Irish Legend 23
   Pre-Christian Ireland 23
   The Irish Gaels and their Celtic Heritage 26
   The Three Collas 30
2. Medieval Ulster 35
   Historical Context 35
   The Sons of Cana 37
   Clanbrassil and Clancann: The Territory of the McCanns 42
3. Tudor Ireland 47
   Historical Context 47
   Political Strife Under Henry VIII and Elizabeth I 48
   The Nine Years' War and the Flight of the Earls 54
4. No Longer Lords of Clanbrassil: The Plantation of Ulster 57
   The Plantation Process 57
   A Brief Note on Land Division 59
   McCanns Included in the Granting Process 60
   The Uprising of 1641 67
5. Cromwell in Ulster 74
   Historical Background 74
6. The Life and Times of Arthur McCann 79
   Were Arthur and Ann from Forkhill Parish? 79
   What was Forkhill Parish Like in Arthur's Time? 80
   The Penal Laws 83
   Hedge Schools: A Typical Irish Response to Adversity 87
   Unrest During Arthur's Formative Years 88
7. The Search for Arthur 91
   Historical Background 91
   Census Substitutes 92
   1821 Census of Forkhill Parish 97
   What is Carrickasticken Like? 101
   Where in Carrickasticken Did the McCanns live? 103
   Which Church Did the Carrickasticken McCanns Attend? 105
8. A New Beginning in Canada 113

Arthur and His Family Make the Voyage 113
The Village of Westport, North Crosby Township 117
Arthur and Ann Arrive 120
Arthur and Ann: Pioneers 124
Arthur Moves 129
Arthur Passes Away 131
Ann Quinn 132
9. The Children of Arthur and Ann 136
Mary McCann 136
Roseanna McCann 147
John McCann 149
Elizabeth (Betty) McCann 153
10. Michael J. McCann and Anne Kearns 159
The Shoemaker 159
Anne Kearns 171
11. The Children of Michael J. and Anne 179
Arthur F. McCann 179
John A. McCann 183
Mary McCann 188
Patrick McCann 189
Anastasia McCann 190
Cecelia 191
Thomas James McCann 191
Michael Jr. the First 194
Michael Jr. the Second 194
Rose Anna McCann 196
William E. McCann 198
Margaret McCann 203
12. Bridget Donnelly and Her Children 205
Anna Bernadetta McCann 208
Teresa Elizabeth McCann 210
Anastasia Magdeline McCann 211
13. Patrick McCann 217
Patrick as a Youth 217
14. Maria Hagan 225
Maria Hagan's Family 225
Hugh Hagan, Mary Flanagan, and their children 229

Hugh Joseph Hagan	232
Jim Hagan	233
Theresa Hagan and the Carty Family	236
Maria Hagan: Wife, Mother, Grandmother	241
15. The Children of Patrick and Maria	245
Monica Cecelia McCann	245
Frances Agnes McCann	249
Cosmo Augustine McCann	250
Mary Veronica (Mazie) McCann	250
Adella Louise McCann	253
Wilfred Charles (Ford) McCann	255
16. Ford McCann	257
Ford McCann, his life	257
17. Henry Allore	269
Henry Allore's Family	269
Henry Allore's First Marriage	274
Henry Allore's Story	280
18. Annie McCoy	286
The Three O'Hare Sisters	286
Annie McCoy's Family	288
Annie McCoy's Children	293
Annie McCoy Passes Away	300
19. Ida Allore and her Children	301
Ida's Story	301
Charles McCann	307
Monica McCann	307
Patrick Henry McCann	309
Mary McCann	310
Wilf McCann	311
Jack McCann	321
Anne McCann	324
Rita McCann	325
Hugh McCann	326
Veronica McCann	327
Michael McCann	327
Patrick McCann	328
Mary Ethelreda McCann	330

  Ellen McCann 331
  Margaret McCann 332
  Oliver McCann 333
  Linda McCann 335
20. Hugh McCann 337
21. Other McCanns 363
  The Foley Mountain McCanns 363
  Thomas and Bridget McCann 366
  Edward and Mary McCann 368
  Sam McCann the Cheesemaker 369
  Patrick McCann and Anne Fitzgerald 371
Post-Amble 377
Acknowledgments 379
About The Author 381
Family Charts 383
Endnotes 387
Select Bibliography 413
Readers' Notes 418
Index 425

ILLUSTRATIONS

Figure

1. Warrenpoint, Newry, Ireland 4
2. Ireland 20
3. The Four Invasions 22
4. Brian Boru 34
5. Bodley Map: Clancann and Clanbrassil 40
6. Armagh 44
7. Shane O'Neill Meets Elizabeth I 50
8. The Rolling Hills of Forkhill Parish 78
9. A Penal Law 82
10. The Hedge School 86
11. The Townlands of Forkhill Parish 90
12. The Graveyard at Urney 106
13. Irish Emigration Ships 112
14. North Crosby Twp., ca 1880 118
15. Soap Making 134
16. Casper J. Speagle 144
17. The Marriage of Elizabeth McCann 152
18. Early Map of Westport 156
19. Michael J. McCann, ca. 1850 158
20. The Apprentice Shoemaker 160
21. The Raftsman 181
22. John A. McCann and Family 182
23. Edith McCann Bollini 186
24. William E. McCann 199
25. Michael J., Bridget, and Daughters 204
26. Anna Bernadetta 208
27. Teresa E. McCann 210
28. Anastasia Magdeline 212
29. Anastasia McCann Flynn 215
30. The McCann House, George St., Westport 216
31. Patrick McCann and Maria Hagan 222
32. Michael Hagan and Bridget Boyle 224
33. Hugh Joseph Hagan 232
34. Jim Hagan and Granny Hagan 234
35. Tom Carty 238
36. Monica C. McCann and Francis McParland 244
37. Frances Agnes 249

38. Johnny and Frances Bulger 250
39. Sister Mary St. John Chrysostom 251
40. Ford and Mike McCann in Peterborough 255
41. Ford McCann 256
42. Ford McCann Advertising Postcard 262
43. The McCann Family, ca. 1935 264
44. Henry Allore 270
45. The Windsor House Hotel 282
46. Thomas McCoy 290
47. Ida Allore, Confirmation Day 300
48. Ford and Ida McCann, Wedding Portrait 302
49. Ida McCann, as I Knew Her 304
50. Charlie McCann 307
51. Monica and her Motorcycle 308
52. Harry McCann 309
53. Mary McCann 310
54. Wilf McCann 311
55. Jack and Claire 322
56. Two Minute Hate 323
57. Anne and Jimmy 324
58. Rita McCann 326
59. Mike 327
60. Pat and Anthea 328
61. Ethel McCann 330
62. Ellen McCann 331
63. Margie McCann 332
64. Ollie McCann 333
65. Linda McCann 335
66. Hugh McCann 336
67. Duke 338
68. Ford and Hugh in Peterborough 340
69. Father and Son 344
70. Hugh and his Tatay 346
71. Samuel T. McCann 369

Preamble

This family history traces the descendants of Arthur McCann, who was born in Ireland about 1777 and died in North Crosby Township, Ontario, Canada in 1852, and his wife Ann Quinn (1786-1864), who was also born in Ireland and died in North Crosby. It pieces together government and church records, tombstone inscriptions, historical references, newspaper reports, oral tradition, and foggy legend into our current best guess as to who we are, genealogically speaking, and where we come from as a family.

Every author should know their target audience, since it will determine style, tone, structure, and many other things that go into the writing and preparation of a book. In this particular case, I have two.

First, *Brief History* is written for my family, as I've made obvious in the dedication. As a result, I'll try to tell you a story, and I'll keep it personal and conversational as much as possible.

Second, this is a history book, as much as I can make it,

and so I've tried to follow, at least on a basic level, the practices of real academics who publish history books for a living. I've tried to follow a basic principle: If you can't document it, you can't use it. As a result, I've made every effort to cross-check my information and record in my endnotes where you can find it if you ever want to go looking for it. I've also included a bibliography in case you want to read some of the sources I've used.

As a result, *Brief History* will hopefully serve as a reference work that you can use to look up specific people or their families. I've included an index to help out with that.

At the same time, although it may sometimes read like the Book of Chronicles—"and So-and-So begat Such-and-Such who begat..."—I've tried to mix in a little bit of an anecdote here and there to keep things interesting. Mostly reference, with a bit of a fireside tale mixed in.

Ultimately, *Brief History* is part Irish history, part family history, part Canadian history, and part memoir.

Now it's time for a bit of an apology. Although the title of this book is *A Brief History*, the thing itself has grown into something closer to a boat anchor than the slim volume I'd originally intended to write. However, a family tree, like any actual tree, has innumerable branches, twigs and offshoots, and once you climb up and start crawling around, you can't just stop and climb down again. There's so much more to see!

To continue the metaphor a bit longer, the view of the tree from one branch can be quite different than the view from another branch somewhere else in the tree. As a result, you'll see that my focus here is clearly defined by the title.

We'll examine the children of Arthur McCann and Ann

Quinn, continue on to their son Michael J. McCann (1830-1910) and his first wife, Anne Kearns (1834-1878), move down the line to their family, and so on and so forth down the generations to me.

Of course, having said that, those of you who have delved into genealogical research yourselves know through hard experience that this kind of stuff is usually like falling down a rabbit hole. Inevitably we end up moving horizontally to follow other paths for a generation or two as the families spread themselves out. Who were these guys, and how do they fit in?

After having begun this research with my father in the early 1980s, relying on a simple family chart put together from memory by my great aunt, Mary Veronica McCann (Sister Mary St. John Chrysostom) in Kingston, Ontario, I think I can say that after forty years this project has suffered its fair share of mission creep.

This stuff wouldn't be so much fun otherwise, though, would it?

Researching Irish records has posed a serious challenge that may come as a surprise to those not familiar with the history of Ireland. Due to the mass destruction of records and cemeteries over time that occurred in Ireland as a result of English occupation, subsequent sectarian strife, and violent revolts, information is scarce, to say the least. Not only in Dublin, but also on the Catholic side in Northern Ireland, where we need to search. What we know about our ancestors in Ireland, then, is rather sketchy.

Not that Canadian records haven't also presented their challenges. Dates and ages of individuals may differ depending on whether you're looking at census records, church records, or cemetery records. Some nineteenth-century Canadian census takers were notorious guessers, or perhaps struggled with the responses of homesteaders with thick Irish brogues who couldn't help the enumerator with the spelling of their surname because they were illiterate. For example, Kearns might be spelled *Cairns*, or O'Hare *O'Hear*, because that's how the fellow was saying it when the enumerator went to write it down.

Occasionally the information found in a census should perhaps be overruled by another source, such as a cemetery headstone. On the other hand, gravestones will often give the age of the deceased but not the date of birth, and when the arithmetic is done it results in a year of birth that varies from other, very reliable information.

Head spinning, I've sometimes been forced to make choices. Gut instinct takes over, I suppose. I've noted differences in information when it seems appropriate, and thereby pass the football off to you, dear reader, to make your own choices as you will.

Finally, it should be noted that I've concluded this family history with only a brief description of my father's generation. We live in a modern society where our personal information is constantly at risk, and identity theft is a threat on a scale that our ancestors couldn't possibly have comprehended. Because I'm choosing to publish this family history as a book with an ISBN and distribution options and so on, rather than merely produce an informal, spiral-bound booklet for private distribution, I've limited the information I'm including here on the final generations I've covered.

As a compromise, I've inserted pages at the end which can be used for notes. My cousins can write down the names and dates of their own children, and their grandchildren, as they wish. In this way, future generations may be documented in complete privacy for the benefit of those who follow.

As a last preambulatory word, and on a strictly personal note, I've dedicated this work in part to the memory of my late father, Hugh McCann, with whom I began this research so many years ago. It was he who obtained the handwritten copy of our family tree from Aunt Mazie and drove us to Westport, where he was born and raised, to retrace his steps through his own past. The penultimate chapter, of course, is his.

I think I've done an okay job of kicking the can a bit farther down the road, Dad. There are many things I haven't been able to learn, gaps I've failed to fill in, but it's the best I can do. I'll leave it here, and we'll see how those who come after us make out taking it the rest of the way home.

Fig. 2 Ireland

Part One

IRELAND

Fig. 3 The Four Invasions

Chapter One

The Mist of Irish Legend

The McCann family from which we descend originated in Ireland, and so our search for our common past begins on the Emerald Isle. Those of us scattered around the world may actually know very little about the history of Ireland, so why not begin at the beginning and see where it leads us?

Pre-Christian Ireland

The story of Ireland may be described as a history of invasions, as wave after wave of people arrived on the island's shores and rolled over its green countryside. Among the earliest traces of human activity in Ireland are those from the Mesolithic period, when hunter-gatherers roamed the Irish countryside around 7000 BC.[1] They may have arrived from Scotland, although no one is certain. They left few traces behind them, being nomadic in nature and more concerned with daily survival than monuments to the ages. It's thought that there might have been a land bridge between Scotland and Ireland at this time, given that the Ice Age had only recently ended, and that these people travelled across it on foot in search of better living conditions.[2]

They apparently worked their way up the Bann River to the shores of the largest lake in Ireland, Lough Neagh. Many stone tools dating from this period have been found scattered about that particular area, including needle points, flake axes, and stone axes.³ The land bridge apparently disappeared by about 5700 BC, and Ireland became the water-bound land we know today. More is known about the Neolithic period, when it's estimated that about 100,000 people lived on the island. This was the Stone Age, when these migrants were gathering in settlements, they were farming the land, and they were building monuments. During this time, beginning at around 2500 BC, they left a legacy of stone megaliths on Ireland such as dolmens and tombs that still fascinate archaeologists and historians today.

One example of a portal tomb that would have been built late in the Neolithic age is located in the townland of Ballykeel, Forkhill Parish, County Armagh. Carbon dating suggests it would have been erected around 1400 BC,⁴ almost 3,200 years before Arthur McCann was born in the same general neighbourhood.

The Stone Age gradually gave way to the Bronze Age and then the Iron Age, which was introduced to Ireland during the period of 700 to 100 BC when a series of invasions by four different groups ultimately led to the arrival of our ancient ancestors.

It's generally accepted that these four groups all came from the broad nation of people known as the Celts. The origins of the Celts extend so far back before recorded history that we can only speculate about them. Scholars suggest that they came from the late Neolithic people referred to as the Indo-Europeans, and that they rode west from the Russian steppes to spread throughout Europe during the last millennium before the birth of Christ. As Peter Berresford Ellis points out, "the Celtic peoples are identified solely by their language and cultures,"⁵ rather than as a single genetic race. And as we will see, differences in their language help us distinguish between the various groups of Celts who arrived in Ireland and displaced one another over the course of several centuries.

Celtic scholar T.F. O'Rahilly describes a possible model for this Iron Age settlement based on his studies of language and mythology.[6] His description, while vigorously debated and contested and argued over by other academics, offers a very colourful picture of this early period in Irish history.

The first wave of invaders to arrive on Ireland before the birth of Christ were the Cruithins, who settled in Ireland between 700 BC and 500 BC. They were an Iron Age people who spoke a form of the Celtic language referred to as P-Celtic, and they may have belonged to the same confederation of tribes known as the Pretani, found also in Scotland and called the *Picti*, or Picts by the Romans, because they practised colourful and terrifying body tattooing and tended to cause the Romans a lot of trouble wherever they showed up. While they were eventually overrun by subsequent invaders, these people remained prominent in the north of Ireland, primarily in Antrim, well into the Christian era.[7]

A second wave of invasion occurred around 500 BC when a Celtic group known as the Erainn arrived from Britain. They also spoke P-Celtic. It is from the Erainn that Ireland derives the name Eire (Erin). A prominent tribe in this wave was the Ulaidh, who dominated the northern part of Ireland and founded the important stronghold of Emain Macha at Navan, near the settlement of Armagh. It is from the Ulaidh that the name "Ulster" is derived.

About two hundred years later the Laginians arrived as

the third wave of invasion. Also speaking P-Celtic, they came from northwest France and captured the southeast corner of the island, which is now known as Leinster in reflection of their influence. They swept westward through Connaught and drove the Erainn off the west coast onto the many small western islands in the Atlantic Ocean such as the Arans.

The Celtic invaders who arrived in the fourth wave were quite different from the first three. Known as the Gaels or Goidels, they swept ashore around 100 BC. They spoke a different version of the Celtic language, referred to as Q-Celtic or Goidelic. This version is thought by some to have been the oldest form of Celtic that was spoken,[8] and it became the foundation of modern Irish. Probably driven out by the Romans from Aquitania, southwest Gaul, or the Basque region in northern Spain, these Gaels arrived in two groups—the Connachta, who swept through the middle of the island and established themselves in Meath, and the Eoganachta, who conquered Munster, the southwestern end of the island.

It is the Connachta Gaels that hold our interest, because the misty legends of Ireland would suggest that our distant ancestors were included in this group.

THE IRISH GAELS AND THEIR CELTIC HERITAGE

What were the Irish Gaels like as a people? We know that they were scrappy and aggressive, for they fought tenaciously to drive the Ulaidh out of central Ireland onto the east coast and in some cases across the Irish Sea to Scotland, and then fought with each other to gain the upper hand in various regions where they settled. Medieval Irish chronicles record innumerable "hostings" or military expeditions, major invasions and minor raids that pitted the Irish Gaels against the Laginians, Ulaidh, Cruithins, and each other.

However, they were not a bunch of bad-smelling, barbaric savages running around destroying everything in their path. In fact, Celts embodied one of the most advanced western civilizations of the Middle Ages. As Thomas Cahill explains in *How The Irish Saved Civilization*, they almost single-handedly preserved Greek and Roman culture—and Judeo-Christian culture—during the culturally dark ages that followed the fall of the Roman Empire. Celtic scholars obtained and copied countless manuscripts and distributed them back into Europe as the "barbarian" tribes settled down in the territories they had conquered from the Romans.[9] And as Alice Stopford Green tells us in her book *Irish Nationality*, Irish teachers in the Middle Ages "had a higher skill than any others in Europe in astronomy, geography and philosophy."[10]

The Celts had a highly organized society in which a group of families from a common ancestry constituted a sept, while a larger group made a clan. Several clans, septs and families were combined to make a tribe, or tuath, which controlled a particular territory or district with its own political and legal administration. Each sept had its own group of warriors, commanded by the sept chief, and several sept armies would band together as needed to defend a tuath. At one time, there were 184 tuaths on the island. The chief of a tuath was referred to as a king, many of whom became the subject of stories and songs celebrating them as the ancient kings of Ireland.

Irish Celts had a highly developed legal system as well. As Alice Stopford Green notes, by 900 AD "the lawyers had produced at least eighteen law-books whose names are known, and a glossary."¹¹ The traditional Celtic legal system was known as "brehon" law. Irish brehon law was based on centuries of common law reaching back as far as Cormac Mac Art in 260 AD and was administered by brehons, or judges. Brehons arbitrated between disputing parties, drawing on the law that was set out in various important documents, and it was clearly understood that even kings were required to obey their judgments.

Brehon law covered every aspect of Irish life, including family law, the all-important areas of land division and tenure of property, and many other areas where legal precedent was required. For example, *Cáin Lánamna,* or The Law of the Couple, was a rather sophisticated document that covered family law.

Their legal system also dealt with the relationship between dominant tribes and their allies among the lesser septs. For example, the document *Ceart Ui Neill,* which translates as *The Rights of O'Neill,* spelled out the legal obligations of septs allied with the O'Neills (who dominated Ulster for several hundred years), including what troops they would supply the king of the O'Neills when he wished to carry out a hosting, or what tribute they would provide as a substitute if they couldn't send warriors. It also clearly spelled out the handling of prisoners and under what circumstances a prisoner might not be stripped of his horse and equipment. As you will see a bit later on, the obligations of the McCann sept to the O'Neills are specifically recorded in the *Ceart Ui Neill.*

Before the arrival of Christianity in Ireland, largely attributed to Saint Patrick in the 400s AD, the Celts had a polytheistic religion with a pantheon of various gods. Their religion was controlled by the druids, an exclusive group of wise men who acted as experts in many fields. The druids spoke confidently about the gods and their actions, they explained the nature of the earth and the movement of the stars and planets, they were authorities in law, and they described the afterlife and claimed to have occult powers enabling them to communicate with spirits, predict the future, and so on.[12]

After Christianity was established in Ireland, the druids were superseded by secular Celtic leaders such as the brehons and Christian scholars and teachers. However, druidism retained a strong influence in Irish culture, and it's interesting to think about the number of modern conventions that we take for granted today, such as Halloween on All Saints' Eve and mistletoe at Christmas, that actually had their origin in druidism and were incorporated into Christian practices over time.

Irish Gaelic naming traditions are also important to understand. As Father Patrick Woulfe explained,

> Irish surnames came into use gradually from about the middle of the tenth to the end of the thirteenth century, and were formed from the genitive case of the names of ancestors who flourished within that period, by prefixing O (also written Ua) or Mac (some-times written Maζ*) ... O literally signifies a grandson, and Mac a son : but in the wider sense which they have acquired in surnames now mean any male descendant. The only difference between a surname commencing with Mac and one commencing with O is that the former was taken from the name

of the father and the latter from that of the grandfather of the first person who bore the surname. Mac-surnames are, generally speaking, of later formation than O-surnames.[13]

Once these prefixes began to be used as surnames and people began writing them down, they might appear as *Mac* or *Mc*, or even *M'* depending on local influences or the patience and energy level of the writer.

One other point that's important to note about early Celtic culture is that it relied on a very strong oral tradition. As Ellis explains, the Celts frowned on committing their knowledge to writing in order to prevent it from falling into the wrong hands.[14] After the arrival of Saint Patrick and the conversion of the Irish people to Christianity in the 400s AD (which, as Green points out, was peaceful and without bloodshed), this prohibition on writing became obsolete in Irish culture. However, it leaves us without written records covering the centuries before Patrick's time. During the four hundred years between the arrival of the Connachta Gaels in about 100 BC and the beginning of documented history in about 400 AD, therefore, we are dependent on legend to tell the story of how our ancient ancestors conquered Ireland.

THE THREE COLLAS

It would seem that in 260 AD the dominant king of the day was Cormac Mac Art, who ruled central Ireland from the Gaelic seat of power at Tara, in County Meath. After his death from choking on a fishbone in 266, power passed through several generations to Muirdeach (Murdoch) Tirech, who encountered numerous difficulties from three of his nephews, the sons of Eochaidh Duibhlein (Dublin).

These three nephews became famous as the legendary *Collas*, or strong men, known as Colla Uais, Colla Meann and Colla da Chrioch. They led their armies in campaigns against Murdoch Tirech, and Colla Uais briefly seized power before Tirech regained control in 327 and drove the Collas off to Scotland to cool down.[15]

They soon returned, however, to rally their forces and eventually defeat him. They then led their armies in numerous campaigns across the countryside to gain control of a large swath of territory, driving out the Ulaidh who still occupied much of this land. In 331 they defeated the Ulaidh on the plain of Farney in Monaghan in a significant victory, and soon after captured the Ulaidh stronghold at Emain Macha and burned it to the ground. These victories sent the Ulaidh fleeing to the east coast, and the Collas established among themselves the kingdom that became known as Arghialla, which has been later anglicized as Ariel or Oriel. It included the present-day counties of Louth, Armagh and Monaghan.

Although modern scholars now debate whether or not the Collas actually existed, many Irish families trace their descent from one of the three Collas based on genealogical records such as *The Book of Leinster* (*Lebor Laignech*, written about 1160), *The Book of Ballymote* (written between 1384-1406) and *The Annals of the Four Masters*, compiled between 1632 and 1636 by Brother Michael O'Clery and others.

(Genealogy was extremely important to the Irish, and one of the roles of poets or bards attached to the household of Irish kings and chiefs was to recite the family history on demand. Thus were preserved hundreds of complicated lineages dating back through the Middle Ages.)

Our interest lies in Colla da Chrioch, also known as Colla Fiochrich, who established himself as the king of the western and central part of Arghialla. His control may have extended from Clogher in County Tyrone to the area immediately around the ruined Emain Macha at Navan. His rule was consolidated and extended by his sons Imchad, Rochadh and Fiachra Cassan.

By the year 400 AD Arghialla was under the control of Niall Noigiallach, or Neill of the Nine Hostages. It's perhaps from his rule that the name Arghialla, which means "hostage-givers," became established. During his reign, each of the nine tuatha that existed at that time in Ulster was required to supply a hostage to him to ensure their loyalty—hence his name.

It's not clear if Niall Noigiallach was in fact the founder of the Ui Niallain, the O'Neill dynasty. He may have actually been a cousin of the Neill from whom the name of the O'Neills was taken. At any rate, the Ui Niallan are understood to have descended from the Colla da Chrioch's son Fiachra Cassan.

The Colla's other son, Rochadh, is the one who's of particular interest to us. Tracing the generations downward as set out in *The Book of Ballymote* and *The O'Clery Book of Genealogies*,[16] his descendants were:

- Deaghaidh Duirnn (Dedhga Durn);
- Feicc (Fiach);
- Cremthainn Leth (his territory was Ui Cremthainn, in modern-day Fermanagh and Monaghan);
- Echdhach (Eochu);
- Cairbre an daimh airgit (king of Arghialla

until his death in 514);
- Nat sluaigh, founder of Clan Nadsluaig of Monaghan;
- Fearghus (Ferghusa);
- Ronan (Cronan);
- Mael Duibh;
- Aitheachda;
- Artrach (in 737 AD "Artrach, son of Aitheachda, Lord of Ui-Meith, died");
- Mael Fogartaigh;
- Ruadhrach (Rory);
- Mael Poil;
- Cerbaill (Cearbhail) (Carroll);
- Laignen; and,
- Mathgamhna.

Thankfully, it's not important for us to remember any of these names. We end the list with Mathgamhna, though, because his sons grew up to found two important family lines that extend to modern times—one of which is ours.

Fig. 4 Brian Boru

Chapter Two
Medieval Ulster

In European history, the Middle Ages are said to have lasted from the fall of the Roman Empire in the 400s AD to the mid-1400s and the rise of the Italian Renaissance. Historians now tend to divide this period into the Early Middle Ages, often called the Dark Ages, from the 400s to the 1000s, and the High Middle Ages, from the 1000s to the 1400s, during which time the darkness was beginning to lift. As we will see below, our family history starts to take on a definite shape in the latter period.

In this chapter we'll begin with a brief survey of the historical context of this time period, the emergence of our family into historical records, and a description of the territory in north Armagh that came to be controlled by our McCann sept.

Historical Context

Many books have been written about the history of Ireland after Saint Patrick's arrival, and it's not in our best interests here to attempt to describe this period in much detail. Our focus is with Ulster, the north of Ireland, where our McCann ancestors settled and carved out a territory for themselves that they held throughout the Middle Ages.

Beginning at around 795 AD the Vikings began to invade Ireland from Norway. In the mid-800s they overran County Louth and penetrated as far west as Lough Neagh, the lake which we've mentioned before. The Irish Gaels battled the Vikings throughout the next two centuries until the Battle of Clontarf in 1014 in which Brian Boru, founder of the O'Briens, defeated the Vikings who were holding Dublin and broke the power of the invaders on the island.[17] It's quite probable that ancestors of ours participated in the wars against the Vikings, but the details, if they exist, are buried very deep in the shadows of time.

The other significant invasion came from the Anglo-Normans. William the Conqueror had successfully captured England after his victory at the Battle of Hastings in 1066 AD, and his followers from Normandy had eventually subdued the English by 1100 when Henry I, son of William the Conqueror, took the throne. Ireland then became a target of Anglo-Normans invading from England during the reign of Henry's grandson, King Henry II, beginning in 1169.

By 1199, King John (creator of the Magna Carta) had consolidated the Norman lordship of Ireland and the Crown of England. There were many battles and political intrigues involving the various Irish Gaelic kings that ultimately led to this political conquest, but those are best told another time.[18]

While the Vikings and Normans were busy trying their hand at conquering Ireland, the Gaels had carved out for themselves numerous kingdoms over which many other battles were fought. These kingdoms, which we've alluded to before, included Connacht, Ailech, Airghialla, Ulster, Mide, Leinster, and Munster. Leaders claiming kingship in them constantly fought one another to expand their territory, as well as to claim the title of *Ard Ri*, or High King of Ireland. Domnall Ui Neill (O'Neill), for example, a king of Ailech, ruled as High King between 955 and 978 AD, as did the aforementioned Brian

Boru, a king of Munster and Leinster, whose reign extended from 1002 to 1014.

In the north, the kingdom of Ailech was initially ruled by the O'Neills, as mentioned. It was situated in modern-day County Donegal. The influence of the O'Neills carried into the territory known as Tir-Eoghain, from which County Tyrone now draws its name. The Cenel-Eoghain was a powerful union of clans controlled by the O'Neills and various off-shoots of the family. Donegal, Tyrone, Londonderry, Fermanagh, Monaghan and northern Armagh fell under the rule of Tir-Eoghain. Although the Cenel-Connail eventually conquered Ailech in the 1100s, the influence of Cenel-Eoghain was already well-established in the north, and the O'Neills continued to dominate.

The Cenel-Eoghain consisted of several septs, including Mac Suibhne (McSweeny), Mac Seain (McShane), O'Doibhilin (O'Devlin/Devlin), Mac Conmidhe (MacNamee), and Mac Eoghain (McKeown). The primary struggles for supremacy, however, took place between the O'Neills and the Mac Lochlainns. O'Neills ruled through several generations from 989 to 1036, and the Mac Lochlainns dominated from 1083 to 1196. During the 1200s they alternated, throwing each other out of power for short periods of time.

With this historical background in mind, we will see the McCann sept finally emerge from the darkness into the indistinct light of Irish written history.

THE SONS OF CANA

Remember Mathgamhna, mentioned on p. 33 at the bottom of the list of descendants of the Colla da Chrioch? He was the king of a territory known as Fernmag, which was located in present-day County Monaghan. According to the *Annals of Ulster*, he was killed in 1022 at Clones by Cathalan Ua Crichain (O'Creighton).[19] His son Domnhaill went on to found the family line known as Mag Mathgamhna, or MacMahon, which dominated Monaghan into the sixteenth century.

However, Domnhaill's younger brother Cana became the founder of another sept, the one that bears our name today.

According to O'Hart, the name Cana comes from the Irish verb "to utter," the word that also means "to sing." (Other sources suggest the name comes from the Irish noun meaning "wolf cub," which was also a term of reference for a young warrior.)

O'Hart lists the following pedigree for Cana's descendants:

> 104. Cana mor: his son;
> 105. Cans, oge : his son;
> 106. Cathal (or Charles) McCann: his son; first assumed this sirname [sic];
> 107. Charles (2) his son;
> 108. Hugh, the Valiant, his son;
> 109. Terence, the wine drinker: his son;
> 110. Donal (or Daniel): his son; lord of Clanbrassil;
> 111. Hugh (2): his son;
> 112. Cairbre oge: his son;
> 113. Neal: his son;
> 114. Neal oge : his son;
> 115. Cairbre mar: his son;
> 116. Hugh mar: his son;
> 117. Hugh (4): his son;
> 118. Terence, of Upper Clanbrassil, in Armagh: his son [d. ca. 1480];
> 119. Cairbre : his son [d. ca. 1510];
> 120. Brian buidhe: his son; lord of Upper Clanbrassil [d. ca. 1540];
> 121. Lochlann: his son; lord of Clanbrassil;

A Brief History

122. Cormac, lord of Clanbrassil: his son;
123. Brian ruadh : his son;
124. Glaisneach McCann: his son; had a daughter named Elizabeth, who was married to John Hamilton, by whom she had six sons, one of whom was killed at the battle of Aughrim, A.D. 1691.[20]

As you can see, O'Hart's list of descendants runs right through to the end of the 17th century. Let's back up, though, as we're not yet finished talking about medieval Ulster and our sept's experiences during that era.

During the 1100s, McCanns were referred to as the lords of Cenel-Aenghusa. A notation in the *Annals of the Four Masters* records that in 1155:

> Amhlaeibh Mac Cana, lord of Cinel-Aenghusa, pillar of the chivalry and vigour of all Cinel-Eoghain, died, and was interred at Ard-Macha [Armagh city].[21]

Information about the Cenel-Aenghusa is scarce. O'Donovan noted in 1862 that "the exact situation of this tribe is unknown."[22] We are left to assume that at some point McCanns seized control of all or part of this territory. During the early 1200s they continued to be referred to in this context in the Annals:

> in 1212 "Donough Mac Cann, Chief of Kinel-Aengusa, died"[23];
> and
> in 1216 "Mag Cana, chief of Cenel-Oengusa, was killed by his own kinsmen."[24]

As the O'Neills moved east from Donegal to carve out Tir-

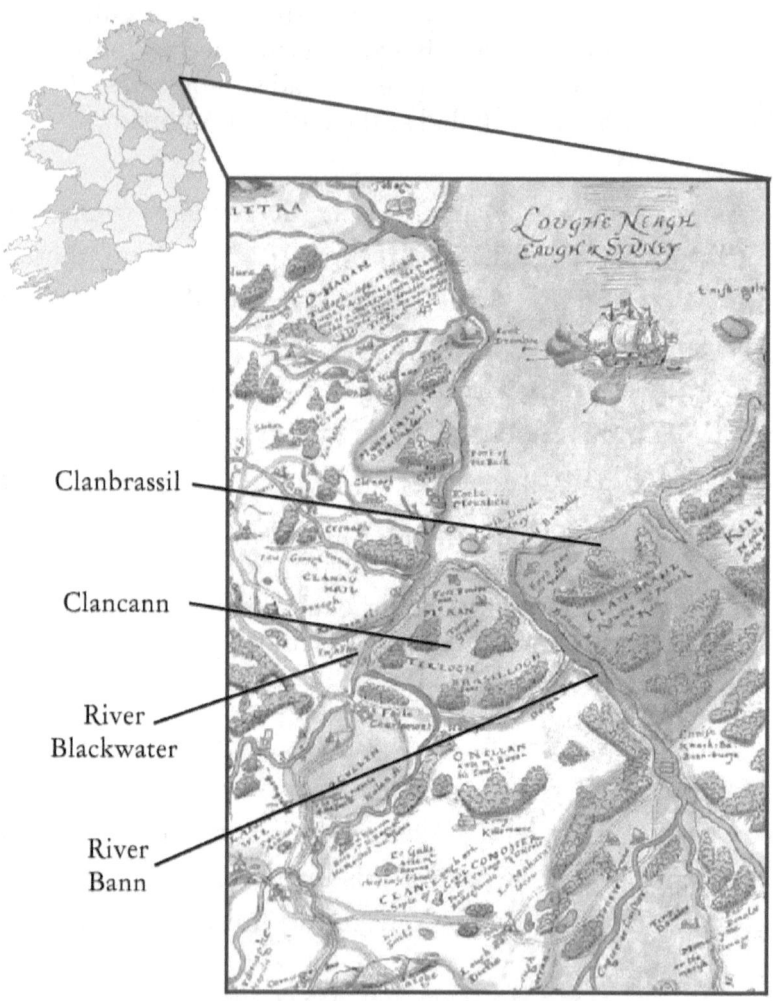

Fig. 5 Bodley Map: Clancann and Clanbrassil

A Brief History

Eoghain (Tyrone), they would have conquered Cenel Aenghusa and thus subjugated the McCann sept. Such septs were referred to as "vassals," which is defined in the *Oxford English Dictionary* as: "In the feudal system, one holding lands from a superior on conditions of homage and allegiance." In this case, as we've noted already, the McCann sept held homage to the O'Neills.

As we've seen, the medieval document *Ceart Ui Neill (The Rights of O'Neill)* spelled out the legal obligations, as per Brehon law, of the various vassal septs to the O'Neills. Although this manuscript dates back to about 1260, scholars assume the obligations themselves predate this written record.[25] Clause nine states:

> 9. The lordship of O Neill over MacCann — hosting and encampment and the equivalent of forty men for military service, and king's money: one third of this is levied on Clann Bresail (beyond the river Bann) and two thirds on this side, and provision for six men.

As a result of this obligation, the McCann sept was often called upon to participate in the wars of succession fought between the O'Neills and the Mac Lochlainns. The *Annals of Ulster* tell us, for example, that in 1167:

> - "Muiredhach Mac Canai was killed by the sons of Mac Lochlainn in reparation to Patrick and the Staff of Jesus, by direction of his own kinsmen."[26]

Then, in possible retaliation for this act, in 1170:

- "Concobhar, son of Muircertach Ua Lochlainn, king of Cenel-Eogain, royal heir of all Ireland, was killed by Aedh Mac Cana the Little and by the Ui-Caracain, Easter [Holy] Saturday [April 4], in the centre of the Great Third in Ard-Macha."[27]

The *Annals* do, however, record some deaths during this period that were more peaceful:

- In 1189 "Eghmily, the son of Mac Cann, the happiness and prosperity of all Tyrone, died."[28]

Not all the violent deaths recorded in the *Annals* came at the hands of the Mac Lochlainns. The McCanns also conflicted on a regular basis with the Ua Anluains (O'Hanlons), who controlled the territory south of their own holdings:

- Lachlainn Ma[c] Cana was slain outside the door of the court of the Lord Archbishop by Eachmarcach Ua Anluain [O'Hanlon], in revenge of [the slaying of] Murchadh Ua Anluain.[29]

CLANBRASSIL AND CLANCANN: THE TERRITORY OF THE MCCANNS

What was the extent of the territory controlled by the McCann sept in the High Middle Ages? Numerous historical sources provide specific descriptions, enabling us to pinpoint on the map with certainty the location of our family's ancestral lands.

As we can see in the reference to the McCann sept's obligations in the *Ceart Ui Neill*, they had come to be referred to as "Clann Bresail," or "Clanbrassil." According to O'Donovan, the Ui Bresail were historically known as a sept descended from someone named Breasal, and in

> latter ages [their] territory was more usually called Clann Breseail ... [but while] the tribe of O'Gairbheth (O'Garveys) were the ancient chiefs of this territory ... in more modern times it belonged to the Mac Canns."

O'Donovan then explains that the territory was "on the south [shore] of 'Lough Neagh,' where the upper Bann enters that lake from which, and from the space given it, it appears to be co-extensive with the present barony of Oneilland East.[30]

During the mid-1200s, when the Irish Gaels in Ulster were contending with Norman invaders from England, the strategic location of Clanbrassil played an important role. In 1260, a coalition of forces led by Brian Ua Neill, at that time the High King of Ireland, fought the Normans at the Battle of Druim Dearg, also referred to as the Battle of Down. The result, unfortunately for our ancestors, was a resounding defeat in which Brian Ua Neill himself was killed along with many of his allies, including Donnsleibhe Mag Cana,[31] who was later immortalized along with the other fallen Irish in the contemporaneous "Poem on the Battle of Dun" by Gilbride MacNamee:

> Want of friends and of wealth
> Is Mac Cana to the Race of Eoghan

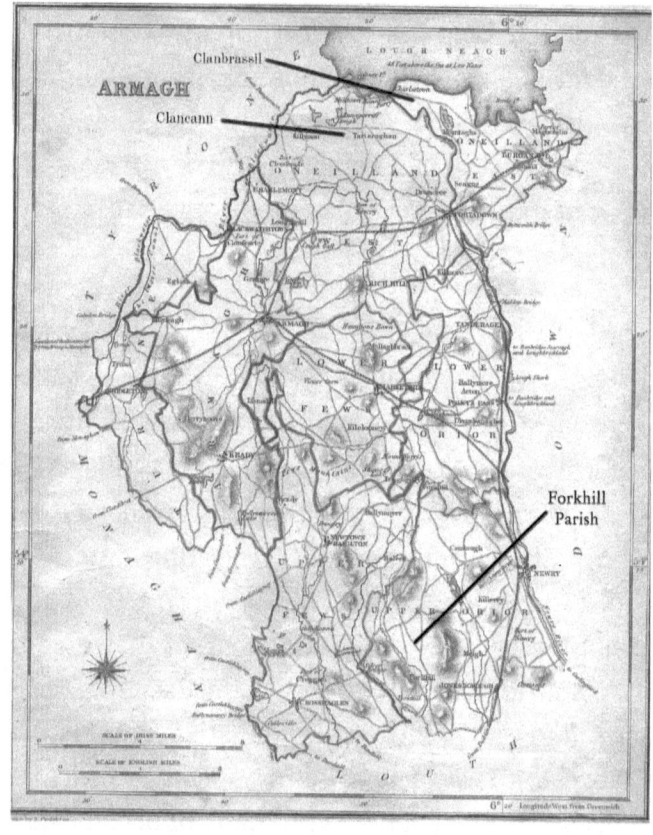

Fig. 6 Armagh

A Brief History

Donnsleibhe Mac Cana the fair-skinned
Is a loss to hospitality and to valor.[32]

As O'Donovan explains in his translation of the poem, the name would have been anglicized as Donlevy MacCann. He was "the head of Clann-Bresail, on the south [shore] of Lough Neagh where it receives the upper Bann."[33]

However, the territory controlled by the McCanns extended on both sides of the River Bann. As we saw in the *Ceart Uí Neill*, the O'Neills expected one third of their McCann tribute to come from the Clann Bresail McCanns on the *east* side of the Bann, while two thirds must be paid by those McCanns on the *west* side of the river.

George Hill, writing in 1877, gave this description of the barony of O'Neilland:

> [it] includes the three Irish territories of Oneilan, Clanbrassill, and Clancann. On an old map of Ulster, of the reign of Elizabeth, Clanbrassill and Clancann are marked as touching the southern shore of Lough Neagh, the former on the east and the latter on the west side of the [River] Bann; whilst Oneilan is placed due south of Clancann, and on the western side of the river. These territories occupy the same positions on the baronial map of 1609... Clanbrassill is represented as being of greater length from north to south than either of the other two territories, whilst Oneilan is much broader from east to west.[34]

So what do we now know? McCann territory in northern

Armagh at this time in history included Clanbrassil, on the east side of the Bann, occupying all or parts of what is now the parishes of Montiaghs, Seagoe, and Shankill; and Clancann, on the west side of the Bann and extending west to the Blackwater River near the Tyrone border, included all or parts of what today is known as the civil parishes of Tartaraghan and Drumcree.

Chapter Three

Tudor Ireland

Historical Context

If we fast forward to 1500, we find the social and political map of Ireland significantly altered. Anglo-Norman invaders had settled down and carved out fiefdoms for themselves, integrating into their surroundings to the extent of adopting the Irish language and many of their customs. The FitzGeralds, for example, became the Earls of Kildare, the Butlers (le Botiller) became Earls of Ormond, while the Burkes (de Burgh) became the Earls of Ulster.

While the English Crown continued to lay claim to the entire island, these newly-minted Anglo-Irish lords ruled their territories with a fair degree of independence. However, as far as the native Irish Gaels were concerned, the north still largely fell under their own control. The O'Neills dominated central Ulster, while the Ui Domhnall (O'Donnell) dynasty still held Donegal, to the west of the O'Neills.

The only territory in Ireland where English law prevailed without challenge was the region known as The Pale. Consisting of the eastern coastal territory from Dalkey, south of Dublin, up to Dundalk in Louth, The Pale represented what was left of the original conquests of the Normans. The name comes from the Latin word *palus*, meaning a stake, and it implies a virtual fence staked out around English territory to separate it from the rest of Ireland, which the English in general viewed as wild and uncontrolled.

Today the expression "beyond the pale" refers to something that is outside the bounds of morally acceptable behaviour, is outrageous, or shows poor judgment. We may each draw our own conclusions as to what this says about language, how it evolves within specific social contexts, and how the English traditionally felt about other cultures they wished to control.

Political Strife Under Henry VIII and Elizabeth I

The Tudor period in English history extended from the reign of Henry VII, the first member of the Tudor family to take the throne in 1485, to the death of Elizabeth I in 1603. During the first 25 years or so of Tudor reign, the situation in Ireland more or less continued as it had been. Once Henry VIII ascended to the throne in 1509, however, the uneasy balance between the various political elements in Ireland changed.

While Pope Adrian IV had named Henry II "*lord* of Ireland" in 1155, albeit under the auspices of the Catholic church, Henry VIII was proclaimed *King* of Ireland, free and clear of Catholic involvement, through the *Crown of Ireland Act 1542*, passed by the English-controlled Parliament of Ireland. This Act required all existing territorial rulers in Ireland, including the Irish Gaelic chiefs, to relinquish their claims of control over their lands to Henry, who would benevolently re-appoint them under his own terms and conditions. It was the beginning of the end for the native Irish kings and their families.

Among the leaders who attempted to comply with this requirement was Conn O'Neill, who was at that time the Chief of Tir-Eoghain. Conn's mother was a Norman FitzGerald, the daughter of the Earl of Kildare. Conn travelled to England in 1541 and surrendered to Henry, who then named him the first Earl of Tyrone. Predictably, this action resulted in chaos within the former Tir-Eoghain that ended up, as we'll see, with McCanns caught up in the turmoil.

Conn's son Feardorcha, known to the English as Matthew O'Neill, was at the same time recognized by the Crown as the heir apparent, and he was named the first Baron Dungannon to provide him with a place in this evolving Irish peerage until he would succeed his father as Earl. However, Shane O'Neill, Conn's younger son, argued that Matthew was an illegitimate child and that he, Shane, should be the successor. Allies of Shane murdered Matthew in 1558, after which Shane ousted his father and drove him off to The Pale, where he died a year later.[35]

By this time, Elizabeth I had succeeded Henry VIII, and Shane petitioned her to be recognized as his father's successor. However, Matthew's son Brian O'Neill was recognized by her viceroy in Dublin as Baron Dungannon and Earl of Tyrone. Shane bitterly disputed this decision and accepted an offer from Elizabeth to travel to England with Brian so that each could state their claims. However, Brian was killed before he could leave Ireland, and Shane was left to make his pitch to Her Majesty unopposed.

It's interesting to read the description of Shane O'Neill's appearance at court, as offered by the English historian

Fig. 7 Shane ONeill meets Elizabeth I

Richard Bagwell:

> The bare rough heads of his gallowglasses [Gaelic warriors], who did not lay aside their axes, their long curls, their wide-sleeved saffron shirts, their short tunics, and their shaggy cloaks of fur or frieze [coarse wool], which in Ireland covered a multitude of sins, made Englishmen stare; not less, says Camden, than they now stare at Chinamen or American Indians. The Ambassadors of Sweden and Savoy were present, and doubtless shared in the general astonishment created by her Majesty's distinguished subject. Shane prostrated himself before the Queen, and then on his knees 'confessed his rebellion with howling,' and made his submission in Irish, which few or none could understand.[36]

The decline and fall of the fortunes of the O'Neills is a fascinating story best left to another time, but the loyalty of the McCann sept to O'Neill would prove to be a constant source of negative attention from the English. For example, their alliance with Shane O'Neill, who ended up falling out of favour with the Crown, unsurprisingly, led to their condemnation in an *Act for the Attainder of Shane O'Neile, and the Extinguishment of the*

Name of O'Neile, and the Entitling of the Queen's Majestie, Her Heyers and Successours to the Country of Tyrone, and to the Other Countries and Territories in Ulster, which passed in 1569, two years after Shane's death:

> IV. And where diverse of the lords and captains of Ulster... the four septes of the Mac Mahounnes, Mac Kyven, and Mac Can, hath been at the commandement of the said traitour Shane ONeyle ... [your Majesty shall now take possession of] the countrey of Clancanny, called Mackans countrey, and all the honours, manours, castles, lands, tenements, and other hereditaments.[37]

After Shane's death, several O'Neills competed for control of *their* territory, one of which was Turlough Brasseil O'Neill, grandson of Conn O'Neill. His middle name, "Brasseil," apparently came from the fact that he was raised by McCanns in Clanbrassil. As Morgan explains:

> In Gaelic society the most important bonds were formed by consanguinity, marriage and the custom of fosterage by which political figures committed the upbringing of their children to others. Such connections with the household families and the ruling families of other Ulster lordships provided the competitors with political and military support in the contest for supremacy in

Tyrone. Turlough Breaselach had the backing of the MacCanns, his fosterers. In 1575 the government estimated their combined strength at forty horsemen and 200 footmen.[38]

It would be fair to assume that the reputation of the McCann sept within the O'Neill power structure remained solid enough, despite all the trouble, that they could be trusted with the upbringing of one of the O'Neills' very important children.

In a peace treaty with the English agreed to on June 28, 1575, Turlough Breaselach renounced his territorial claims east of the River Bann. The treaty nonetheless "gave him the overlordship of McCann and McGuire" septs.[39] As the Bodley map of 1609 shows (Figure 5), his territory remained in his name, immediately south of Clancann.

How were the McCanns generally perceived at this point in history?

A number of Englishmen during the period spent time in Ulster and wrote reports of their experiences. In 1586, Sir Henry Bagenal, who was marshal of the army of Queen Elizabeth I in Ireland at the time, provided the following descriptions:

> *Clanbrasell* is a very woodie and boggie countrey, upon the great Loghe's side called Eaghe [Lough Neagh]; it hath in it no horsmen, but is able to make 80 kerne [footsoldiers].
>
> *Clancan* is a very stronge countrey, allmost all wood and deep bog; it is invironed on th' one side with the aforesaid great Loghe, and of th' other side with a greate bogge and 2 deepe ryvers, th' one called

the Blackwater, and th' other the Little Bann, both which in this countrey do fall into the foresaid Loghe. In this countrey are no horsmen, but about some 100 kerne, who lyve for the most parte uppon stealthes and roberies.[40]

Bagenal's objective, as we can guess from these remarks, was to record the relative strength of Irish forces in Ulster in preparation for future actions against them. A little slander never hurt either, apparently.

Another document by an unknown author that was published as *The Description of Ireland and the state thereof as it is at this present in Anno 1598* offers a nearly identical description. However, the estimated number of "kearnes" in Clanbrassil had increased in the 12 years after Bagenal's report to 160, while in Clancann there were now 150. This individual was also not impressed with the behaviour of the inhabitants of Clancann, echoing Bagenal's statement that they "live for the most part in tyme of peace upon Stealth and Robberies."[41]

THE NINE YEARS' WAR AND THE FLIGHT OF THE EARLS

While McCanns apparently spent much of the late 1500s as an accomplished guerrilla force defending their territories against incursion, or as an unseen rabble lurking in the forest and waylaying stray Englishmen passing through, depending on one's perspective, the situation came to a head in 1593 with the Nine Years' War, also referred to as Tyrone's Rebellion.

By this time Hugh O'Neill, a son of Matthew O'Neill and

grandson of Conn, was recognized as the second Earl of Tyrone. He led a number of insurrections before joining forces with Hugh Roe O'Donnell, and by 1593 was in the middle of a full-scale war against England engulfing the region.

That the McCanns bore the brunt of this conflict is not in doubt. Sir Arthur Chichester, the commander of English troops who was notorious for his scorched-earth approach to warfare, wrote in 1601:

> I have beaten Brian MacArt over the Bann, who is in Tyrone with all his goods and people. He cannot return until O'Neill have leisure to give him assistance. He holds a strong fort in Killultagh [in nearby Antrim], which I must in this busy time take from him. I came this day from before it, having been in Clanbrassill, from whence I fetched such cows as were left on this side the Bann, killed such people as we lighted upon and cut as much corn as possibly we might for the time and number. I found all that country as plentifully stored with corn as any part of England, and I will labour by all means to destroy it, which will cut their throats faster than our swords, from which flight keeps them.[42]

His brutal destruction of the McCann territory of Clanbrassil, which the English had to cross on their way to O'Neill in Tyrone, was typical of the kind of warfare historically conducted by the English in Ireland.

In February 1603 Elizabeth I offered terms of settlement

to O'Neill. After her death a month later, O'Neill submitted to these terms, which were later ratified by Elizabeth's successor, James I.

When Chichester went on to become Lord Deputy of Ireland, his war against O'Neill moved into a more political sphere, and by 1606 O'Neill's position had become very difficult.[43] His ally O'Donnell was planning to flee to Spain after having been named as a conspirator against King James. Things fell apart for O'Neill, word of his impending arrest circulated, and on September 4, 1607, O'Neill, O'Donnell and others left Ireland for Spain.

This escape became known as the Flight of the Earls, and it's seen as a watershed moment in Irish history, when the ancient Celtic leadership of the native Irish people ended for good.

Chapter Four

No Longer Lords of Clanbrassil: The Plantation of Ulster

The Plantation Process

Once the native Irish leadership in Ulster was out of the way, Chichester lost little time consolidating his gains. Land was confiscated across the region and plans were immediately drawn up to dispossess the native Irish and to transplant settlers from Scotland and England who were loyal to the Crown and would, theoretically, transform Ulster into a pacified colony.

Chichester quickly appointed Sir Toby Caulfield to receive on behalf of the Crown all rent that used to be paid by native Irish to O'Neill and the other earls and chiefs. Then in the fall of 1608 a commission was formed by Chichester to study "what places are fittest for fortified posts ... what legal claims any Irish or English have to any portions, and what natives had best be pacified by grants."[44] The jury commissioned to carry out the study included 17 native Irish, among them Carbery McCann, who would have been recognized then as a chief and no doubt was someone whom it was politically wise to pacify.[45]

The result of this commission was a plan to divide the land into lots of 1,000, 1,500 and 2,000 acres which would be distributed to "English and Scottish planters, servitors, and natives" nominated by the King.[46] Included in the final outcome, as Chichester later reported, was the note that

> The countries known by the name of M'Cann's country and Braslowe [Brasilegh] are within this county [Armagh], which are possessed principally by gentlemen, who claim the freehold thereof. They would gladly be tenants or freeholders to the King, and would pay a good rent to His Majesty.[47]

We see, then, that the McCanns had seen the writing on the wall after the flight of O'Neill and the other earls and were signaling to the English that they would attempt to make the best of a poor situation.

A second commission was then convened in 1609 to complete a survey of the real estate in question, mark out the boundaries of the subdivisions, identify church lands excluded from the exercise, and to mark good sites for English settlements, castles with battlements, and other features.[48] Maps were drawn up reflecting the findings of this commission, including the Bodley map (Fig. 5).

In June 1610 the King gave Chichester the go-ahead to convene a third commission that would officially hand out the prizes to undertakers, servitors, and native Irish identified as grant recipients, and to relocate the natives who were not so fortunate as to be included in their plans. Some of this last group were to be moved to designated lands, similar to reserves set aside for aboriginal natives in North America much later.

Others, however, were told by proclamation in 1611 that "they must prepare themselves to depart with their goods and chattels, at or before the first day of May next, into what other parts of this realm they please, where they may find best conditions of being."[49]

In other words, they would be removed from their homes and turned loose to find new places to live in a countryside that was being divided up without them.

A Brief Note on Land Division

Today we're used to measuring land in acres or hectares, but in early seventeenth century Ulster land was commonly divided into ballyboes, seisereaches (sessighs), and ballybetaghs. Unfortunately for the precision-minded among us, these units of measure were not uniform and exact. They varied according to whether one was measuring pasture for grazing or arable land for growing crops. They also varied depending on the county in which the unit of measure was being applied.

Generally speaking the ballyboe was the primary unit in Armagh. The word is said to come from the Irish *baille* (anglicized as bally) which in this time period meant "town," and *bó*, which some scholars think meant "cow" and others, "house." In any event, it was a land division for pasture, and it referred to the amount of land on which a herd of cows could be kept. It's important to remember that an Irish native's wealth was traditionally measured by how many cattle he owned, and so it was natural to extend this thinking to parcels of land.

Clancann was said to have equalled 79 ballyboes and Clanbrassil, 76.[50] Sullivan tells us that according to documents published at the time, "the *Ballyboe* was of three different extents in the county of Armagh: in Orior one hundred and twenty acres, in Clanbrassil and Clancan sixty; and in all other parts two hundred."[51] We'll see these amounts reflected in the grant statements quoted below.

A seisereach corresponded to plough land, and may have derived from the words *seisr*, "six," and *each*, "a horse." The belief is that a seisereach was equivalent to the amount of land a team of six horses could plough in a year, at so much per day.[52] The term was not used in Armagh at this time, so we won't worry about it too much. Meanwhile, the ballybetagh was a larger unit of measure that probably included about 16 ballyboes.[53]

McCanns Included in the Granting Process

Although Clancann and Clanbrassil ended up being granted almost exclusively to English or Scottish settlers, there were some McCann chiefs who were included in the granting process. According to Hill, there were only 39 native Irish in Armagh who received grants, and these were all grouped together in the barony of Orior:

> These persons are all designated in their several grants as "gentlemen," and belonged to the respectable native classes through the county, but very few of them were able to retain their former standing when removed from their homes and deprived of the lands on which they had pastured their cattle. The surnames that prevailed most among these natives, removed from various districts of the

county, and placed in Upper Orior, were O'Hanlon, MacAna or McCann, O'Neill, O'Hagan ...[54]

Why were they not just left in peace on their traditional lands? Hill tells us they were moved on the suggestion of Chichester, who wrote:

> It is very difficult and dangerous to remove and transplant such a number of barbarous and warlike people into any parts of the kingdom ... Therefore, the remedy, I conceive, will be to appoint them some one part of the plainest land of their own country; or to intermix their town reeds with ours in plain countries, where they may be environed with seas, strongholds, and powerful men to overstay them, and then to proportion those lands indifferently unto them upon meet rents and conditions to keep them in subjection.[55]

On that note, let's look at the grants given to McCanns.

Carbery McCann

> Grant to *Carbery McCan*, gent., Ballitullinacross, Reaghan, and Ballycullin [Ballytullin], one balliboe each; in all, 360 acres. Rent 3l, 16s, 10d.[56]

As we saw above, Carbery McCann was selected as one of the natives who would be allowed to participate in the commission process to identify worthy grantors. Carbery was a lord of

Clanbrassil, but these grants removed him from his traditional land and relocated him in Ballymore parish, Lower Orior, immediately west of the modern-day village of Poyntzpass. They correspond to the current townlands of Tullynacross, Ballyreigh, and Tullylinn.

The problem with this grant, aside from its small size, is the fact that this land was the traditional territory of the O'Hanlons, historical rivals of the O'Neills and therefore also of the McCanns. (You may recall that Lachlainn MacCana was killed in Ard Macha by Eachmarcach O'Hanlon in 1268 to avenge the slaying of Murchadh O'Hanlon.) Well, despite the fact that the O'Hanlons had likewise been uprooted, these grants would have effectively relocated Carbery into hostile territory. It's not surprising then, when Pynnar came along to conduct his survey in 1618-1619, he found that "Carbery McCann, chief of his name, has sold his portion in Oryer and is removed to Clandeboy [in County Antrim] where he has lands of Conn O'Neale."[57]

Donnel McCann

> Grant to *Donnel McCan*, gent., the parcel of Coronare, being 1/3 of a balliboe, 80 acres, rent 17s, 2 d[58]

Donnell McCann was referred to by Hogan in 1598 as "chief of Clanbrassil," and was probably one of the last in the sept to be known by that title.[59] He participated with Carbery McCann in the final commission that awarded the grants, and so was recognized by the English as another native important enough to be pacified by a show of "generosity."

While there were several notable Donnell McCanns, this one had previously made it into poetry. The Irish bard Aengus

O'Daly had been hired by Sir George Carew in the early 1600s to travel around Ulster and write a satiric poem critical of native Irish leaders, as an attempt, it would seem, to demoralize them. However, O'Donovan notes in the introduction of *The Tribes of Ireland* that while O'Daly savaged many such leaders, "he had not the stomach to satirize Mac Cann of Clann Breasail at the upper Bann, because he did not deserve it":[60]

> Mac Cann of the dun mansion!
> Compare no one to Donnell;
> The apple tree and its blossom betray him;
> And all are not tired of his accumulation.
>
> Bear my blessing across the Bann,
> Where dwells Mac Cann, head of the hosts,
> It is hard for us not to free him,
> A man who was never condemned before us.[61]

O'Donovan explains that "Mac Cann's residence at that time was situated close to Lough Neagh, in the barony of Oneiland East, on the east side of the upper Bann, where that river enters the lough.[62] Since "dun" means "fort" in Irish, it's quite possible that Donnell McCann occupied a fort known in Irish at that time as *Bun an Bhealaigh*, or Bun na Banna, meaning "at the foot of the Bann," near the modern-day village of Bannfoot, Derryinver townland, Montiaghs civil parish.

Donnell's grant of the ballyboe of Coronare relocated him to the parish of Loughgilly, Lower Orior, just to the southwest of the grants awarded to Carbery McCann. Located just to the north of present-day Forkhill, Loughgilly was also well-known as a former O'Hanlon stronghold, and one of their fortified castles was located there. Again, a McCann was transplanted into hostile territory, and to a particularly small parcel of land.

Rorie McPatrick McCann

> Grant to *Rorie McPatrick McCan*, gent. The balliboe called Carricknegawna, containing 120 acres. Rent 1l, 5s, 8d;

The Bodley map of 1609 (Fig. 5) shows that Rorie McPatrick McCann had lived in Clanbrassil on the south shore of Lough Neagh. His middle name tells us he was the son of a man named Patrick McCann.

Rorie's grant was located in Upper Orior, in what is now Forkhill parish. It's quite a bit south of the grants given to Carbery and Donnell, and smaller, once again, than what he held in Clanbrassil. Additionally, it was once more situated in territory traditionally belonging to the O'Hanlons.

His son, Toole McRory McCann, was said to have been in possession of Carricknagavna in 1627.[63] He's also known to have had two other sons, Bryan McRory McCann and Patrick McRory McCann. As we'll see later, Toole McRory McCann was a leading figure in the uprising of 1641.

As a further note, because Rorie McCann was relocated to what is now Forkhill parish, it's quite possible that he and his family were the ancestors of the McCanns who went on to populate Forkhill extensively in the next two hundred years, including the parents of Arthur McCann, who is the focus of this *Brief History*.

Hugh McBrian McCann

> Grant to *Hugh McBrian McCan*, 1/3 part of the balliboe of Lissenuske,

and half the balliboe of Drom-hernie, containing 80 acres. Rent, 1L, 1s, 4d;

Hugh McBrian McCann was another participant in the Plantation commission, along with Carbery and Donnell McCann. For his troubles, he received 80 acres. Lissenuske was immediately to the west of Carbery McCann's grant in Caronare, in Loughilly parish. Dromhernie must have been mistaken for Drumilt (Drummult), which is immediately south of Lissenuske. This is a fairly safe guess, since the acreage is listed as a single amount, suggesting the ballyboes were contiguous.

Carberie Oge McCann and Toole McFelim McCann

Grant to *Carberie Oge McCan* and *Toole McFelim McCann*, Shraghanaran, and 1/4 part of Brackelagh, containing 160 acres. Rent 1L, 14s, 4d.[64]

These two grants have defied discovery so far. The "oge" in Carbery oge McCann's name was a common Irish adfix meaning "young," and it may have meant he was related to Carbery McCann, above, but was the younger one.

Carbery oge's son, Bryan McCarbery oge McCann, was caught up in the 1641 uprising, which we'll talk about below, and he gave a deposition to inquisitors after his capture that tells us that he lived in the townland of Gallconcuck (Gallrock today) in Tartaraghan (Clancann). It also tells us that his father, Carbery oge, lived in the townland of Cannagolla Beg by that time.[65] This was a ballyboe in Clancann that was granted to an Englishman, as we'll see, and so it looks as though Carbery oge gave up his grant, wherever it was, to move to a townland where he likely lived before 1610, accepting the necessity of paying rent to an English landlord rather than live in a place to which he had no connection.

At the end of the day, native Irish were granted portions of land that were only a fraction of the size of what they had previously controlled. As Hill explains,

> These natives, although holding such small portions of land, held them on the same terms as the other more fortunate undertakers, i.e. as of the castle of Dublin, in common socage, and subject to the conditions generally of the plantation of Ulster. They got their patents for the most part in 1610, but a few of those mentioned above did not obtain them until the beginning of 1612 ... From the foregoing list of grants to natives, we find that only a very few of such in each county were admitted to partake in the plantation scheme, and that whilst they had previously held the rank of gentlemen—so styled, indeed, in their miserable patents—they were obliged to accept the merest shreds of their own soil. [66]

Many of the patents were only for their lifetime, and could not be passed down as an inheritance, and others were soon contested by nearby English settlers, often before the Irish natives had had the good grace to pass away.

The Uprising of 1641

The Plantation of Ulster having been completed, the next few decades saw a fair amount of turmoil in the former Clanbrassil and Clancann territories as the English undertakers attempted, with varying degrees of success, to fulfill their obligations to displace the native Irish with Protestant settlers, build new communities, and replace traditional Irish ways of doing things with a new society that would be more pleasing to the English Crown.

In Ireland as a whole, the decades following Plantation were very hard for the natives. Dispossessed from their land, they endured an economic downturn in the 1630s and simmering religious tensions that persisted between native Catholics and transplanted English Protestants. Conditions were ripe for the outbreak of rebellion by the Catholic population in Ireland in October 1641.[67]

Ultimately leading to the Eleven Years' War, the uprising began as a failed attempt to capture Dublin Castle by Rory O'Moore and Sir Phelim O'Neill. It quickly spread north into Ulster, where O'Neill called upon the septs still bound in fealty to his family, including the McCanns, to join the rebellion.

Without getting into a lot of detail about the uprising and the Eleven Years' War, we need to take a brief look at the participation of the McCanns, as it was extensive and significant.

How do we know what happened? In the aftermath of the uprising, two different commissions were formed to take depositions from English victims, witnesses, and accused Irish rebels. One round took place in 1642 and the other in the early 1650s. The 1642 depositions are considered unreliable by most historians because they depended heavily on hearsay and second-hand accounts, while the later round is considered somewhat more accurate.

There were two very serious events that took place in 1641 involving McCanns, one at Portadown bridge and the other at Lurgan. There were also other incidents that were identified in the depositions that we'll look at as well.

The Massacre at Portadown Bridge

When news of the rebellion first reached Armagh, many of the native Irish mobilized and began converging on the houses of English and Scottish settlers. The idea was that these people would be rousted from their homes, herded to locations where they could be held, and then forced to leave the country so that the Irish could repossess their lands.

In November of 1641, a group of Protestant settlers who were being held at a church in Loughgall with this idea in mind were marched under armed guard about six miles to Portadown. When they reached the Bann, they were stopped by their captors and thrown off the bridge into the river. According to most accounts they were stripped and robbed first. The number of people killed varies from between 60 to 160.

Who were the leaders of the Irish responsible for this massacre? William Clarke, a survivor, stated in his first deposition in 1653 that the local rebels were led by Manus Roe O Cane [Kane].[68] However, Philip Taylor, an eyewitness, stated that earlier he was taken prisoner in Portadown by "Toole McCann now of Portadown gent. a notorious rebel and commander of a great number of rebels" who led an army of 100 soldiers in the capture of the castle at Portadown, then assaulted and pillaged the town and burned all the houses on the far side of the river. He was then responsible for the drowning of the Protestant victims at the bridge.[69]

Toole McCann was also blamed by several other deponents. Captain Valentine Blacker, a settler brought in by the English landowner William Brownlow, was allegedly victimized in the sacking of Lurgan, which we'll look at in a moment. Blacker told inquisitors that Elizabeth Simons and Sara Hobkins told him that Toole McCann was responsible for what had happened at Portadown.[70] As well, Humphrey Stewart stated that he'd been likewise told that Toole oge McToole dall McCann was the leader of the rebels at the bridge, but that others had told him Toole McRory McCann was the actual leader.[71]

While Toole McCann has been given a place in infamy for the Portadown massacre, Micheál Ó Siochrú and Mark S. Sweetnam point out in a recent article[72] that deponents actually placed the blame on a number of different people. They note that William Clarke claimed that only one of the perpetrators was still alive—a man named Rory McVaugh. Since Toole oge McToole McCann was known to be still alive when Clarke gave his deposition, it casts doubt on the veracity of other witnesses, who may have hated Toole for other things and decided to lay the greatest burden of blame for Portadown bridge on him as well.

Before leaving Portadown to look at what happened at Lurgan, one other deposition should be noted here, because it paints quite a vivid picture of the times.

When Anthony Williams Workeman was deposed in February 1652, he was around the age of 21. He testified that during the uprising in 1641 he was 12 years old. He and his family lived in a house about a mile from Portadown. He and his father were swept up in a convoy to the town, but along the way Bryan McRory McCann promised them safe passage anywhere if they would pay him money. The boy's father pledged to pay him if he would take them safely to Lisnagarvey, where settlers were being assembled for deportation. Bryan agreed, so they returned to the Workeman house to get the money.

When they arrived, they found Toole McCann and other Irish had taken the Workeman family to Portadown in a separate convoy. Mr. Workeman paid Bryan the promised money but the following morning, expecting the safe passage promised to him, he found that Bryan and his brother Patrick McCann were gone, although "the house was full of Irish."

Toole McCann soon returned and herded them off to a bog a half mile away, where they were allegedly drowning their prisoners. According to Anthony's testimony, Mr. Workeman was killed by Edmond McCarbery McCann, Edmond Roe McArdle and others, but young Anthony was spared by the intervention of McArdle's young son, who was the same age as Anthony.[73]

Although it's impossible to know whether this story is true or false, it reminds us that rebellion is a brutal and dirty business. How frightening it must have been for the boy to have been caught up in such chaos that cost the lives of his family. There is never any glamour in resistance or retaliation when civilian settlers are made the targets of such violence.

The Sacking of Lurgan

Lurgan was a thriving village within what was now known as Brownlow's Derry, within the former Clanbrassil, when the uprising reached it. Not surprisingly, accounts varied regarding what actually happened. When depositions were taken in 1652 and 1653 as some of the failed rebels were put on trial, William Brownlow and some of his settlers told one story while other witnesses and the rebels themselves told another. However, Brownlow was given the opportunity to prepare English witnesses before their testimony, so it's not a great surprise that most of their accounts tended to agree with his.[74]

According to Brownlow, an army of Irish rebels attacked Lurgan around the 23rd of October 1641 and "with fire and sword burnt the town and murthered several of the Protestant inhabitants."[75] Brownlow named Toole McCann, Toole McRory McCann, Art oge McGlasny Magennis, Edmond Boy McGlasny Magennis, Glasny oge Magennis, Ohee O'Hanlon and others as the leaders and main perpetrators. Seven settlers in particular were named victims by Brownlow, who claimed he had no firearms or weapons with which to defend his castle or the town. (Apparently, however, he'd previously received arms from the government in anticipation of unrest, so he may have been lying to the commission about his lack of firepower.[76])

Brownlow told inquisitors that he agreed to surrender his castle in exchange for safe passage to Lisnagarvey, where settlers were being assembled for deportation, but that the rebels reneged on the agreement, looted the place, murdered a number of people, and burned much of the village to the ground.

Events may have actually unfolded in a slightly different

way. When the rebels arrived at Lurgan, they apparently first offered Brownlow the opportunity to surrender the town and castle, and to escape. According to rebel Neece McConville (McConwell), Brownlow's response to this offer was that

> the said Art oge Maginis and all his party
> should be hanged like rogues and thieves,
> as they were, before that he would deliver
> either town or castle unto them.[77]

After this rebuff, the rebels advanced to burn the town. Brownlow sent out forces to repel the invaders, and skirmishing took place. Brownlow's men retreated back into the castle, and the rebels began a siege. While Brownlow had suggested that he and his people submitted meekly to the rebels, the evidence suggests they put up a stiff fight before surrendering.

Brownlow, his family, and the settlers were herded across Armagh under armed guard and ended up in Dungannon. After his release, he was a witness in the trials of several rebels, including Toole McCann. Toole was charged with the murders of seven men in connection with the sacking of Lurgan. Although it's apparent now that these men were killed during the skirmishing and were "casualties of war, not victims of cold-blooded murder,"[78] Toole McCann was convicted and executed at Carrickfergus in July 1653.

Although Toole McRory McCann was also active at Lurgan, he does not seem to have been charged. When he was examined by the inquisitors in 1653, the record states he was 50 years old. If we assume, then, that he was born in about 1603, he would have been a child of seven or eight years old when his father, Rory McPatrick McCann, was removed from Clanbrassil and transplanted to Carricknagvna. Toole McRory admitted he knew Toole oge McToole McCann but denied he was under his command or that he commanded armed rebels himself. He stated that he lived five miles from Portadown, and that he'd heard about the massacre at the bridge but wasn't there.[79]

Interestingly, a local settler named Nicholas Williams stated in his deposition that he was one of those who had left their homes to seek refuge in Brownlow's castle when the uprising began. He testified that Toole McCann led the rebels but that Toole McRory McCann was also there, "for that he had a pretension of right to the castle of Lurgan."[80] This statement would suggest that perhaps Rory McPatrick McCann had lived in this location before being forced out, and that Toole McRory felt he was fighting to regain his legacy.

From this point forward, the prominence of the McCann sept diminished, and they joined the ranks of thousands of other Irish families living out their lives as itinerant farmers, linen weavers, or townspeople.

No longer were they the Lords of Clanbrassil.

Chapter Five
Cromwell in Ulster

Historical Background

After the 1641 Uprising, events back in England became rather tangled. King Charles I, who had married a Catholic, was executed in 1649 as a result of the English Civil War. An interregnum dominated by Oliver Cromwell and the English Parliament ended in 1660 when James II, the son of Charles, returned from exile to restore the monarchy.

James was the last reigning English monarch who was a Catholic, and although his term on the throne is now known for its attempts at religious tolerance, Protestantism became ascendant once more when he was deposed in favour of his daughter Mary II and her husband, William III of Orange.

In August of 1649, a decade before the Restoration, Cromwell had landed in Ireland and, with an army of about 20,000, proceeded to re-conquer the island in a campaign characterized by massacres and "unnumbered acts of burnings and hangings . . . the slaughter of ecclesiastics, and the merciless treatment of prisoners."[81] The English completely re-occupied Ireland by 1652, and in August of that same year *An Act for the Setling of Ireland* was passed.[82]

This new law was nothing less than a pretext for a renewed plantation exercise, this time with planters largely drawn from army veterans receiving their reward for having participated in Cromwell's nightmarish and bloody conquest.

To facilitate this new land grab, Englishman William Petty was commissioned to carry out yet another survey of lands to be confiscated from Irish Catholics deemed to have participated in the rebellion and thereby forfeiting their rights as freeholders. Conducted in 1655 to 1656, Petty's efforts are known as the Down Survey. Legend has it that those to be dispossessed were told they could either "go to Hell or to Connaught." In the end, many were relocated to reserves in County Clare, effectively pinning them down between the Shannon River and the Atlantic coast.[83] Others were dispatched in ships to the West Indies as indentured servants to work on British-owned sugar cane plantations.[84]

The mechanism by which this latest land grab was carried out was yet another commission, referred to as the Cromwellian Inquisition of 1657. The report of the Inquisition was transcribed by T.G.F. Paterson in 1927, and it includes lists of the townlands that were a part of each parish.

Since our focus is on Forkhill, we need to note that it did not exist as a parish at this time, as we'll discuss in the next chapter. Cromwell's report is useful to our research, though, because it shows us that townlands later identified as a part of Forkhill were encompassed in Loughgilly parish at this point in time. We'll take a closer look at this information later.

Before we leave the 17th century, there's one more source of information we should consider.

Hearth Money Rolls

The Hearth Money Rolls were an exercise in taxation first

undertaken in 1664. This bright idea was intended to move the burden of revenue generation away from landowners (many of whom were now transplanted English and Scottish Protestants) onto the general population (predominantly Irish Catholics).[85] It placed a tax of two shillings on every hearth "or other place for firing" discovered in each household. It was enforced across religious and economic levels indiscriminately, and it was universally unpopular.

It was a tax, after all.

As the late Rev. L.P. Murray explains, the latest 17th-century rolls that we have in existence are from 1665-66. The original rolls were destroyed in the infamous Record Office fire of 1922. "As they provided us with the only fairly complete Census Records previous to 1821, it was deplorable that they were never printed."[86]

Thankfully, Murray himself had visited the Record Office and made a full copy of the Armagh rolls before the fire. The county was divided into five baronies: Orier; Armagh; Torhany (Tirrany); Fews; and Onealand. Orier is the one that particularly interests us, because it contains Forkhill parish.

Within Orier, we find the following listings for McCanns:

- Donnell McCann (Botten; one hearth);
- Collowe McCann (Mullaghedatt; one hearth);
- Bryan McCann (Dymon; one hearth);
- Edmond McCann (Ballyknock; one hearth);
- Connor McCann (Lissadyne; one hearth);
- Murtagh McCann (Ballintample; one hearth); and,
- Patrick McCann (Latty & Coragh; one hearth).

Botten is now known as Bolton townland, and it's in

A Brief History

Loughgilly parish, just north of Forkhill. Mullaghedatt, also known as Mullagheddy and Mullyhead, is in Kilmore parish, just south of Portadown and well north of Forkhill. Dymon, a.k.a. Deamoan, from the Irish *Déagh-Móin*, meaning "Good Bog," is in Ballymore parish, again, north of Forkhill. Ballyknock, from the Irish *Baile Cnuic*, meaning "townland of the hill," is also in Kilmore parish. Lissadyne is in Loughgilly as well. Latty and Coragh, neighbouring townlands, are in Killevy parish, as is Ballintample, also known as Ballintemple.[87]

Unfortunately, we still lack the information to make concrete connections between them and the McCanns who lived in Forkhill parish in the next two centuries. However, if we look more closely at Forkhill, we may detect a few clues that could be followed forward at some future time.

Fig. 8 The Rolling Hills of Forkhill Parish

Chapter Six

The Life and Times of Arthur McCann

What was Forkhill Parish like when Arthur McCann lived there? What conditions did his grandparents and parents face that would have affected how he was raised?

Were Arthur and Ann from Forkhill Parish?

First of all, we must establish that before immigrating to Canada, Arthur McCann and his wife Ann Quinn were residents of Forkhill Parish in County Armagh.

In the church register now kept in the St. Edward the Confessor Catholic Church in Westport, Ontario, we find a record of the marriage of "Peter Carberry, son of Brian Carberry and Bridget McGouch of the parish of Forkhill, Ireland to Elizabeth McCann, daughter of Arthur McCann and Mary Quin of the same parish." This marriage took place on February 1, 1853, and the record was entered into the register by Father John Foley.[88]

We'll look more closely at Elizabeth McCann later in this family history, but for now the importance of this entry is that it establishes the fact that the family lived in Forkhill Parish before emigrating. Many of the settlers who arrived in North Crosby Township in the 1840s were also from Forkhill.

We don't know for certain where Arthur's grandparents and parents lived, or from which line they came. It's possible that Arthur descended from Rorie McPatrick McCann, who was, as we saw earlier, transplanted south from Clanbrassil to Carricknagavna, Upper Orior, during the Plantation process. His son Toole McRory McCann continued to possess this land grant in 1627, and it's possible his other sons, Bryan McRory McCann and Patrick McRory McCann, likewise settled in the area, which is now part of Forkhill parish. It's possible, then, that this was the lineage from which the various McCanns in Forkhill descended, including our own family.

What was Forkhill Parish Like in Arthur's Time?

Writing in 1837, Samuel Lewis described Forkhill as a post-town and parish with a total population of 7,063. It was formed as a civil parish in 1771, just before Arthur was born, by separating twelve townlands from Loughgilly parish. Comprising the western half of Forkhill, they included (north to south) Aughanduff, Tullymacreeve, Cashel, Mullaghbane, Shanroe, and Shean, among others.

In 1773, eleven other townlands were separated from Killeavy (Killevy) parish to join Forkhill. Paterson's transcription of the Cromwellian Inquisition lists them as having belonged at that time to Creggan parish. These include Carrickasticken, Tievecrom, Longfield (Leaukill), Clarkhill (Clarekill), Ballykeel, and others.[89]

As Canadian historian Kyla Madden explains, "Despite the best intentions of the Crown, the seventeenth-century scheme of

Ulster plantation failed to penetrate much of south Armagh."⁹⁰ A poll tax return from 1659 recorded fewer than 200 English or Scottish transplanted settlers in Orior compared to nearly 700 Irish. Forkhill townlands such as Carrickasticken, Shean, Mullaghbawn, and Clarkhill showed only Irish.

After changing hands several times, the land was eventually purchased by Richard Jackson in 1750. Only 28 years old at the time, he found himself the landlord of a rural wilderness inhabited by hundreds of impoverished tenants.⁹¹ As time passed, he tried to improve the area by setting up a weekly market and annual fairs, and he placed ads in Belfast newspapers trying to entice linen drapers and weavers to relocate. Linen was an important industry in Ulster at a time when there wasn't much else, and the local economy of Forkhill would have benefited from its growth in the area.⁹²

When Jackson died in 1787, the Belfast newspaper reported that a great number of his tenants and labourers were present at the gravesite.⁹³

His will left the Forkhill estate in trust to a group of Church of Ireland (Protestant) bishops and rectors who would manage it on a daily basis. A portion of the interest generated by the estate would be spent on the education, health, and welfare of tenants (Catholic) in the parish. Money was set aside to purchase looms for the poorest tenants so that they could work in the linen industry, and to provide winter coats to the oldest tenants.⁹⁴

His legacy also funded charity schools in the parish, and by 1821 there were eight such free schools, all supervised by Protestant schoolmasters or sewing mistresses. The first one opened in Shean townland in 1790, followed by two others in

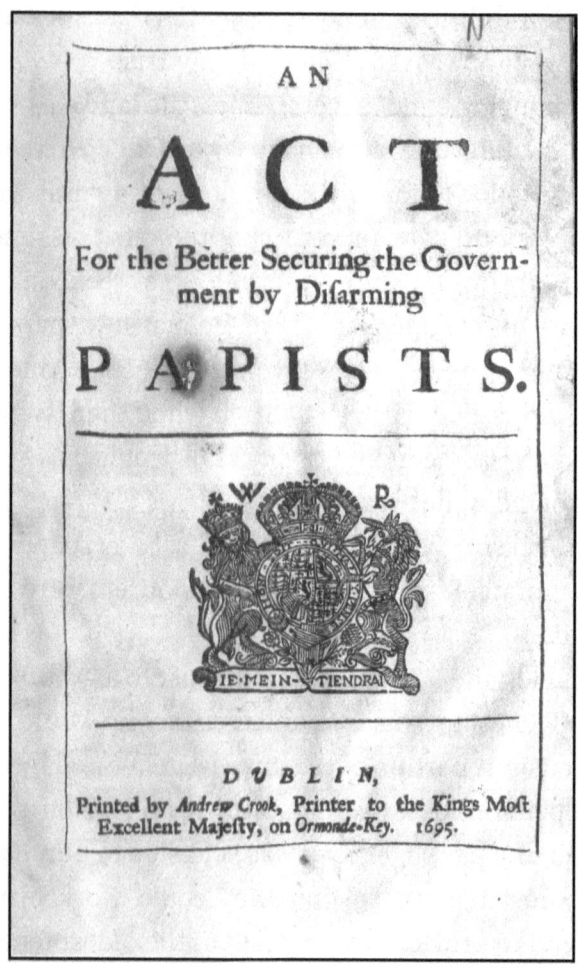

Fig. 9 A Penal Law

Mullaghbawn and Aughadanove townlands.[95]

Would Arthur, who was about 13 years old when the Shean school opened, have attended one of the Jackson charity schools? To answer that question, we need to step back for a minute to look at a series of laws that were passed at the beginning of the eighteenth century that would have affected his schooling—and almost everything else.

THE PENAL LAWS

England never missed an opportunity to squeeze the Irish Catholic population, and a good example of this compulsion was found in the notorious Penal Laws. Passed by the Irish Parliament during the reigns of William and Mary, Anne, George I, and George II, this series of laws regulated the status of Irish Catholics in almost every aspect of their lives.

For example, *An Act to Prevent the Further Growth of Popery* (2 Ann c.6), passed in 1703, introduced strict prohibitions regarding Catholic land tenancy. Catholics were

> rendered incapable of purchasing lands of inheritance, but were allowed to take leases of 31 years, with the proviso that if the farm yielded profit to a Papist amounting to more than one-third of the rental, any Protestant informer could eject the Catholic and claim the holding as his own.[96]

This Penal Law also changed the way in which land could be passed down by a Catholic when he died, re-imposing on Catholics a system of equal subdivision among surviving sons. The idea, of course, was to reduce the size of plots leased by successive generations of Catholics to miniscule parcels.

Although it was ultimately repealed in 1778, just after Arthur was born, the law's effects were quite real. By the beginning of the Great Potato Famine in 1845 (shortly after Arthur and his family left for Canada), 24 per cent all Irish tenant farms had been reduced to between one and five acres in size, while 40 per cent were of five to fifteen acres.[97] Since potatoes tended to be the only crop that could be grown in enough quantity to provide sufficient nourishment to a family living on such a small plot of land, it's obvious why the Famine was so devastating.

Of course, the English had thoughtfully provided a loophole to this particular Penal Law. If the eldest son converted to Protestantism, he would inherit his father's entire property and not have to subdivide it among his brothers.

Another Penal Law that had significant consequences for Catholics was *An Act to Restrain Foreign Education* (7 Will III c. 4), which was passed in 1695. On its face it was another attempt by the government to limit contact between Irish Catholics and their continental allies, but more significant in terms of domestic policy was the provision that

> "No person whatsoever of the popish religion shall publickly teach school, or instruct youth in learning, or in private houses teach or instruct youth in learning within this realm from henceforth . . . up on pain of twenty pounds, and also being committed to prison, without bail or mainprize, for the space of three months for every such offense.[98]

Again, this provision had more than one objective in mind. First of all, it outlawed Irish Catholic teachers. If they wished to avoid prison and a serious fine, Catholic teachers were expected to be wise enough to find another profession. Second of all, it virtually ensured that all Irish children would from that point on be educated in the English language by Protestant teachers. The Irish language would hopefully dwindle away, the values and ethics of the Protestant religion would be taught to Irish children, and gratitude and loyalty to England would hopefully be cultivated in young Irish minds at the same time.

As Antonia McManus points out, although Edmund Burke and W.E.H. Lecky claimed that the objective was to "reduce Catholics to a state of ignorance and servitude," it was instead a move to force them into "an education guaranteed to train them up to be loyal Protestant subjects."[99]

Other Penal Laws were passed to exclude Catholics from holding public office, to ban their ownership of firearms, to take away their right to vote, to prevent them from becoming lawyers or judges, and to ban the ownership of a horse worth more than £5. As well, in the rare instances where Catholics were allowed to build a church, it could be constructed only of wood and not of stone. (Presumably so that it would be easy to burn down, should the need arise.)

While today we might look at these prohibitions as ludicrous and outrageous, we must understand and appreciate the pressure they exerted on Irish Catholics to accept their lot as a subjugated and conquered population.

Fig. 10 The Hedge School

Hedge Schools: A Typical Irish Response to Adversity

Let's return now to the question we posed a few paragraphs ago about young Arthur's schooling.

If Arthur received an education at all, it's possible he might have attended what was known as a hedge school. Since Irish Catholic teachers were forbidden to teach without being declared outlaws and wild desperadoes, they created their own underground education network.

Schoolmasters convened secret classes for Irish children that were conducted outdoors, often behind the long hedges that divided fields in the countryside, or in barns or ruined buildings. Most attempted to deliver a full curriculum, including science, mathematics, Greek and Latin, spelling, poetry, and the Catholic Catechism. Since the books available to hedge school instructors were primarily in English, most of the teaching inevitably would have been conducted in that language as well as in Irish.[100]

Since teachers were subject to fines and imprisonment if caught, "students took turns acting as lookouts, ready to warn the schoolmaster if any suspicious person approached, giving the class time to disperse."[101] While it may sound like something out of a dystopian science fiction novel to us today, it was a grim reality at the time.

Hedge schools were not free. Parents paid a stipend to the schoolmaster to provide a Catholic education to their children. In return, boys and girls received a personalized method of learning that some nineteenth-century writers compared to Plato's approach.

One of the most famous hedge school masters was the

renowned poet Peader O'Doirnin. Born about 1700 in Faughart parish, County Louth, which is immediately south of Forkhill parish, he was a well-established scholar and poet who set up hedge schools in the 1730s and 1740s. One such school was in Forkhill, where he was said to have competed for students with another famous poet and scholar, Muiris Ó Gormáin. O'Doirnin died on April 3, 1776.

Given the assumption that Arthur's family lived in the southern part of Forkhill, perhaps in Carrickasticken, it's quite possible that his father was tutored by O'Doirnin or Ó Gormáin, just as it's possible Arthur himself also learned his letters behind a hedge.

Unrest During Arthur's Formative Years

When Arthur was about 21, yet another uprising tore the countryside apart. Kyla Madden provides a very good summary of the background and events of the Rebellion of 1798, and as she points out, Antrim and Down were the principal locales in which unrest took place in Ulster.[102] The year before, however, an uprising was brutally suppressed in Forkhill, and as a young man, Arthur could very well have been involved.

Two years earlier, in 1795, a military barracks was established in the parish, under the command of an English soldier named Colonel John Ogle. Married to a niece of Richard Jackson, Ogle received permission to form the Forkhill Yeomanry in order to counter organized rebels already active in the area. A group called the United Society of Irishmen had spread its influence through the parish, and a Catholic priest named Father James Coigly, who was based in nearby Dundalk (Louth), was one of the leaders. Several times Ogle wrote to the authorities at Dublin Castle that he had been shot at by United Irishmen.

In May 1797 a violent clash took place in Forkhill between a mob of several hundred people and a regiment of the Ancient British Fencibles. Many rebels were either killed or taken prisoner. After this incident, martial law was declared, and the military conducted a prolonged and brutal campaign through the area to confiscate weapons and quell any movement toward trouble. The network of United Irishmen in Forkhill was smashed, and Ogle wrote to Dublin Castle in June that the countryside was now quiet.[103]

Arthur would have been at an age where such turmoil would have had a great effect on him. Did he participate? Or did he try to stay clear of all the trouble? We'll never know for sure, but we can be certain that one way or another it would have profoundly shaped his view of life and of his homeland.

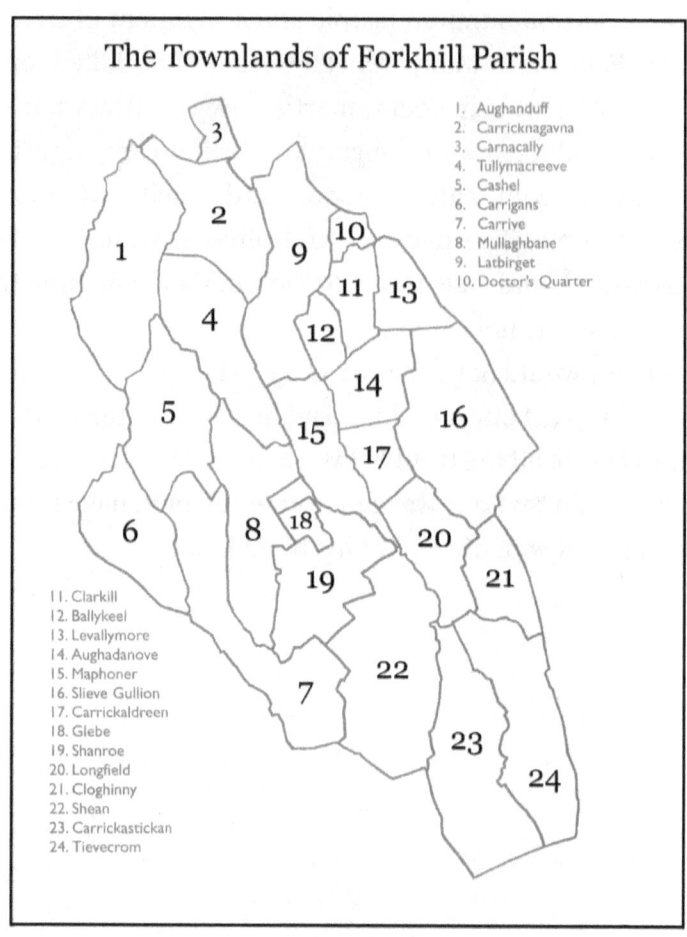

Fig. 11 The Townlands of Forkhill Parish

Chapter Seven
The Search for Arthur

Historical Background

The genealogist's best friend is the census. Tied to a specific geographical location, it enumerates every person residing there—head of the household, spouse, children, and anyone else living in the residence, including boarders or family elders. It usually records each person's age, which enables us to estimate dates of birth. It may also note occupations, and the relationships between parents and children often permit us to track forward and backward through other censuses to build an understanding of the generations. Working with nineteenth-century Canadian censuses is fairly easy and rewarding this way, particularly when families stayed put long enough to establish patterns.

Unfortunately, as we mentioned before, Irish censuses are nowhere near as helpful. In fact, as Kyla Madden notes, most copies of the 1821 census were destroyed in the aforementioned fire that devastated Dublin's Four Courts in 1922, along with countless other precious records.

As a result, genealogists are often forced to make do with other sources of information, however skimpy they may be. We'll take a brief look at these sources, and we'll also examine in a little more detail Madden's gift to all of us who are researching ancestors in Forkhill parish.

Census Substitutes

Many of the nineteenth-century Irish census returns that do actually exist are unreliable or incomplete. As an alternative, genealogists are often forced to investigate Irish tax records as possible substitutes for information on local populations. While they lack the extensive family information available through a census, tax records can at least provide a name and location. On such slender threads are many theories constructed when it comes to family history research.

We've already consulted the Hearth Tax Rolls as a substitute source of seventeenth-century information. It proved to be of minimal usefulness, but let's see if we have any better luck with eighteenth-century offerings.

Flax Growers List

This one was also called the Spinning Wheel Premium Entitlement List. As we mentioned, linen production had become an important industry in Armagh in the 1730s, and in the 1760s Richard Jackson had made an effort to attract drapers and weavers from Belfast to Forkhill as part of his effort to stimulate the local economy. Thirty years later, the government launched a program intended to encourage farmers to plant flax, in order to expand the front end of the linen industry.

In 1796 the Linen Board announced the following offer:

> To the person who should sow between the 10th day of March and the 1st day of June 1796, with a sufficient quantity of good sound flax seed, any quantity of land, well prepared and fit for the purpose not less than 1 acre –

4 spinning wheels, 3 roods – 3 ditto, 2 roods – 2 ditto, 1 rood – 1 ditto. And to the person who should sow in like manner any quantity of like land not less than 5 acres, a loom, or wheels, seeds or hatchells to the value of 50 shillings, and for every five acres over and above the first five a premium.[104]

By this time Arthur McCann would have been about 19 years old and likely still living at home with his parents. The Flax Growers list shows an Arthur McCann in the parish of Keady as having qualified for the program, but none of the 15 assorted McCanns in the list was located in Forkhill.

Interestingly, though, the list for County Louth includes an Arthur McCann in Faughart parish, immediately south of Forkhill and somewhat closer to where our Arthur probably lived. Once again, tantalizing information that doesn't lead us to the promised land.

Freeholders Lists

While the infamous Penal Laws of the early 1700s had prohibited Catholics from voting, legislation eventually came into force between 1793 to 1829 that granted voting rights to all men, Protestant and Catholic, who owned their land outright or held a lifetime lease for land that had a worth of at least 40 shillings. Referred to as freeholders, their particulars would appear either in registers or in poll books in advance of an election. After 1829, the qualifying amount was raised to 10 pounds, effectively creating a rule by well-off propertied freeholders.

The Public Record Office of Northern Ireland (PRONI) has digitized about 5,500 sheets from the registers and poll books and made them available online with a useful search engine. A query for the surname "McCann" yields 578 records, most of them ranging between the years 1795 to 1839.

If we filter these results so that we only see those from County Armagh, we're left with 434 hits. If we further filter these to set aside the records from northern Armagh and focus only on Orior entries, Upper or Lower, we reduce our workload to 95 hits.

If we sort them once again to isolate on Arthur McCann, we are left with a total of 14 records relating to three individuals:

McCann	Arthur	Clarkill	Upper Orior	Armagh	1817
McCann	Arthur	Clarkill	Upper Orior	Armagh	1826
McCann	Arthur	Clarkill	Upper Orior	Armagh	
McCann	Arthur	Cross	Upper Orior	Armagh	1818
McCann	Arthur	Cross	Upper Orior	Armagh	1818
McCann	Arthur	Cross	Upper Orior	Armagh	1818
McCann	Arthur	Cross	Upper Orior	Armagh	1818
McCann	Arthur	Cross	Upper Orior	Armagh	1825
McCann	Arthur	Cross	Upper Orior	Armagh	1825
McCann	Arthur	Cross	Upper Orior	Armagh	1825
McCann	Arthur	Cross	Upper Orior	Armagh	1839
McCann	Arthur	Cross	Upper Orior	Armagh	
McCann	Arthur	Duburren	Upper Orior	Armagh	1828
McCann	Arthur	Duburren	Upper Orior	Armagh	1828

Of the three, two lived outside of what is now Forkhill parish. Cross is located in Killevy parish, at the foot of Camlough Mountain about a kilometre south of Camlough village.

Duburren is also in Killevy parish.

Clarkill (Clarkhill or Clarekill), on the other hand, is in the northeastern quadrant of the parish. This Arthur McCann, who owned land worth enough to qualify him to vote, becomes a definite candidate for further consideration.

Unfortunately, there are no entries for Arthur McCann in Carrickasticken.

Tithe Composition Books

Another tax imposed on the Irish population was brought into effect by the *Tithe Composition Act* of 1823. This tax was religious in nature, in that all occupiers of land, Catholic and Protestant, were required to pay to the Church of Ireland (Protestant) an annual tithe (10 per cent) of their revenue generated through agricultural production. As a result, Tithe Applotment books were maintained between 1823 and 1837 to record the particulars of all individuals required to pay this tax.

Kyla Madden notes that this tax was not terribly popular in Forkhill parish. Unrest caused by the tithe flared in 1832 and 1833. In July 1832 a meeting was held at the Mullaghbawn Catholic church in which a number of petitions to Parliament were drafted in opposition to the tithe, after which everyone went home peacefully.[105]

In August, the Church of Ireland clergyman in Forkhill complained that most residents refused to pay, and he was forced to involve the "local constabulary," including the tithe proctor, Archibald Murdoch, and two special constables. As they trooped around the parish to collect from defaulters, they were met by angry mobs armed with pitchforks and other implements, blowing horns at them and threatening them with harsh language. The special constables were paid visits in their homes. Additional police were summoned to the parish to supplement the local force.

In February 1833 a large mob of between 800 and 2,000 people assembled on the Forkhill-Louth border with an objective of intercepting the police as they went around serving summonses and confiscating goods or livestock in lieu of the expected cash payments. Many participants in the mob were from the townlands of Carrickasticken and Carrive, where a number of McCanns resided. While no one was apparently injured in this uprising, it was, as Madden notes, a serious indication of the opposition to this tithe in Forkhill.[106]

With all of this background in mind, a reading of the *Tithe Composition Book of the Parish of Forkhill*, dated April 1828, scanned and made available online by PRONI,[107] turns up two Arthur McCanns—the one we've already encountered in Clarkhill in the Freeholders Lists, and a second one in Carrickasticken townland.

The entry for the Clarkhill Arthur McCann groups him with three other McCanns: Bryan, Patrick, and "Widow Macan." According to the copy book, the three properties occupied by Arthur, Bryan and the Widow all were assessed at 7 pounds, 1 shilling, and 6 pence. The property occupied by Patrick was assessed at 3 pounds, 0 shillings, and 38 pence. We can guess from this data that Widow Macan was perhaps Arthur's mother, Bryan was a brother, and Patrick was a son of one of the two men.

Carrickasticken is a slightly different matter. Arthur McCann is recorded three times, once for land at 5£/1s/2p, again for land at 6£/2s/12½p, and a third time at 6£/3s/21½p. The recorder noted against the second entry that it was a "2nd Holding." Presumably this Arthur was assessed for three separate farming properties altogether.

There are three other McCanns with him in the townland. John McCann was assessed at 3£/1s/14p, Neal McCann at 13£/0s/25p, and Tole (Toole) McCann twice, at 3£/1s/14p and at 4£/3s/17½p. Once again using the size of the assessment as a rough guide, we might guess that Neal McCann was either the father of the others or an eldest son who inherited the largest property; Arthur was next in line, holding properties about half as productive; and John and Tole were lower on the totem pole with land that was half as productive again.

The Forkhill Tithe Composition book, then, gives us two possible candidates for the Arthur McCann we're looking for. First, it confirms the existence of Arthur McCann in Clarkhill and provides the names of extended families' members. Second, it brings to light a second Arthur McCann living in Carrickasticken townland.

1821 Census of Forkhill Parish

The story of how Kyla Madden came across the only known copy of the 1821 Forkhill Parish census is the sort of tale that haunts the dreams of amateur genealogists. While rummaging around through the study of the south Armagh Church of Ireland rector, she pulled out a bound manuscript from a pile of old folios and discovered a transcript of the 1821 census for Forkhill that enables us now to intensify our search for Arthur McCann and Anne Quinn.[108]

As she explains, the census of 1821 was the first general enumeration undertaken in Ireland. A previous census had been attempted between 1813 and 1815, but the enumerators were constables and the period in which it was conducted was once again a time of turbulence and unrest. Few Irish were likely to open their door to the constabulary under any circumstances, and only 10 districts across the country handed in completed returns while a further 26 provided defective returns.[109]

For the 1821 census, the enumerator selected for Forkhill parish was a well-known Protestant farmer named Robert Ballmer. He lived in Tiffcrum (Tievecrom) townland, down at the south-eastern end of the parish, and was expected to know the district fairly well. Unfortunately, he was also a local constable,[110] but nonethless the results of his work are fairly comprehensive.

Madden provides an excellent analysis of the census in *Forkhill Protestants and Forkhill Catholics*, and I recommend you read it for a comprehensive sense of the demographics and tendencies of the parish at the time. For our purposes here, we're interested in what the census returns tell us about our ancestors.

The census was published locally in 2003 by the Mullaghbawn Community Association as *Kick Any Stone*, a collection of historical documents collated and edited by Kevin Murphy.[111] In it, we find two Arthur McCanns. The first one was included in the returns for Ballykeel townland:

A Brief History

Surname	Name	Relation	Age	Occupation	Acres
McCann	Arthur	Head	50	farmer	6
McCann	Mary	wife	46		
McCann	Miles	son	23	Labourer	
McCann	Patrick	son	20	Labourer	
McCann	Michael	son	12		
McCann	Bryan	son	14		
McCann	Peter	son	4		
McCann	Isabella	daughter	19	spinner	
McCann	Bridget	daughter	8		
McCann	Mary	servant	30	servant	

If we look at maps for the much later Griffith's Valuation survey,[112] we can see that there are McCann properties within a few hundred metres of each other on either side of the Ballykeel-Clarkhill townland boundaries, connected together by a narrow lane that can still be seen today on Google Maps running north from Ballykeel Road. There's little doubt that these properties all belonged to the same family, which might account for this Arthur McCann being sometimes listed in Clarkhill and other times in Ballykeel.

Now, however, the 1821 census finally gives us family information to study, and it tells us right away that this Arthur McCann is probably not the one we're looking for.

While his wife's name is listed as Mary, this is not particularly troublesome, because Ann Quinn is referred to in some Canadian sources by the same name. It's probable her name was Mary Ann and that occasionally "Mary" predominated over "Ann."

The fact that their third-oldest son is named Michael, however, casts a shadow over our analysis. This individual would have been born in 1808 to 1810, and we know that

Michael J. McCann, the son of Arthur and Ann who became a shoemaker and merchant in Westport, Ontario, was born in 1830. Furthermore, the 1864 Griffith's records show Michael McCann as one of the most active property lessees in Ballykeel and Clarkhill, along with Arthur McCann (perhaps another son, unless the 1821 Arthur was still active in land management at the age of 90, which is possible, but not probable). This Michael clearly was still alive in 1864 and living in Forkhill parish rather than Canada.

The other Arthur McCann found in the 1821 census resides in Carrickasticken:

Surname	Name	Rel.	Age	Occupation	Acres
McCann	Arthur	Head	50	Farmer	14
McCann	Anne	wife	42		
McCann	Bryan	son	23	carpenter	
McCann	Richard	son	21	Labourer	
McCann	Charles	son	19	Labourer	
McCann	Stephen	son	13		
McCann	Hugh	son	7		
McCann	Margaret	daughter	19	spinner	
McCann	Anne	daughter	9		
McCann	Eleanor	daughter	8		
McCann	Eleanor	daughter	2		

This Arthur is also listed with an age of 50, meaning he would have been born around 1771, and his wife, Anne, is listed at 42, suggesting a birth year of around 1779. Comparing these dates to what we have in Canadian records, they seem to be off by about six years in each case.

None of their children enumerated here is mentioned in Canadian records, suggesting that if this is the Arthur and Anne we're looking for, their oldest children may have remained behind. Griffith's Valuation data includes Stephen and Hugh, which may be their sons.

The only possible exception is at the very bottom of the list. As you can see, the enumerator recorded two children by the name of Eleanor. In the original copy book, which is reproduced in *Kick Any Stone*,[113] we see that he ran out of room at the bottom of the page and was forced to carry over the entry for the final child to the top of the next page.

This is the sort of thing that can drive an amateur genealogist crazy, because Canadian records tell us that Mary, the daughter of Arthur and Anne, was born right around 1819, which would have made her 2 in 1821. Did the enumerator make a mistake? After filling in all his header information at the top of the next page, did he absent-mindedly record the name of the previous child a second time instead of writing down Mary's name? Is this the smoking gun we are to be denied through all eternity?

Putting hysterics aside, we must conclude that while Arthur McCann of Carrickasticken is a most likely candidate to have been the Arthur for which we have been searching, we cannot conclusively declare him The One.

Welcome to my world.

What is Carrickasticken Like?

Although we lack the evidence to declare the search for Arthur and Ann in Ireland a success, it looks as though the family enumerated in the 1821 census in Carrickasticken is our best bet.

Having said, that, what was their home townland like?

Referred to in Irish as *Carraig an Staicín*, which means

"pointed rock," Carrickasticken is located on the border with County Louth, Republic of Ireland. Its size is just under 3.5 square kilometres, or just over 850 acres. So, not an overwhelmingly large place. Longfield townland lies to the north, Tievecrom to the east, and Shean to the west, including the town of Forkhill only a kilometre or so across the line.

Today, it's part of what's called the Ring of Guillion Area of Outstanding Beauty, a designation of the U.K. Department of the Environment that enables resource management and facilitates tourism. Slieve Gullion is an extinct volcano that provides the highest point in County Armagh, and its surrounding ring of lesser mountains and hills makes the area rugged and beautiful by turns. Nevertheless, Carrickasticken is known for its "species rich grassland with herbs and orchids, retained due to traditional farming methods."[114]

It's also known for its many raths, or ring forts. Small, circular earthworks perched on a hill or a slope, they were more important to the people who built them as agricultural structures than as military forts, although they did provide a measure of security. Wooden structures at the centre were protected by a circular ditch and a built-up earthen bank. Livestock were kept inside the enclosure, and various trades such as iron working and woodworking went on in there. It's difficult to date these structures, because archaeologists are mostly dependent on whatever artifacts they find within, such as pottery, tools, or personal items like brooches and pins. Some raths are said to go back to the 8th century A.D., while others might be later.[115]

According to O'Hart, local Irish had a superstition that it was extremely unlucky to mess with the raths. They believed they were inhabited by fairies, the so-called "good people," and any meddling with the enclosures or surrounding embankments would result in misfortune. This belief might explain their continued existence after so many centuries.[116]

WHERE IN CARRICKASTICKEN DID THE MCCANNS LIVE?

The census of 1821 did not provide specific information about where each family lived. The households are numbered, the way they are in almost all censuses, but we lack corresponding co-ordinates to locations within the townland. The same must be said as well for the Freeholders entries in the PRONI database.

We do, however, have an ace up our sleeve.

The Griffith Valuation is a census substitute often used by genealogists searching for nuggets in the shadows. This 19th-century initiative was conducted by Sir Richard Griffith for the government to assess the value of property in Ireland. It was carried out in three phases: the first, between 1825 and 1837, consisted of yet another boundary survey; the second, from 1829 to 1844, assessing the values of land and buildings; and the third, from 1852 to 1864, a general valuation survey.[117]

The reason why the Griffith Valuation data is so interesting is because it names names and tells us where these folks lived. The reason why it's of minimal value to us, however, is because we can establish, as seen below, that Arthur McCann and his family emigrated from Ireland right around 1842. Griffith, then, can only tell us where he *wasn't*. The corollary being that Arthur McCanns in the data were *not him*.

Just the same, we all love information that has our family name attached to it, and the Griffith data is interesting enough to mention here.

The website *Ask About Ireland* has a section dedicated to Griffith's Valuation, and it's well worth a look. Its search engines allow queries by "Griffith's Names," "Griffith's Places," and others.

Querying "Carrickasticken" in the latter will lead to a map provided by Google Maps that has historical data overlaid on top. This data displays the boundaries of each household in the townland and provides an identifying number that links the households to information that Griffith wrote down in the register.

For instance, we can cross-reference the two sources to see that Mary McCann was the head of household #59, leasing from landlord Henry Alexander, on a property just over two acres in size. Susan McCann leased two portions of #63, one that was four acres and another that was two. Hugh McCann occupied #62, Stephen McCann #65, Thomas McCann #66, Henry McCann #68, and John McCann #69. Rep. James McCann had two properties, #52A and B, sandwiched between those of Hugh on one side and Stephen and Thomas on the other.

James McCann's property was valued as a "cottier's house and land," suggesting he held it under the system known as *cottier tenure*, where land was leased on a yearly basis, according to the *Oxford English Dictionary*, directly to labourers who used it to cultivate crops. Perhaps, given the location of these parcels in the midst of other McCann households, the previous lease had somehow failed to transmit down to the next generation after a death, and landlord Alexander was following a yearly arrangement permitted him by law.

Unfortunately, copyright law prevents me from reproducing

the map I'm looking at right now as I write this section. I can say, though, that these properties are clustered together in the western half of the townland within walking distance of the Louth border, perhaps 3.5 kilometres from the southern tip of the townland.

The map also shows us that there was a rath, a ring fort, on one of Susan's properties, #63A. A portal to Ireland's ancient past, perhaps close enough for Arthur to stare at (from a safe distance) and dream about.

So, was this Arthur's family, those sons and daughters-in-law who chose to remain behind when the rest immigrated to Canada? It's possible. Carrickasticken Arthur's son Stephen was 12 years old in 1821, and Hugh was 7. They would have been 32 and 27, respectively, when Arthur left, likely with their own family and a wife who preferred to stay. It's possible that these are the same men, recorded in the Griffiths Valuation when they were in their late forties or early fifties.

Which Church Did the Carrickasticken McCanns Attend?

Before we leave Arthur McCann of Ireland, it's interesting to consider the question of churches and Carrickasticken. While the main Catholic church in Forkhill parish, located in Mullaghbawn, would have been about six kilometres away from the Carrickasticken McCanns, the ancient Urney chapel and graveyard is less than a kilometre away, just across the border in Dungooley townland, County Louth. Walking distance.

Legend traces its origin all the way back to St. Patrick, and the church bore his name until 1900 when it was renamed in

Fig. 12 The Graveyard at Urney

honour of Bridget of Faughart. Throughout its history, "it does not seem ever to have been a parish church properly so called, but only a chapel."[118]

However, before it was replaced in 1794 by a new church in Kilcurry (Louth), "Urnai was the place of worship for all the country round about. To this tiny edifice, only twenty-eight feet by sixteen and a half internally, they came in their hundreds for Mass, indifferent to the weather from which but few of them could have protection."[119]

The site fell into disrepair, and as John P. Clarke wrote in 1965, "The earliest legible inscriptions [in the graveyard] are, in fact, all late eighteenth-century; the names which occur most frequently being: Hollywood, Muckian, Smyth, Coburn, McCanna (McCann), O'Hanlon and Ferency."[120] Clarke found nothing in a legible condition that predated the eighteenth century, and as photographs taken by Eric Jones in 2019 indicate, the headstones continue to deteriorate as the years pass.[121]

Thankfully, Reverend Diarmuid Mac Iomhair had previously provided a transcription of headstones while some were still legible.[122] In his list of inscriptions we find:

- Mc CAN—Aged 76 yrs Here lieth the body of Bryn Mc Can who depad [sic] this life May ye 12th also his son Petr who died ye 23d day of sd month aged 26 yrs anno humanae salutis 1790 erected by his son Robt all of Carive (53). (The stone has the emblem IHS with a cross rising above the H and a heart below it, the whole contained within a chevron and circle ; to the left of the circle is a hand with extended fingers);

- McCANN - This stone was erected by Michael McCann in memory of his father, Neal McCann, who departed this life December the 7th, 1785, aged 74 years;
- McCANN - Dedicated in memory of Robert McCann of Shanrow who died - Feb -, aged 8[?]0 years; also his wife, Cathrine[?] McCann;
- McCANNA - Here lieth the body of Mattew McCanna who departed this life April the 21st, 1795, aged 21 years; also the body of Rose O'Hanlon (his mother) who departed March the 19th, 1795, aged 61 years. Requiescant in pace. Amen. Erected by Bernard McCanna.[123]

As we can see, McCanns from as far away as Carrive and Shanroe worshipped at Urney, so it's hardly a stretch of the imagination to guess that Carrickasticken McCanns also joined the hundreds who attended mass there.

One last story about Urney, which comes to us from Rev. Mac Iomhair:

> On April the 5th, which was the Wednesday following Low Sunday in the year 1769, there was carried here [to Urney] down the narrow road from Forkhill the body of an old schoolmaster, whom his pupils had found dead in his sleep two

days before. This was the scholar, wanderer and poet, Peadar Ó Doirnin. He was buried at the north-east wall of Urney Graveyard in the County Louth ... in the grave with his mother. ... There is a small stone with Greek lettering (number 52). ... Convenient to it there has now been erected a monument as part of the commemoration held in honour of "*Ó Doirnin na gcuach is na siollaí mín*".[124]

Do the remains of our ancestors lie in this ancient graveyard in the company of the famous poet and hedge school teacher? Perhaps. However, their tombstones would now be wiped clean by time and weather, or they lie beneath the surface, covered by grass and soil, lost to us.

PART TWO
CANADA

Fig. 13 Irish Emigration Ships

Chapter Eight
A New Beginning in Canada

Our story now moves ahead to the early 1840s, when Arthur and Ann board a ship with their youngest children and set sail for the New World and a very risky chance at a new beginning on foreign soil.

In this opening chapter of their immigrant experience we'll look at what the voyage might have been like, what their destination held in store for them, and their arrival there.

Arthur and His Family Make the Voyage

Arthur and Anne decided around 1840 to pull up stakes and immigrate to Upper Canada, or Canada West as it was currently known. Their daughter Mary (the second Eleanor in the 1821 census?) had taken the big step with her husband, Michael McArdle, a few years earlier, and perhaps she'd written back to them that there was land available and a fresh start to be made.

Emigrating from northern Ireland cost money, and Arthur would have needed enough to pay for the family's passage. Money would also be needed at the other end of the voyage to pay for transportation from their port of entry in the New World all the way to their final destination. Perhaps Arthur liquidated all his assets in order to finance the journey.

One small consolation is that he would have avoided by a

few years the terrible ordeal of the potato blight that destroyed almost all the crops in Ireland and resulted in the Great Famine of 1845 to 1849. If he'd waited, he likely would not have been able to raise more than pennies on the pound for whatever holdings he had to his name.

It's likely they would have sailed from Newry or Warrenpoint, seaports that were only a few kilometres away from Forkhill. In Newry, which they may have visited from time to time, they would have seen numerous advertising placards posted everywhere in town listing sailing dates, destinations and costs for passage on any of the many packet ships making the journey back and forth between Ireland and Canada.[125]

The average voyage in the early 1840s to Quebec lasted about 45 days, and could have cost as much as £4 per person. For this price our family would have been crammed in the cargo hold of the ship with other emigrants, clutching their meagre possessions. They would have been required to bring their own provisions, probably consisting of a sack of potatoes and a sack of flour. Water would have been provided to them, but for steerage passengers spending almost all of their time in the dark, dank confines of the cargo hold, it would have been dirty and unsanitary.

In addition to food, they may have brought a few personal possessions with them. In order to economize, they would not have brought furniture or other such large items, as the cost of storage space in the ship would have been far beyond their means. More likely they brought a few tools and implements, such as an axe or hatchet, a shovel and a scythe blade, and a few knives, a pot or two for cooking and perhaps a few dishes and utensils. They may have also brought small personal items such as a watch or clock, warm clothing, thread and needles, and perhaps one or two mementos of their former life in Ireland. They would have been limited to whatever they could carry.

Under these difficult conditions it was very common for passengers to die during the voyage. Some of the ships became sailing coffins as cholera swept through the holds. Typhoid fever, measles and other diseases killed a great many people hoping for a new beginning in Canada. Grosse Isle, in the Gulf of St. Lawrence, became a graveyard for many of these unfortunate emigrants.[126] Whether anyone in our family passed away during the voyage is unknown. Thankfully, the principal members of our family survived, or there would be no story to tell.[127]

Arthur would have been about 65 years old when he undertook this journey, and Ann would have been about 56. Of the children we know about who travelled with them, Roseanna would have been about 17; John, 16; Elizabeth (Betty) 14; and Michael J., 12.

Packet ships from Ireland normally landed at Quebec City and discharged their passengers, from which point immigrants boarded a steamboat travelling from Quebec to Montreal, where they disembarked once more.[128]

At Montreal it was necessary then to face the difficulties posed by the Lachine Rapids, which disrupt the St. Lawrence River as it wraps around the south shore of the island of Montreal. The rapids historically made it very difficult to travel west from Montreal up the river. In the past, the ten-mile stretch between the port in Montreal and the lower end of the rapids at Lachine had to be travelled either on foot or by wagon, if one could be hired. Peter Robinson's first group of Irish settlers, for example, walked this stretch in 1823, carrying their belongings with them. By 1833, however, a stage was operating during the summer months.

Once at Lachine and looking westward up the St. Lawrence, however, the journey was still complicated. Two possible routes were available to travellers. One route involved following the Ottawa River inland to Ottawa, known as Bytown at that time, and then down the Rideau Canal system, which had opened in 1832, to Kingston. The other route involved following the St. Lawrence River to Prescott, Brockville and Kingston. Our family may have gone either way.

Disruptions to travel along the St. Lawrence caused by the Americans during the War of 1812 had encouraged the authorities to develop the Ottawa River route as a safer approach. Four problem spots, one at St. Anne's passing île St. Perrot, another at Carillon, a third at Chute à Blondeau, and a fourth at Grenville were overcome with canals and locks that were open for business by 1842. Durham boats or steamers travelled this route as far as Bytown and then headed southwest down the Rideau Canal. If they took this route, they would have disembarked at Newboro across the Upper Rideau Lake from Manhard Mills, as Westport was known at the time.

As far as the other route is concerned, travellers proceeded from Lachine up the St. Lawrence River in a steamboat that carried them 36 miles to Coteau-du-lac, where they disembarked and boarded a stage that carried them 90 miles along the river to Prescott. At Prescott they could continue by stage along the road to Brockville or Kingston, or they could travel by steamboat to Kingston.

From Kingston travellers could then take a steamboat up the Rideau Canal system to Newboro, where a boat could take them across Upper Rideau Lake to Manhard Mills.

At this point, no matter which route they had taken, they would have been thoroughly exhausted by their travels, as well as much lighter in the purse. Mary and Michael McArdle may have met the weary travellers and taken them home for a while until they had a chance to get settled on land of their own. Or Arthur may have made arrangements in advance for a particular piece of property to occupy, and they may have travelled there on foot, carrying their possessions with them.

Either way, they would have passed through rough wilderness along routes that were barely more than cleared pathways through the forest, a far cry from the roads and highways that we know today.

The Village of Westport, North Crosby Township

Today, Westport is a quiet little village with a population of about 700 people. It's a very popular destination spot for tourists, particularly American boaters. A public wharf on a man-made island has dock space for up to 30 vessels. The harbour also has a picnic area, barbecues, and sewage pumping facilities. My father often told me that as a boy in the late 1930s he loved to hang around the docks and watch the boats come and go. He liked to joke that during the summer there were more Americans in the village than hometown Westporters. He found the Americans friendly and generous, and said they were always welcomed in Westport by the people who lived there. No doubt in part because they were good for business.

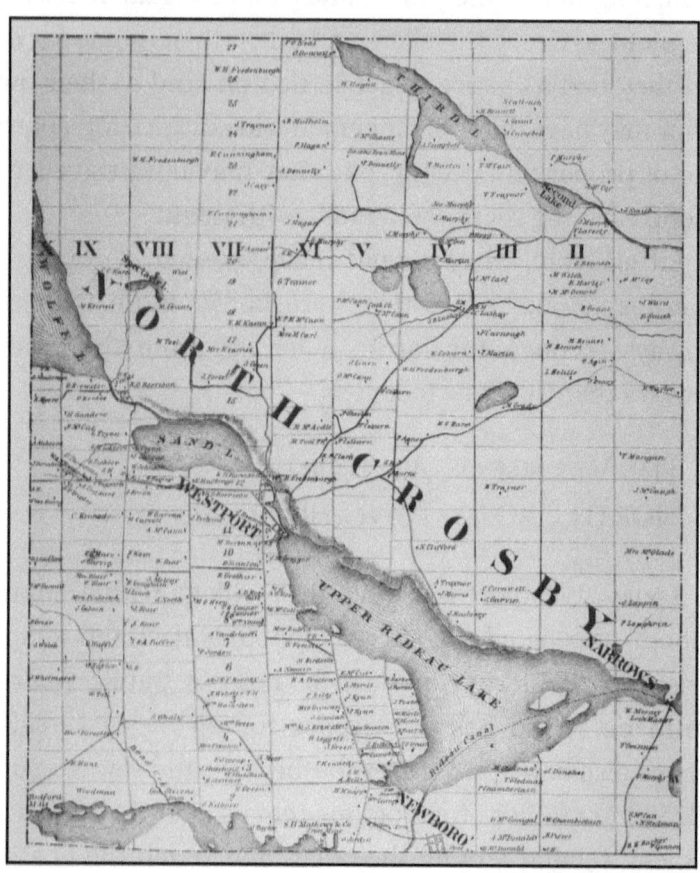

Fig. 14 North Crosby Twp.

A Brief History

The settlement of Westport had its origin about 225 years ago, when Governor Haldimand initiated a series of surveys in the 1780s in order to establish townships along the north shore of the St. Lawrence River. These townships were needed to accommodate the many United Empire Loyalists streaming north after the conclusion of the American Revolution. Known as the Johnstown District, this area covered just over one million acres at the time. Beginning in 1783, the surveys blocked out a series of townships of about 10 square miles each. Each township was then divided into concessions about one and one-quarter miles across, and each concession was then divided up into rectangular lots of about 200 acres each. By the time that Leeds County was created within the Johnstown District, it included the townships of Burgess and Bastard, North Crosby, South Crosby, Elizabethtown, Elmsley, Escott, Kitley, Front of Leeds and Lansdowne, Rear of Leeds and Lansdowne, Front of Yonge, Rear of Yonge and Escott, the incorporated villages of Gananoque and Newboro, and the town of Brockville.

Arthur and his family ultimately ended their journey in North Crosby Township. The area was originally surveyed by Reuben Sherwood, who received in an 1803 grant the land on which the village was built. The first settlers in the township had already begun to arrive between 1810 and 1820. In 1817, Sherwood sold some of his land to Sheldon Stoddard, and he and Stoddard built a large sawmill at the foot of Sand Lake. In 1827, three Manhard brothers settled in the area and built another saw mill and grist mill just across the bay from the village.[129]

At this point in time, the small community growing up in the middle of North Crosby Township was known as Head of the Lake, but it soon became known as Manhard Mills. In

1840 Robert Rorison, a successful lumber dealer, purchased the mills from the Manhards. Meanwhile, Aaron Chambers and Gabriel Forrester had established a business moving logs and square timber on the Rideau from Manhard Mills to Ottawa and Montreal, engaging large crews of French, Scottish Canadians, and local raftsmen. It was Chambers and another local merchant, Lewis Cameron, who in 1841 changed the name of the village to Westport, reflecting its location at the west end of Upper Rideau Lake.[130]

Arthur and Ann Arrive

It was into this burgeoning community in the early 1840s that Arthur McCann and his family arrived. The first appearance of Arthur in Canadian records is in a clergy reserve inspection report of 1844, in which Arthur McCann is listed as a claimant and occupant of eight acres of clergy reserve land on Lot 22 of Concession 2, North Crosby Township, in Leeds County, Canada. It would appear that he had been occupying the land since 1842. As a result of this inspection report, which was undertaken by the Commissioner of Crown Lands, occupants were given an opportunity to purchase the clergy reserve land on which they were living. The report listed all those making an offer, and Arthur McCann is included in the list.[131]

The concept of the clergy reserve lands should be explained. At this time in Canadian history, land was being handed out to settlers in a number of ways. Loyalists who had fled north in the late 1700s after the American Revolution were given free grants of land to reward their loyalty to the British Crown. The Brockville and Perth areas were heavily settled by such individuals. Lord Durham's famous report in 1839 stated that a total of 3.1 million

A Brief History

acres were granted to United Empire Loyalists in Upper Canada. As well, veterans received about 450,000 acres in land grants after leaving military service. Persons contracted to perform surveys received a total of 262,000 acres. The heirs of General Brock alone received a grant of 12,000 acres. In addition, some land was held back as Crown Reserves, so that as its value rose as a result of increased settlement in the area it could be sold by the government at a decent profit.[132]

Furthermore, the *Clergy Reserve Act* passed in 1791 by the British House of Commons set apart one-seventh of all unsurveyed land of Upper Canada "for the support of a Protestant clergy." The Church of England was expected to rent the land to settlers as a source of income. However, many settlers were reluctant to rent when they could get their own land through other means, and so the Church quite often ended up selling the land outright.

The assessment rolls for North Crosby Township, which record the amount of tax paid on land in the township, show that Arthur paid £11 (English currency still being used in Canada at this time) in land tax in 1844. The terms of his agreement are not known, but prior to 1844 they usually amounted to 10 per cent down and the balance to be paid in equal amounts over the next nine years. Perhaps operating on a similar sort of deal, Arthur continued to faithfully pay his assessed taxes each year in addition to his "mortgage" payments. The taxation assessment rolls record that he paid £6 in 1845, £4 in 1846 and £3 in 1847.

Lot 22 of Concession 2, North Crosby Township, is on what is known today as the upper mountain, just northeast of Westport. As you can see on the map in Figure 14, half the lot is taken up by Little Crosby Lake, which is between Crosby Lake and Pike Lake. At the time, Little Crosby Lake was known as Second Lake. Today, Cedar Bridge Road is a side road running through the lot coming up from County Road 10, also known as the Scotch Line Road. It's little more than a single-lane gravel track winding up and around very hilly terrain covered with hemlock, birch and juniper. It's rocky and rough property that Matthew Connor, the enumerator of the 1851 census, did not particularly like. Struggling through the snow that still lay deep around the township in the early part of that year, he wrote the following comments in his census book:

> The whole of the land on this sheet is on what we call The Mountain. It has been valued by the Assessors at from 1/8 to 2/6 per acre. At this season of the year it is difficult to value land, but if we may estimate it by the circumstances of the people and the general appearance of things, I would say the above is high enough. Much of the land which has been cleared is not cropped owing to its barrenness. . . .[133]

and

> As there are so many on one lot, I found it a matter of impossibility to give the quantity each person holds or whether it is rear or front or what portions they hold in the following concessions 1, 2, 3, 4, 5, 6, 7, 8 & 9 of this township of North Crosby. Particularly in this season of the year when the snow is very deep and no path from the houses in this wilderness.[134]

Matthew Connor's low opinion of this portion of the township and its value for taxation purposes in 1851 echo what appears to have been a downward trend in the value of the property overall. In the early stages of settlement, land was sometimes valued sight unseen, working from a map without benefit of actual eyeball contact with the property itself. It was only once people actually settled on the land and tried to clear it for crops that its true worth (or lack thereof) became apparent.

Why did Arthur and Ann choose this particular spot to settle in?

Their daughter Mary and son-in-law Michael McArdle had preceded them to Upper Canada as we mentioned, and in the early 1840s they were listed as residents of North Burgess Township, only a kilometre or two away in next-door County Lanark.

There were other McArdles already living in North Burgess who may have been related to Michael. We'll discuss the McArdle family in a bit more detail later, but for now the information interests us because it's a possible reason for Mary McCann to have immigrated with her husband to this township, and for Arthur and Ann to have followed them there.

While it would likely have been family that drew Arthur and Ann to this area, it was certainly not the quality of the land. The enumerator of the 1851 census of North Burgess was as unimpressed as his North Crosby counterpart, Matthew Connor:

> The general character of the land is very rocky and unfit for cultivation with a few exceptions. This part of the township contains 22 freeholders

and tennants [sic] the remainder of the inhabitants are squatters and mostly poor.[135]

Although Forkhill parish had its fair share of rocks and hills and mountains, it would seem that the landscape north of Westport village was possibly worse.

Arthur and Ann: Pioneers

What was it like to settle on land like this in the 1840s? Writers such as Susannah Moodie, her sister Catherine Parr Traill, and Anne Langton wrote about the harshness of the Canadian wilderness and the difficulties encountered in clearing the land, planting crops and raising a family. These accounts were written, however, by English women whose husbands were educated gentlemen with at least a small amount of capital to invest in a decent dwelling, ploughs, livestock, seed, and hired help. Robert Leslie Jones tells us that a man who had £100 in his pocket "had a bare minimum. It would take £20 buy a pair of oxen, a yoke, a logging chain, and a harrow, £8 for a cow and a couple of pigs, £22 for a year's provisions, and £50 for erecting buildings and for hiring labour to assist in chopping and logging."[136]

While Arthur may have had some money left over after his voyage from Ireland, and he was doing well enough to be able to afford to pay £11 in taxes in 1844, it's doubtful he had the kind of money on hand that Jones mentions. Arthur and his family must have been faced with an extremely difficult situation.

The first order of business would have been to clear a spot for their home and for crops that would hopefully get them through the fall and winter. If a natural clearing existed, then a great deal of trouble might be saved. If not, he and his sons were faced with a backbreaking job right at the outset.

Today a building lot in the bush is cleared with heavy equipment. With the use of a bulldozer, a backhoe, a chipper and a few grouchy men with chain saws, a decent building site can be cleared in a couple of days. In the 1840s, however, the prospect of clearing the land for habitation was much more daunting. For this reason, the government imposed on settlers the condition that land be cleared at a particular rate over a given period of time when they accepted a grant. With respect to clergy reserve land, actual settlement was a condition of sale, which meant that someone such as Arthur had no choice but to proceed with the clearing job and the construction of a home.

In the absence of bulldozers and chain saws, Arthur's primary tools would have been an axe and fire. Brush would be cleared, stacked in piles, and burned. Trees would be cut down, chopped into moveable lengths, and hauled aside. Stumps would be burned in order to weaken them enough for removal from the ground. Some fortunate settlers might have access to oxen and a logging chain or rope to pull the stumps out. Advanced technology! In many cases, though, a new arrival was forced to rely on the axe they had brought with them from Ireland and the strength of their arms.

The settler Samuel Strickland described a logging bee in which twenty neighbours with five yoked oxen helped him clear a site in Peterborough County in 1826. According to his estimate, a team of four men and oxen should be able to clear and burn an acre a day. The settler Thomas Need hired someone to do his clearing for him at something over £3 a day. On the other hand,

Mrs. Jameson recounted a settler stuck doing the entire thing himself, ending up with only five acres cleared after five years of lonely hard work.[137]

It would seem that Arthur McCann was able to clear eight acres on Lot 22 during his time there. Thankfully, our elderly ancestor would have had two teenagers to help him, along with a son-in-law and perhaps a few other family members.

Once clearing had reached a certain point, the next step would have been to build a shelter, something for his family to live in. At that time in Canada West, Irish settlers would build a log shanty. While log homes today are beautiful, rustic affairs, there was absolutely no romance to be found in a settler's shanty in the 1840s.

A shanty was a single storey, single room structure that might be only about 12 by 14 feet in size. It had a single door in the front and may or may not have had a window. The floor was dirt and the spaces between the logs in the wall would have been filled with mud. The hearth and chimney were built from field stones, a good use for rocks turned up while ploughing.[138]

Shanties were often built during another bee. While logging bees would generally have been just a lot of hard work with plenty of sweat, fire, and smoke, a bee to build a shanty would have been a bit more of a social event at which families gathered, and food and drink (often alcoholic) were served. If enough participants stayed sober long enough, the shanty would be up and ready to inhabit by the time the festivities were over. It's quite possible that McCanns and McArdles, and perhaps a few neighbours, participated in the construction of the first McCann log shanty on Lot 22.

Later on, a loft might be built inside for a sleeping area, or partitions erected in an attempt at privacy, but in only about 170 square feet of living space options were very limited and privacy was not a realistic wish. Materials for partitions or floors were also a challenge, as it was time-consuming to split logs into slabs or planks to build interior surfaces. The front door would have been made of straight slabs of split cedar and hung on wooden pin-and-block arrangements that substituted for iron hinges. The roof would initially be made of bark or sod, and would leak like a sieve until shingles could be split or purchased.[139]

More chopping and splitting were then needed to make the first furniture for the shanty. Early beds were often built into a corner of the shanty by boring holes into the log walls and fitting six-foot poles into them along with a crosspiece and an upright leg. The "box spring" might be made of slender poles woven with elm bark or hemlock boughs. Someone desiring a bed that could be moved about the shanty, however, might build one from four posts and four crosspieces.

Chunks of logs were used as stools until chairs or benches could be made. Chairs were often made of pine, with seats of split elm or willow bark. Tables would be bulky affairs like a modern butcher's block. Winter would be the time of year when someone who was handy with wood might build a few pieces of furniture to while away the snow-filled days. If they were particularly hopeless at furniture making but had a bit of cash set aside from their crops, they could always purchase a chair or table from a local craftsman.

Once an acre or so was sufficiently cleared, the next step would be to plant crops. If the family arrived late in the year, the work of building a shanty and clearing land for planting would have left no time to plant before the onset of frost, other than perhaps some winter wheat sown among the stumps. If this were the case, their first Canadian winter would have been an ordeal, spent living on hoarded provisions and the bounty of others.

The next spring, once the snow was finally gone for good, Arthur, John and Michael would have studied their clearing and assessed their chances of growing enough to survive another year. Seed potatoes would be an absolute necessity to purchase, along with implements to work the soil. The family may have brought a few tools with them, such as a hoe or adze, and a spade or a shovel. Jones tells us that settlers might have made or acquired an A-shaped harrow made of heavy logs and iron teeth to use as their only labour-saving device. Wooden teeth might have been substituted for iron, and the harrow would have been dragged between what stumps still remained in the field to scratch up enough soil to receive a crop.

Potatoes would have gone into the ground that spring without question, and perhaps some buckwheat in another part of the field. One unexpected problem a settler would encounter after clearing a field is that weeds and other undesirable plants would very quickly invade and establish themselves, including brambles, buckthorn, thistles, milkweed, couch grass, and tamarack and birch saplings.[140] Since buckwheat is known to choke out other growth as well as provide a useful product for subsistence, it could have been a staple crop as part of the overall clearing and planting process.[141] A scythe or sickle would be used to harvest the crop, and a home-made thresher would separate the wheat from the chaff.

Arthur Moves

At some time before 1848, Arthur decided to leave the clergy reserve lot on Concession 2 and try his luck elsewhere on the mountain above Westport. Accordingly, in the census of North Crosby taken in 1848 we find him listed as the occupant of Lot 16 of Concession 8. The census identifies it as a 200-acre lot, with three acres "under tilling" and 197 acres in woods or wilderness, 120 acres of which is listed as "unfit for civilization."

As you can see on the map in Figure 14, this is a spot about 10 kilometres southwest of his original settlement. It's situated off Mountain Road, also known as County Road 36, right about where Pollard Road intersects with Porter Road on its way to Wolfe Lake. The lot would have been accessed from Porter Road, below the intersection.

This location could not exactly be described as prize real estate any more than was his previous place. Today it has gone back to bush and woods, but the remnants of a clearing are visible when looking from overhead in Google Maps. If you visit the site, you'll immediately see outcroppings of bedrock close to the edge of the road, with only a thin layer of topsoil. Getting out of the car for a closer look, you'll realize you're not really sure what he was thinking when he came down here. Nevertheless, this is the place he chose to make a second attempt at a home in North Crosby.

According to the census, there were seven people living in Arthur's household in 1848, one of whom was not a family member. This survey didn't provide names, unfortunately, but listed individuals according to age. There is a married male between 40 and 59 (Arthur would have been about 70); a single male 18 to 21 (John); a single male 14 to 18 (Michael); a married female older than 45 (Ann Quinn, who was about 65); two single females 14 to 45 (Elizabeth and Roseanna, who married in September of that year); and a single female 5 to 14. This last person was the individual classified as not being a member of the family. Who she was remains a mystery.[142]

Arthur is listed as a "non-proprietor," meaning he didn't own this property. Lot 16 of Concession 8 had been granted in 1797 to Jean McLean, wife of Alexander McLean and daughter of George Gardner, the son of United Empire Loyalist refugees from Vermont. Mrs. McLean lived in Yonge township and had no interest in relocating.

The land ended up in the possession of Allan MacNab, likely the son of Sir Allan Napier MacNab, a soldier and politician who was heavily involved in land speculation, particularly in the southern part of the province (especially Hamilton).[143] MacNab held title to Lot 16 from 1833 to 1852, and would have been Arthur's titular landlord.

The census for 1848 tells us that in the previous year Arthur planted two acres in oats, harvesting 40 bushels, and one acre in potatoes, harvesting 50 bushels. He produced 30 pounds of maple sugar, and he owned three cows and a pig. Hopefully the pig wasn't one of the nasty, vicious, half-wild porkers known as landpikes, that were probably more useful as guard dogs than as a source of pork. They were skinny, big-eared shoats widely known to be far more trouble than they were worth.[144]

When the census of 1851 was conducted, Arthur was listed as living on 50 acres of the rear portion of Lot 17 in Concession 8, having apparently moved over from Lot 16. According to North Crosby land copy books, this lot was Crown land.

A Brief History

Remaining on Lot 17 was his son, John, now married to Sarah Coburn, and his son-in-law Michael Toole, who had married Arthur's daughter Roseanna. This would put them on the south side of what is now Pollard Road, right at the intersection with Porter Road.

While in 1848 Arthur was listed as a "yeoman," in 1851 the enumerator, Matthew Connor, categorizes him as a labourer. At the age of 73 or so, his farming days would no doubt have been easing down just a bit.

Nonetheless, the agricultural portion of the 1851 census records that Arthur had 12 acres under cultivation here, with two acres in wheat yielding 24 bushels, two acres in oats worth 59 bushels, an acre of rye yielding 12 bushels, an acre in potatoes for 40 bushels, and the rest in hay. He also produced 70 pounds of maple sugar (a man after my own heart). His livestock included two oxen, a milk cow and three calves, two sheep, two pigs, and he was listed as having produced 200 pounds of pork.

Although an elderly man by this time, it's obvious Arthur wanted to stay busy on his farm.

Unlike the 1848 census, the 1851 returns recorded the names and personal information of family members. Ann Quinn is still here, and so is Michael, a single 19-year-old, and Betty, who was 17 at the time. Also enumerated is a single, 18-year-old female named Ann, who was perhaps the unrelated female from 1848!

Arthur Passes Away

While the census of 1851 paints a picture of an old man still active and involved in his farm, the winter of 1851 must have been difficult for him to get through. On March 18 the following spring, the day after St. Patrick's Day, he passed away at the age of 75. He was buried in St. Edward's Roman Catholic Cemetery outside Westport. His headstone reads:

> Arthur McCann
> Died
> Mar. 18, 1852
> Aged 75 years

ANN QUINN

Other than knowing that she was born in 1786 and came from Forkhill parish, we have very little information about Ann Quinn. Anecdotal information suggests that she was the daughter of Arthur Quinn (born 1760) and Catherine Donnelly (born 1760). Quinn is a common surname and there were many of them in the 1821 census of Forkhill Parish, but no Arthur Quinns to be seen.

A few Quinns settled in the Westport area. The 1848 census of Upper Canada lists Peter Quinn in North Crosby, occupying Lot 17 of Concession 1, and just a few kilometres away in North Burgess Township, Lanark County, were a number of Quinns including Bernard, James and Owen Quinn, all middle-aged Roman Catholic farmers who may have been brothers. Many of these Quinns are buried in the St. Bridget Cemetery in Stanleyville, between Westport and Perth.

As well, there was another Ann Quinn in the area. This was the wife of Owen Kearns. One of her daughters, Bridget Kearns, married Thomas McCoy. Thomas and Bridget McCoy play an important role in this family history at a later date.

Ann was about 56 years old when they emigrated from Forkhill, and her responsibilities as the adult female in the family would have been almost overwhelming. Susannah

Moodie described in some detail how daunting were the tasks faced by pioneer women in the early days of settlement. Moodie's situation was somewhat easier, as she was English and part of a social network that could provide financial or moral support when needed. Her proximity to a large settlement like Peterborough also helped matters somewhat.

Ann Quinn, on the other hand, arrived in an isolated environment with a very different social network around her and very little in the way of a safety net. She had two teenaged daughters at home to help her, but there's no doubt the three of them would have been busy from sunrise to sunset.

Ann would have helped in the fields because it was necessary to do so. She would have gathered ash from the brush fires and overseen the repulsive task of leaching lye from the ashes and combining it with fat and bones saved from meals –no doubt a stinking mess– in a kettle to make soap. There was maple sugar to boil, wool to spin, clothing to make or mend, pork to salt, grain to thresh and grind into flour, and a thousand and one other tasks to perform as part of the challenge to survive from one day to the next through harsh Canadian winters, the likes of which no Irish would have ever seen before.

The lives of pioneer women were far from easy. They were women of fortitude, determined not only to win the fight to survive against the Canadian wilderness but to beat it and prosper, and to help their husband build a better future for their children and grandchildren. For her resolution and perseverance, I'm thankful to Ann Quinn for her Irish spunk and her refusal to quit, because, of course, without her I wouldn't be sitting here writing this book right now in a warm, safe home of my own. Across the generations, I owe her a debt of gratitude.

SOAP-MAKING IN THE EARLY DAYS

Fig. 15 Soap Making

Ann outlived Arthur by 12 years. After his death she continued to live with Michael, even after he moved into the village and established himself as one of the leading tradesmen in Westport. She passed away on August 4, 1864, and was buried alongside Arthur in St. Edward's Cemetery. Her headstone, shared with Arthur, reads:

>Also his wife
>Ann Quinn
>Died
>Aug. 4, 1864.
>Aged 78 years.

Chapter Nine

The Children of Arthur and Ann

Over the course of their marriage, Arthur and Ann had a number of children, and if they are the Carrickasticken couple there were nine born to them who may have remained behind in Ireland in addition to the five we know who immigrated to Canada West in the early 1840s. Who were these five, and what became of them in the New World?

A quick note before we begin. This is the point in our *Brief History* where the information becomes a little more dense. Well, a lot more dense. It's the point where I have to walk a fine line between telling a story about these people who came before us and providing you with as much genealogical information as I can. The only chance I stand, I think, of walking that line between boredom and a decent reference work is to structure the rest of this thing in subsections that organize the data in a consistent and accessible way.

Wish me luck.

Mary McCann

The eldest of Arthur and Ann's children on record here in Canada, Mary McCann was born in Ireland about 1819. Again, as always, the possibility looms before us that she was the second Eleanor recorded in the 1821 Forkhill census as being the two-year-old child of Arthur and Ann McCann of Carrickasticken.

Mary apparently married before she emigrated from Ireland, at least one year before the rest of her family followed. Her husband was Michael McCardle, whose name is variously spelled as *McArdle, McCarel, McCarl* and *McCarrol*. Please forgive me if I toggle back and forth between the first two, depending on how the documents have it.

Michael McCardle was born in Ireland in about 1813. According to O'Hart, the MacArdles were descendants of Colla da Chrioch, along with the McCanns, MacMahons, and others with roots in County Monaghan, as well as one of the "chief clans who possessed Louth."[145] McArdle remains a common name in Armagh, Louth and Down.

It's probable that Michael's parents were John McArdle and Catherine McCann, who lived in the townland of Carriff in 1821.[146] The census records that their son Michael was eight, confirming an 1813 birth year. This McArdle family emigrated from Armagh at some time around 1840, as the register of St. John the Baptist Catholic Church in Perth lists the marriage of their daughter Catherine McArdle to James O'Brian of South Sherbrooke, on May 29, 1841. Five years later, their daughter Ann McArdle married Antoine Cluthier [Cloutier] from North Crosby in 1846. Acting as a witness to this marriage was Michael McCann, likely Catherine's father.

There were a number of other McArdles living in North Burgess and North Crosby at the time, and they may also have been relatives of Michael McCardle.[147]

As mentioned, evidence shows that Mary and Michael likely

emigrated before her parents. The parish records of St. John the Baptist Church in Perth show the following baptismal record for their first child, Anne McCardle:

> On this 7th day of November 1841 I the undersigned Priest of this Parish have baptized at Perth Anne two months old of the Lawful marriage of Michael McArdle & Mary McCann of Burgess. Sponsors James McArdle & Ellen Quinn. M.J. McDonaghey[148]

They were still living in North Burgess in 1843 when their second child, Catherine, was baptized by Father McDonaghey on December 17. But while their third child, Isabella McCardle, was also baptised by this priest in Perth on October 6, 1845, the register records their residence as "Crosby," indicating that they had moved across the line into North Crosby Township.

Michael McArdle is enumerated in the 1848 census of North Crosby while living on Lot 16 of Concession 6, which is on the other side of Mountain Road from where Arthur and Ann were living in Concession 8. A short walk, as it were. He's listed as a labourer, and there are five individuals in the household at this time, three of whom were born in Upper Canada (Ann, Catherine, and Isabella). The agricultural portion of the census shows no production whatsoever and no livestock other than a single pig. It's probable that Michael worked for his father-in-law Arthur at this time.

On July 4, 1848, Mary gave birth to another child, Mary Ann McCardle, who was baptised by Father Foley in North Crosby. The sponsors were Michael Kearns and Betty McCann, Mary's sister. Then on January 24, 1851, Bridget McCardle was born.

She was baptised the next day to parents Michael McCarroll and Mary McCann.

The 1851 census once again provides personal family information, and we can see that Michael McCarel's age is listed as 38, which again conforms to the 1813 birth year, while Mary McCann's age is given as 29, which would suggest an 1822 birth year, about three years away from 1819. Ann is now 11, Catherine is 10, Isabella is seven, Mary Ann is six, and Bridget is two.

Sadly, Ann McCardle was not well. Matthew Connor, the enumerator of the 1851 census, records that she was deaf and dumb. In the column for "Lunatic or Insane" he made a check mark, and he wrote "Lunatic – very helpless."[149]

Mary and Michael continued to grow their family. On October 24, 1853, John McCardle was born. He was baptised the same day by Father Foley. Sponsors were Philip Shevelin and Mary Martin. Eleanor (Ellen) McCarroll was born on May 11, 1856 and baptised the following day, sponsored by Michael Toole and Ann McCarroll.

Moving ahead a decade, when the census of 1861 was conducted, Michael McCardle's age was listed as 48, which again coincided with an 1813 birth year, and Mary McCann's was 42, which is a birth year of about 1819, right where we're looking for it. Ann was 20, and again listed as both "deaf and dumb" and a "lunatic or idiot." Isabella was 16, Mary Ann was 13, Bridget was nine, John was seven, Ellen was four, and a new addition, Michael McCardle, was one.[150]

A decade later, when the next census was conducted in 1871, Mary and Michael had left North Crosby. Where'd they go?

The McArdles Immigrate to the United States

Once the American Civil War ended in 1865, that country began a westward expansion that coincided with successive campaigns by the U.S. Army to remove the Indigenous populations from the Midwest plains.

In Canada, recent settlers who'd been stuck with poor land were bombarded by newspaper advertisements and posters promising fertile land at affordable prices, and many were convinced to pull up stakes once again:

> The immigrant into Canada, confronted with a choice between clearing a farm in a remote region or paying a high price for more desirable land, often preferred to continue his journey to Illinois or Wisconsin. Many native-born Canadians showed the same preference.[151]

On June 1, 1871, Michael McCardle appeared in the Circuit Court of Pierce County, Wisconsin, to declare his intention to become a citizen of the United States.[152]

Eighteen years later, in 1889, he appeared in district court in Pipestone County, Minnesota, and swore the same oath.[153] These declarations would have been necessary in order to apply for patents on land for settlement. On the second document, we see that he signed with an X, confirming the notation in the 1861 census of North Crosby that he was illiterate. He also declares on the Pipestone document that he had originally crossed into the United States through the Port Huron, MI, crossing in July 1856. We know that he was still in North Crosby in 1861, so perhaps this was a scouting expedition, or an aborted attempt to leave home.

In 1874 their daughter Mary Ann married Miles Fleming, a farmer, and in 1880 they were enumerated in the census for Gillford, Wabasha County, Minnesota. We discover that her mother, Mary McCann, is living with the young couple and their three young children. [154]

As for daughter Isabella, who was born in 1845, we must first turn back the clock to 1851, when she was six and living with her family on the Perth Road in North Crosby. Across from them was William Covoyoung, who lived on a farm with his wife, four children, and his younger brother Francis, who was 20 years old. [155]

It's easy to guess that the families were friends. Eventually Isabella married Francis in about 1864, when she was 19 and he was about 33.

They appeared in the North Crosby census of 1871, living at Concession 3, Lot 17, with their two children, Margaret J. (6) and Mary (4). At some point after that, they followed the other McCardles to the United States. Isabella passed away on February 29, 1896, in Emmet County, Michigan, and was buried in Saint Francis Cemetery, Petoskey, Michigan. [156] Just over a month before, Francis had passed away on January 23, and was buried in the same cemetery. [157]

The One Who Remained Behind

Catherine McArdle was Mary's second child, born in North Burgess in 1843. Remembering that her older sister, Ann, had severe disabilities, we can presume that many expectations were placed on Catherine as the next oldest.

We've seen that in 1856 her parents may have travelled to Port Huron, Michigan, to begin the process of immigration to the United States, but they were back in North Crosby before the next census was taken in 1861.

Whatever the dynamic within the family might have been, Catherine set off on her own by marrying James Speagle on February 14, 1860. She would have been about two months past her sixteenth birthday.

The Speagle family was very interesting, and while it's true that mission creep is certainly to be feared in a family history, it behooves us to pay Catherine the respect she is due as Mary McCann's daughter by describing the family into which she married, and the children she raised in North Crosby with her husband James.

The Speagles (sometimes spelled Speigle or Spiegle) were one of the older pioneer families in Lanark County. In the early days of settlement, before 1820, a number of military regiments were disbanded in Upper Canada and the discharged soldiers were given land grants to enable them to settle. Among these military corps was the "De Watteville" Regiment, which consisted of German and Belgian soldiers in Napoleon's *Grand Armee* who had been captured by the British. The remnants of this regiment negotiated their freedom by agreeing to fight for the British in Upper Canada against the Americans in the War of 1812, and once that conflict had ended they were discharged, many of them accepting land grants in North Burgess Township.[158]

Among these was a young German private named Casper Speagle, who had just over three years' service with the regiment when he was granted land on Concession 3, Lot 13

(West) of Bathurst Township, located a few kilometres north of Stanleyville above what is now Christie Lake Road. The son of Johann Spiegle and Catherine Dearing, he received his land on June 11, 1816, and promptly settled down. Nearby were comrades-at-arms such as Jacob Tormiller, who was granted the eastern half of Lot 13 next door to Casper, Joseph Witzal, Soloman Fischer and Ferdinand Brondel, all privates in the De Watteville Regiment. Most of these men did not stay long, but Casper remained, determined to forge a new life with the opportunity that had been given to him.

On April 24, 1824, Casper married Ann Byrnes, the daughter of Henry Byrnes and Elizabeth Nugent, at St. John the Baptist Catholic Church in Perth. Their children included Elizabeth Speagle, James Speagle, and Catherine Speagle.[159]

James Speagle was born on May 27, 1831, so he would have been around the age of 29 when he married the 16-year-old Catherine McCardle. He had established himself as a carpenter, and after their marriage they settled on property on Concession 6, Lot 15, in North Crosby Township, very close to the McCardles, where they lived for the rest of their lives.

Their children included Mary Ann Speagle (born in 1860), Adella Speagle (1861), Laura Speagle (1864), Casper J. Speagle (November 15, 1864), Anna R. Speagle (1865), Elizabeth Speagle (1868), James Speagle Jr. (March 16, 1873), Michael J. Speagle (about 1876), John Speagle (about 1878) and Isabel Speagle (March 21, 1881). With a family of six daughters and four sons, Catherine McCardle found herself at the head of a substantial household.

Their son Casper J. Speagle became a successful carpenter, and he built a prosperous contracting business, specializing in churches and other large projects. He was involved in the construction of 11 churches in eastern Ontario, including Sacred Heart of Jesus Roman Catholic Church in Lanark[160] and St. Philip Neri Catholic Church in Toledo in 1907.[161] He was also responsible for the design and construction of a new three-storey public library in Perth, at the corner of Basin and Gore Streets, which opened its doors in 1907. The project was funded in part by a grant of $10,000 from the Andrew Carnegie Foundation.[162]

He also built many of the homes in Westport, as well, specializing in brick construction. Among his projects were the rectory of St. Edward the Confessor Church, the Knapp residence on Whelan Street, the Wing residence next to the town hall, the residence of Dr. Dwyre, the McNally house at

CASPER J. SPEAGLE
Contractor.

Among the many of Westport's sons who have reached the top of the ladder in their chosen avocation, none perhaps, enjoy a more enviable reputation than Mr. C. J. Speagle, contractor. When quite young, Mr. Speagle learned the carpenter trade, and by his industry and aptness soon became one of the best in the district. Some years ago he branched out into the contracting business on a small scale at first, and by carefulness and superior workmanship gradually obtained the reputation which now makes the name of Speagle stand for everything that is best in the building trade. His specialty is church contracts or other large and similar buildings. He has completed eleven churches in various parts of Eastern Ontario, also the public library at Perth, and the Model School, Athens. His work in this line is his best recommendation. Mr. Speagle is deservedly popular and for several years was an energetic member of Westport's municipal council. In politics he is a staunch Liberal, and in religion he is a consistent member of St. Edward's church.

Fig. 16 Casper J. Speagle

Rideau and Main Streets, the home that he built for himself at 5 Bedford Street and later sold to his brother James, and the house at 36 Spring Street that he built for his second cousin, Arthur F. McCann, as we will see later.

James Speagle died in 1903 at the age of 73, and Catherine McCardle died 26 years later, in 1929, at the age of 85.

Mary Passes Away

Returning to Michael and Mary, it would seem that at some point they went their separate ways, and the trails split between Minnesota and Wisconsin.

Their daughter Bridget McCardle, born in North Crosby in 1851, married a man named Thomas Kinney in Pipestone, Minnesota, and had at least two children there, Aaron Kinney (1887) and Lila Kinney (1891).

Other family members, however, moved on to Wisconsin. Their son William Michael McCardle received a land patent on June 6, 1890, for 165 acres in Bayfield County, Wisconsin, the northernmost county in the state, on the shore of Lake Superior. His wife Maggie Mooney McCardle, whom he'd married in Pipestone on December 26, 1887, received a patent after payment for a further 160 acres in Bayfield County on August 28, 1893.

His sister Julia McCardle, who'd recently married a man named William Davey in nearby Ironwood, Michigan, in August 1893 at the age of 25, joined the fun with another 160 acres carved out of Bayfield County on April 27, 1894. Finally, on March 13, 1895, just over 68 acres were registered to Mary herself. Her residence was listed on this patent as being at

Port Wing, Wisconsin, a small town right on the shore of Lake Superior.

When applying for her patent, Mary was required to complete a document of testimony and an affidavit. For example, she declares that she had resided on the land and cultivated it since September 15, 1878 (perhaps a white lie) and that she immigrated in July 1856, as Michael had also declared. The document confirms that she, too, was illiterate.

Written in the margin of her testimony questionnaire:

> My husband who is still living deserted me and my family many years ago since which time I and my children have been wholly dependent upon ourselves for support and which they are large enough to help me . . . [the rest is illegible]. [163]

Only a year after completing this land transaction, Mary passed away on March 30, 1896. According to her Canadian death certificate, she was 77, the cause of death was "la grippe" or influenza, and she was a widow. Michael McCardle, evidently, had pre-deceased her, perhaps in Minnesota.

Her body was returned to North Crosby and she was buried in St. Edward's Cemetery with her parents. Her inscription on the family headstone reads:

> Mary McCann
> Wife of
> Michael McCardle
> Died
> Mar. 30, 1896
> Aged 77 years.

Roseanna McCann

Roseanna McCann, or Rose, was born in Ireland either in 1825 or 1829. The uncertainty is due to the fact that in 1851 Matthew Connor listed her age at her next birthday at 22, meaning that she would have been born in 1829. However, Agmond Roe recorded an age of 37 for her only 10 years later. As Connor's information seems to be a little less reliable – he made obvious estimates of the ages of older people that could be off by more than 10 years—we should probably assume that Roseanna was born about 1825, making her the second oldest of the known children of Arthur McCann.

Roseanna married Michael Toole, the son of Mark Toole and Mary Kierans or Keeron, on September 8, 1848.[164] Michael was from Carrive townland in Forkhill, and he's present in the 1821 census with his family, living with his 63-year-old grandfather, Patrick Keeron. Mark Toole was 30 at the time and was listed as a weaver, while Mary, 34, was a spinner. Michael's age is listed here as 1, giving him an approximate birth year of 1820.

A brief word on the surname Kierans. It derives from the Irish *ciar*, meaning black. The family name *O Ciaráin* was common in County Mayo and County Donegal. It has appeared over the centuries as Kierans, Kearns, Kearons, Cairns, and so on.[165] All the people whose surnames have been anglicised in one of these ways could be said to have had a common origin, but I don't think we can directly connect Michael Toole's mother's family to the Kearns family we'll look more closely at later.

In 1851 Michael and Roseanna were living on the other half of Lot 17, Concession 8, with Arthur and John McCann, as mentioned earlier. They built a log shanty and cleared six acres for wheat and potatoes, and a pasture for a cow and a pig.

On June 27, 1849, Roseanna gave birth to Peter Toole. The sponsors of Peter's baptism were Roseanna's brother John McCann and her sister Betty. Mary Jane Toole was born May 8, 1851 (sponsored by Laughlan Grant and Anne Kearns); Anne Toole was born on September 4, 1853; Mark Matthew Toole was born in 1855; and little Roseanna Toole was born about 1860.

After 1861 the Toole family left North Crosby. They settled in Buchanan County, Iowa, where Michael passed away on August 27, 1877. He was buried in Saint John's Catholic Cemetery, Independence, Iowa.[166]

Their son Peter, who'd married Alta May Flint, died on May 18, 1915, at the age of 65, and was also buried in Saint Johns Catholic Cemetery in Independence.[167] Their daughter Mary Jane, who'd married a man named Patrick Toomey, died in 1894 and was buried in the same cemetery. Daughter Anne, who'd married Cornelius Toomey (Patrick's brother?), passed away on April 11, 1919, at the age of 65 and was buried in Saint John's as well. Finally, their son Mark Matthew Toole, who'd married a woman named Julia Galvin, died on October 7, 1919, at Sanborn, Iowa, and was buried in the Saint Cecelia Cemetery.

Roseanna passed away on January 10, 1886, at the age of 58. Buried in Independence with the rest of her family, the inscription on the marker she shares with her husband reads:

> Roseanna
> Wife of
> M. Toale
> Died
> Jan. 10, 1886
> Aged
> 58 years.

JOHN MCCANN

John McCann was born around 1826 and would have been about 15 or 16 when he immigrated to Canada with his parents and siblings. He worked with Arthur to clear the land, build the shanty, and plant the crops on their first farm on Concession 2, and no doubt he carried much of the physical burden himself, given his father's age. He would have taken the lead once again when the family moved down to Lot 16 of Concession 8, several years later.

At the age of 22, John married Sarah Coburn on November 28, 1848, in St. John the Baptist Catholic Church in Perth, two months after the wedding of his sister Roseanna to Michael Toole. Also born in Ireland, Sarah was the daughter of Thomas Coburn and Ann Lock. Thomas Coburn was an Irish stone mason born around 1797.

After their marriage, John McCann built a log shanty on Lot 16, establishing his own farm for his new family. The following autumn, on October 19, 1849, John and Sarah proudly watched as their twin sons, Patrick McCann and John McCann Jr., were baptized in St. Edward the Confessor Church in Westport. The sponsors of this double baptism were Mary McCann McCardle and Philip Shavelin, who was the schoolmaster at the church and school on the Parish Road. The twins are not listed in the census of 1851, though; perhaps they didn't survive infancy. [168]

John raised crops on four of the six acres of land cleared around his log shanty. The agricultural portion of the 1851 census tells us he grew wheat on one acre and harvested about 24 bushels, which was good production given that the average among wheat-producing farmers in Ontario (or Canada West, as it was known at that time) was not quite 16 bushels per acre.[169]

He also grew rye on one acre and harvested about 15 bushels, again above the average yield in Canada West, which was 6.5 bushels per acre. Rye was not a very popular crop among farmers at this time. It was considered more appropriate for poor, light land rather than soil better suited for more valuable crops. It was not much used for bread except in areas with a significant German population and was mainly grown "to satisfy the demand of the distilleries."[170]

At this point in history, about 85 per cent of the rye grown in Ontario was produced in the Belleville area and was sold to a distillery in Kingston. In North Crosby Township there were 72 farmers who dabbled in rye, producing a total of 808 bushels (just better than 11 bushels an acre). Only one of these farmers, the Irish Catholic Edward Bulfin, was a serious rye producer, harvesting 100 bushels on five acres, and his crop likely ended up in Kingston as well. As for the others, their rye may have made its way to this distiller or it may have ended up in stills much closer to home.

John dedicated another acre to oats, from which he harvested about 25 bushels (the average for Canada West was 27.6 per acre). Oats were considered a much more important crop than rye, as they were fed to horses and to Scotsmen in areas such as Glengarry County.[171]

Finally, he kept an acre in potatoes and took about 40 bushels from it, which was good production and would have enabled him to sell what the family didn't need for their own consumption. From the other two acres he took about a ton of hay, according to the census, which was a small amount compared to his neighbours. However, John did not keep many animals, limiting himself to two beef cows, a milk cow and two pigs. He had salted 150 lbs. of pork that year. He also made 20 lbs. of maple sugar, a fairly small amount compared to others.[172] (You may recall that his father produced 70 lbs. that year.)

In all, John was clearly a hard-working and rising farmer for a young man in his mid-twenties just starting to make his own way in the world. He seems to have made a decision to concentrate first on establishing and cultivating cash crops before devoting very much time to animal husbandry. He no doubt planned to clear other acreage later for pasture.

Meanwhile, his family was growing. On May 28, 1851, Mary McCann was baptized, witnessed by John Grant and Aunt Betty McCann. On August 14, 1853, the family grew again with the addition of Michael McCann, whose baptism was sponsored by his grandfather Thomas Coburn and by Rory Grant.

In the following year, however, disaster struck. On February 6, 1854, John McCann died at the age of 28, two years after the passing of his father, Arthur. The cause of his death at such a young age is not known, whether it was through a farming accident or from illness.

Six years later Sarah remarried, on January 30, 1860, to Stephen McElevay, age 40, born in Ireland and residing in Perth, the son of John McElevay and Mary McNeil. The marriage was conducted by Father Foley in North Crosby. McElavey was a stone mason in Westport who likely worked with Thomas Coburn.[173] Stephen and Sarah moved away from Westport between 1866 and 1871, as they were not included in the census of 1871 for North Crosby or Westport.

John was buried in St. Edward's Cemetery next to his father.

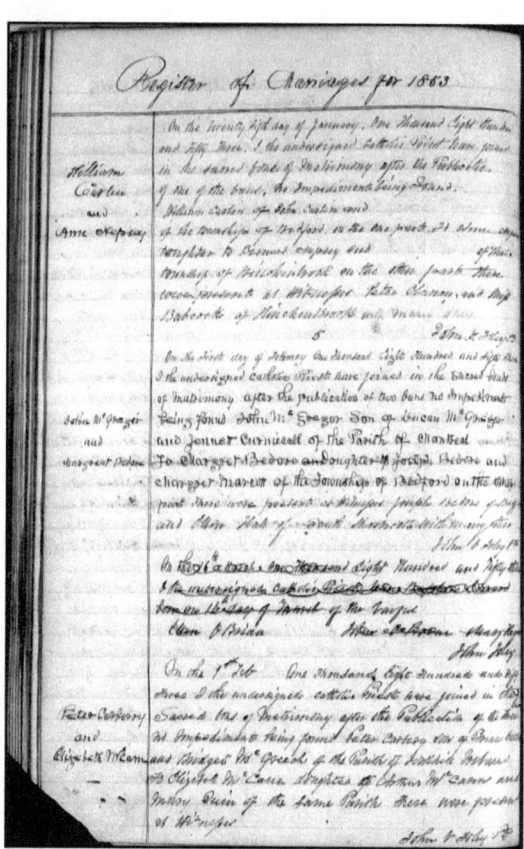

Fig. 17 The Marriage of Elizabeth McCann

Elizabeth (Betty) McCann

Elizabeth McCann was a young girl of about thirteen years of age when she accompanied her parents and brothers and sisters in the long voyage from Ireland to Upper Canada. Born about 1828, Betty, as she was known (or sometimes Betsy), is recorded by Matthew Connor in the 1851 census as being 17 years old on her next birthday, but this would not be correct. She would have actually been about 22. She was about 23 years old when her father died in March of 1852.

On February 1, 1853, she married Peter Carberry, the son of Brian Carberry and Bridget McGreech of Forkhill parish, Armagh. As we've noted earlier, the entry in the St. Edward's register recording Betty's marriage identified Arthur and Ann as having emigrated from Forkhill as well (see Fig. 17).

On April 18, 1854, Betty gave birth to Bernard Carberry. His baptism at St. Edward's church was sponsored by Betty's brother Michael J. McCann and her sister, Mary McCardle. Bernard became a carpenter and immigrated to the United States. He died on June 9, 1905, at the age of 51 in Hartford, Connecticut and was buried there in the Mount Saint Benedict Cemetery.[174]

On February 20, 1856, Peter Carberry Jr. was baptised at St. Edward's church. His sponsors were Michael and Bridget Kearns.

In 1861, Bridget Henrietta Carberry was born. She married a man named Francis A. Quinn and passed away on January 25, 1893, at about the age of 32. She's buried in Saint John's Catholic Cemetery in Gananoque, Ontario.[175]

On March 26, 1863, Betty gave birth to John Joseph Carberry. John became a painter, and he lived in Brockville for 33 years. He passed away from Bright's Disease, also known as nephritis (chronic kidney inflammation), on February 12, 1924, at the age of 60.

On November 9, 1864, Francis H. Carberry was born. Elizabeth is referred to as "Betsy" in the baptismal record. Sponsors were James Speagle and Michael McCann. Francis immigrated to the United States later in life, where he married Sarah Kingston in Hancock, Houghton County, Michigan, on March 13, 1895. His age on the marriage register is listed at 24, but he would have actually been around 30. His bride's age is given as 19.

On January 25, 1870, Betty's husband Peter Carberry passed away. He was buried in St. Edward's cemetery. Her brother Michael J. McCann was present with her at Peter's graveside.

She continued to live in the village after his death, with Bernard, who was 17 in 1871; John, 15; Bridget, 13; and Francis (Frank), who was 11.

Betty passed away on April 30, 1877, after a 15-day battle with asthma. Bernard soon married and was working as a cabinet maker. The 1881 census tells us that he and his wife had a son, Wilford Carberry, born about 1880, and Bernard's brother Francis, 16 at the time of enumeration, was living with them.

Elizabeth was interred in St. Edward's cemetery, and her inscription on the family headstone reads:

> Also Elizabeth McCann
> Died
> April 30, 1877.

Michael J. McCann

The youngest of the children who accompanied Arthur and Ann when they emigrated from Ireland was Michael J. McCann. Michael J. was born in September 1830, and was about twelve years old when he made the voyage with his parents to Upper Canada. As it is from him that my family descended, we'll devote the next chapter to him.

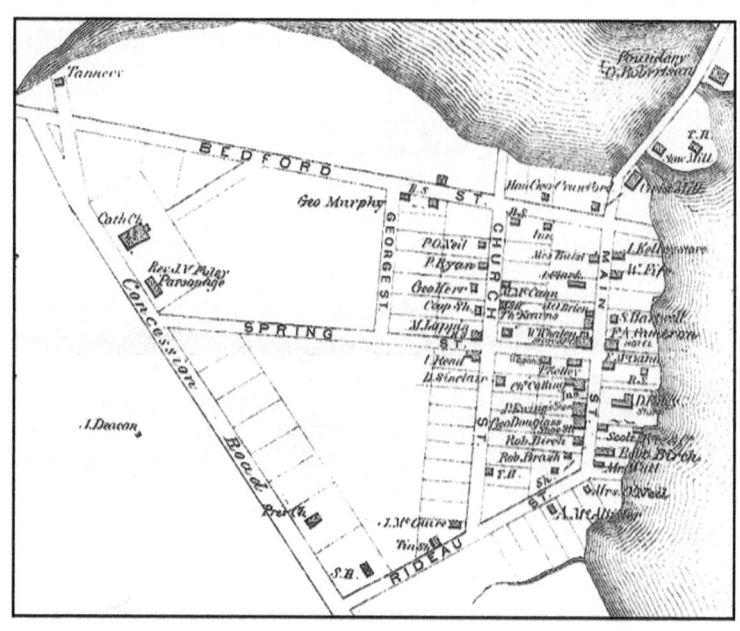

Fig. 18 Early Map of Westport

PART THREE
WESTPORT

Fig. 19 Michael J. McCann, ca. 1850

Chapter Ten

Michael J. McCann and Anne Kearns

When Arthur McCann passed away in 1852, his son John was married and raising a family on an adjacent farm, and so it fell to the youngest, Michael Joseph, 22 years old, to assume responsibility for his father's household.

His mother, Ann Quinn, was about 66 years old. His sisters Mary and Roseanna had already married and moved out, but Betty was still at home, not to marry until the following year. Also in the household was the mysterious Ann, whom we surmise was the unrelated person recorded four years ago in the 1848 census, as we've mentioned before.

Michael's date of birth was September 29, 1830, in Armagh, Ireland.[176] As the youngest, he no doubt did his best to assist his father and brother as they cleared the land and established two separate homesteads, but I suspect he didn't enjoy the lifestyle very much. Once his father passed away, Michael soon took steps to divest himself of the property and to follow his own chosen career path down in the village of Westport.

The Shoemaker

One wonders how the family would have turned out had Michael J. remained on the farm. Many farming families in North Crosby Township passed on the agrarian way of life

Fig. 20 The Apprentice Shoemaker

through several generations down into the twentieth century, and had Michael J. chosen to follow in his father's footsteps, subsequent generations would have had a much different upbringing.

Records indicate that he assumed responsibility for Arthur's portion of Lot 17 after his father's death. Assessment rolls for 1856 show that he paid tax on 50 acres, and the Clergy Reserve Sales Register records that he completed the purchase of the property in 1858.

However, Michael decided at some point during the 1850s that he was not meant to be a farmer. He was a small man, and he may not have had the physical strength and stamina to endure the endless hard work of clearing land, planting and harvesting crops, building fences, chasing cattle and snappy landpikes, and all the other labour-intensive, physically demanding tasks involved in operating a farm. He did, however, have large hands with thick, strong fingers that made him well-suited for a skilled trade. It is not surprising, then, that in the late 1850s he became an apprentice to learn the shoemaker's trade.

In 1851 there were a number of shoemakers at work in North Crosby. Very near the original McCann homestead, up close to the border of North Burgess Township, was a 31-year-old Catholic shoemaker named John Smith who likely functioned as an itinerant shoemaker,[177] meaning that he would travel from farm to farm to make shoes for the families in his area. He would carry with him a selection of tools including a shoemaker's hammer with a wide flat head and elongated claw, an assortment of knives for cutting and trimming the leather, heavy needles and thread, awls for punching holes in the leather, and shoe nails. In addition he would carry wooden shoe forms, called lasts, around which a shoe would be made. He might have only a small assortment of lasts with him, small ones for children and larger ones for adults, and after taking each family member's measurements he would tack small scraps of leather onto the last to accommodate different sized feet. John Smith may have paid Arthur McCann a visit when the family lived on the next lot over and left a lasting impression on young Michael.

At that time, there were several other shoemakers, including Edward Kenney, a 34-year-old Catholic, and F.A. Cameron, a 39-year-old Methodist who soon afterwards changed careers and operated the Westport Stage House Hotel and livery stable at the corner of Main and Spring Streets. Additionally, two sons of the tanner Stephen McEathron, James and Daniel, were putting their father's product to good use as shoemakers.

Michael likely apprenticed with either John Smith or Edward Kenney. It was the nature of nineteenth-century Ontario that Protestants and Catholics tended to look after their own (the Orange Order played a large role in assisting Protestants to establish themselves in business or in a trade, for example),[178] and it's probable that Michael would have been accepted as an apprentice by either of these two Catholic tradesmen.

Most probably he was taken on by Edward Kenney in town, which meant that he left the farm behind and moved to Westport. The timing of this move is not certain. Although he continued to pay for Lot 17 and ultimately purchased it in 1858, as mentioned, this doesn't necessarily mean that he and his family continued to reside there. We can only say that he had moved to Westport before 1861.

With a young wife and five young children, Michael now

had a family of his own to feed, clothe and house. He must have perceived that the farm was not going to permit him to raise his family with a quality of life that was acceptable to him. Perhaps he also realized that he did not have the interest in or aptitude for farming that his older brother John had had. Whatever his motivations, Michael J. made his decision and quickly established himself as a shoemaker whose products and services were soon in demand in Westport.

In 1861, he was one of five shoemakers in North Crosby. In the village, F.A. Cameron had already traded leather for hotel rooms while George Douglass, an Anglican, had appeared on the scene to take his place. Other Catholic shoemakers in town besides Michael J. were John O'Brien and James Kelly.

Michael lived and worked in a building on Lot 4 of Church Street East next door to Thomas Kearns the Protestant furniture maker and across the street from George Kerr, the cooper. He employed three men and a woman, and he produced $400 worth of boots and shoes a year. For the sake of comparison, John O'Brien produced $300 worth of product and James Kelly $200, while George Douglass led the community by selling $600 worth of shoes and boots to his largely Protestant clientele.

At the back of Michael's building, as was common at the time, there was a stable and pig stye where he kept a horse, three pigs, and a cow. There was also room in the stable to keep his pleasure carriage, to which he hitched the horse when travelling around. The carriage was valued at $50.

The shop occupied the ground floor of the building, and above it were living quarters for his growing family. In 1861 he was already a proud father of five children, including Arthur F., who would soon be eight; John A., seven; Mary, five; Patrick, three; and the baby, Anastasia. In addition, his mother Ann Quinn lived with him, along with a boarder, James Murphy, a 28-year-old bachelor who must have been Michael's employee.

One oddity in the 1861 census is that his household also lists "Elizabeth McCann," a 30-year-old single woman. We know that Elizabeth married Peter Carberry in 1853, and they had their own home, so this entry is an anomaly that has yet to be explained. Our best theory is that Elizabeth was visiting when the enumerator arrived, she got swept up in the count, and was mistakenly identified as single.

The 1860s were prosperous years for Michael. By the time the census was taken again in 1871, he'd become the leading shoemaker in the township. There were six shoemakers altogether in North Crosby. Two, Robert Bell and Henry Bolton, were both in Newboro village and the other four, George Douglass, Alexander McAllister, Patrick Murphy and Michael J., were in Westport. The days of the itinerant shoemaker would seem to have ended, and it's probable that by 1871 people came into town to get their shoes. When they did, they apparently preferred to buy them from Michael J.

Statistics for the four Westport shoemakers tell an interesting story:

Name	Fx Cap	Flo Cap	Emp	Wages	Raw Materials		Product	
					Quant	Val	Quant	Val
McCann	100	1000	2	400	180 sides	$750	360 pairs	$2,000
Douglass	200	600	2	600	150 sides	$750	470 pairs	$1,172
McAllister	200	100	1	300	30 sides	$300	250 pairs	$1,000
Murphy	n/a	100	1	313	30 sides	$300	313 pairs	$939

In the last ten years Michael had reduced his employees to two men, paying $400 in wages a year. George Douglass was the only other shoemaker to have two employees, and he was somewhat more generous, paying $600 in wages. Michael produced almost double the value of footwear to Douglass, although his volume was lower. Apparently Michael charged more for his goods, an average of $5.55 a pair compared to $2.49 for a pair of Douglass offerings. McAllister averaged $4.00 a pair and Murphy $3.00.

Quality of material may not have made a difference in price, as Michael used leather worth $4.17 a side while Douglass paid $5.00 a side for his material, and McAllister and Murphy paid a whopping $10.00 a side. The local supplier of leather was Matthew Scott, who had replaced Stephen McEathron in the tannery on the other side of Bedford Street. Scott was doing very well for himself, and his inventory included 600 hides worth $2,000 ($3.33 per hide). Either Michael had negotiated a better price for himself with Scott than the others based on a higher volume, or his competitors were importing more expensive leather from outside the township. Either way, Michael was the most successful at keeping his overhead low. The difference in price must have been a result of quality of workmanship. To generate the amount of business that he did with prices higher than his business rivals, his boots and shoes would have had a reputation for quality, style and durability beyond the competition.

The story of Michael's productivity in 1871 does not end there, however. Unbelievably, the family managed to grow 50 bushels of potatoes on their quarter-acre property. They no longer had a horse but they still owned a pig and a cow for milk and 100 lbs. worth of butter. On top of this, they had added 10 sheep from which they not only took mutton but 30 lbs. of wool to make 30 yards of material. It would seem that the agrarian way had not entirely been left behind.

By comparison, their next-door neighbour Thomas Kearns the Protestant furniture-maker was growing potatoes on a half-acre lot but only harvested 20 bushels. He produced the same amount of butter from two milking cows that the McCanns did with one, and he preferred to do without the swine and sheep, keeping a horse instead. While having a horse and milch cow in the village was as common then as having a large dog is today, it would seem that the McCann family felt quite comfortable stretching the agricultural productivity of their village lot to the maximum. Michael had been born and raised a farmer's son, and while his children were town-dwellers from birth they obviously were not going to reach adulthood without knowing something about agrarian self-sufficiency.

The family continued to grow as well during that decade. The 1871 census records that after Anastasia was born, Cecelia McCann followed in 1862, Thomas J. McCann (T.J.) in 1864, and Michael McCann Jr. in 1866. Michael died in 1869 and the next child, born in the same year, was also named Michael Jr. Rose McCann followed in 1871, not long after the census was taken.

Absent from the count that year was Michael's mother, Ann Quinn, as she'd passed away in 1864. Also absent, when compared to 1861, was Betty, who was now head of her own household after the death of her husband, Peter Carberry, in 1870.

As the 1870s progressed, the family prospered. Michael's oldest child, Arthur F. McCann, married Margaret Leonard. As we'll see below, Michael and Anne were blessed with the arrival of three grandchildren during the decade.

Their second son, John A. McCann, also married during this time, to Margaret Ann O'Brien, the daughter of John O'Brien. Two more grandchildren arrived.

They were not finished with parenthood themselves, as Anne gave birth to another son, William Edward McCann, on February 6, 1874, two months before she turned 40, and a daughter, Margaret Jewel McCann, on New Year's Day, 1877.

Sadly, Anne Kearns passed away on September 12, 1878, and Michael was left with a house full of children that must have seen strangely empty without his friend and partner of more than 25 years. He found solace in family, friends and the church to which he was faithful.

Michael was tested again in 1880. His daughter Anastasia passed away from tuberculosis at the age of 20. The oldest girl in the house at the time, she must have carried much of the load when it came to looking after the younger children while her father continued his business as the town's most prominent shoemaker.

As it happened, Michael had become close to another strongly devout parishioner, Bridget Donnelly, the daughter of Arthur Donnelly and Anne Kelly. Five months after Anastasia's death, and two years after Anne passed away, he married Bridget in September 1880, just before his 50th birthday.

They soon began a family of their own, as Bridget gave birth to Anna Bernadetta McCann a month before her stepson Patrick's wedding. Teresa Elizabeth followed in 1884 and Anastasia Magdeline, perhaps named for the late Anastasia, in 1888.

Michael's business sense remained keen. As the 1880s

progressed and Michael passed into his fifties, he looked for other opportunities to expand from his shoe business and ultimately found one with the family of his former friend and rival shoemaker, John O'Brien. O'Brien had died in 1862, leaving his wife and family behind in the shop and home on Main Street, just in back of Thomas Kearns' property next door to Michael.

In 1871 his widow Mary O'Brien was still living there with her three children, Margaret Anne, Edward and John. A few years later, Michael's son John A. married Margaret Anne. The families remained close over the years, although the O'Briens apparently left Westport before 1881, perhaps to move to Ottawa where John and Margaret Anne were living. Ultimately when it came time for the O'Briens to sell the property on Main Street, Michael presented them with an offer that John O'Brien Jr. accepted on behalf of the family. On September 30, 1887, Michael purchased the property for $140.

Two years later, the *Perth Courier* reported that "James Broskin of Iroquois has rented M.J. McCann's new building on Main Street for groceries."[179] Although Broskin himself does not seem to have ever established himself in Westport, Michael apparently had a profitable supplement to his income.

It would seem that the family operated the store themselves, in fact. The *Eastern Ontario Gazetteer 1898-99*, the next best thing to a telephone book at the turn of the previous century, not only lists "McCann MJ, shoemaker" for Westport but also "McCann MJ Mrs, grocery." And as late as the 1901 census, taken when he was 70, he was still listed as a shoemaker.

By this time, his first family had all moved on with their lives, and he and Bridget lived in what would have been a much quieter household with their three daughters. Anna would be approaching her 19th birthday, while Teresa would be 16 and Anastasia 12.

Arthur F. had passed away, John A. was living in Ottawa, and Mary, Rose and Margaret had all married and moved away, but William was living on Spring Street and working as the church sexton, Michael Jr. was living with his wife and mother-in-law on Bedford Street, and Patrick was conducting a successful business as a house painter and decorator while raising his family in the house on George Street that he had built almost 20 years before.

The village had changed around him, the empty lots being filled with new buildings as the years passed. The faces and names were much different, as well. A comparison of the censuses of 1871 and 1901 shows that the population of North Crosby Township as a whole had actually dropped slightly, from 2,176 to 2,030, as the gradual ebbing of the lumber boom and migration to the West had combined to slow the township's growth over the years.

The demographic makeup of the township had shifted, as well. In 1871, 46 per cent of the population of North Crosby were Roman Catholic, and 41 per cent were Irish Catholics. Indeed, 13 per cent of the township were Irish Catholics who had been born in Ireland. By 1901, however, only 37 per cent were Catholics, 34 per cent were Irish Catholics, and just under 3 per cent were Irish Catholics born in Ireland, a drop of 10 percentage points. As Michael looked around, he saw that the number of Irishmen like himself had dwindled from 274 to only 58 in a space of three decades.

Canada was changing and North Crosby, that had once

resembled a home away from home for so many Irish, was changing with it. And yet, if he wanted to hear the sounds of home, he needed only to leave his shop and walk a block over to George Street, walk past Patrick's house and continue on down the street to 16 George Street where, taking a cup of tea in the kitchen of Henry and Mary Bennett, Irish-born Catholics who were also still getting used to the idea of being in their 70s, he could hear once more the sweet sounds of the Irish language.

Henry and Mary were those extreme rare birds, Irish who still spoke Irish as their mother tongue. Indeed, the 1901 census of Ireland itself showed that only 14.4 per cent of the population could still speak Irish, down from 15.1 per cent in 1871. Having emigrated from Ireland as a 12-year-old boy with his family in 1844, Henry and his family farmed on Lots 18 and 17 of Concession 2, at the end of Kelly Road not far from the farm of Michael Kearns. Henry's father had died in 1850 at the age of 60 from tuberculosis and it had fallen on Henry, then just 21, to run the farm for his mother Mary Bennett along with his younger brothers Michael, Peter and Patrick Bennett. Now living a life of quiet retirement in the village in 1901, Henry could share a common past with the elderly shoemaker Michael J. McCann, who was the last surviving member of his own family born in Ireland.

Tragedy struck in 1907 when Michael J.'s son Patrick died. By the next year, he himself had taken ill. It probably started as a small malady that he attributed to old age, but over the course of the next two years the tumor that had started to grow in him gradually asserted itself until it took his life on December 16, 1910, at the age of 80. His physician, Dr. A.B. Singleton, had visited him the day before and no doubt could offer nothing more than comfort and the advice that the priest, Father Michael O'Rourke, should be summoned.

Michael was buried in St. Edward's Cemetery with his parents, his brother John and his sisters Betty and Mary, not far from the gravesite of Anne Kearns. On the marker just below the inscription for Mary was engraved the following:

>Michael J. McCann
>Died
>Dec. 16, 1910
>Aged 81 years
>A Faithful husband
>And a loving father.

Anne Kearns

If I could have had one wish come true during the long decades of researching this *Brief History*, it would have been to have found the marriage record of Michael J. McCann and Anne Kearns. Unfortunately, the register for St. Edward's church in Westport was damaged at some point, and it looks as though the page where it would have been written down was torn out. Other possible sources of this record have also come up empty.

If I had one other wish that could have come true, it would have been to come across a photograph of Anne Kearns. If Ann Quinn was the pioneer woman who ensured our family's survival in the barren landscape of North Crosby, then Anne Kearns was the matriarch of our Westport McCanns, the mother of 12 children and grandmother of many. I'm so very curious to see what she looked like and what traits would have passed down through the generations from her.

Assembling information on the Kearns family for analysis in our *Brief History* has proven to be a challenge. Data is spotty and inconsistent in the censuses, for example. Another challenge, predictably, comes in the spelling of the family name, which ranges from Karnes to Kierns to Kerns to Kearney to Cairns to Kearns. Also misleading was the presence of a Kearns family in Westport we've already encountered next door to Michael J. McCann on Church Street—Thomas Kearns, the Protestant furniture maker, and his sons and daughters.

Nevertheless, a few things become clear. There were several Kearns men who settled in the township that were all of the same generation, having been born within a few years on either side of 1800, and also a number of Kearns men and women who followed after. Here's what I've been able to find.

Owen Kearns

Owen Kearns, who was born in County Louth, Ireland, about 1787, was a farmer who died at Westport on September 17, 1868, at the age of 81. His farm was located on Lot 20 of Concession 2, which was far up on the Mountain at Perth Road North and Byrnes Road, just the other side of the highway from Arthur's original homestead.

In the 1851 census, enumerated as Owen Kains, he was listed as being 64 years old, but he must have been older. His wife, the other Ann Quinn, was listed as being 40. Also in the household were their daughter Bridget Kearns, 14, and another Ann Kearns, age 45. Everyone was born in Ireland, and their house was listed as a log shanty.

Owen occupied 65 acres, 12 of which he had under crops

including wheat, oats, buckwheat, hay and potatoes, and 16 were in use as pasture for his sheep.

Elsewhere in the 1851 census, a 24-year-old Peter Kearns was working a farm on Concession 9, Lot 17, along with his wife Mary, 34, and his son John, 5. He was next door to Arthur McCann and in the cluster of families including John McCann and Sarah Coburn, Thomas McCann and Bridget Kelly/Keily, and Michael Toole and Roseanne McCann.

Since the unknown Ann in Arthur McCann's household was probably Anne Kearns, Michael J.'s future spouse, it's quite possible that Peter was her older brother and that they were both children of Owen Kearns and Ann Quinn. A theory that holds some water, since Owen lived right across the road from Arthur's original homestead on lot 22 of Concession 2, as already mentioned. Peter and Anne would have had plenty of opportunity to get to know the McCann family before they moved.

Records at St. John the Baptist Church in Perth show that their son, Thomas Kearns, was born August 22, 1843, and was baptized on November 18.

Owen Kearns died in 1868 and was interred that September 18 in St. Edward's cemetery in the presence of his widow, Ann Quinn, and Michael Kearns.

Ann Quinn Kearns lived to the age of 94, when she died on October 10, 1898. Before her death, we see in the 1891 census she was living with James Ryan and his wife Mary McCann, the daughter of Michael J. McCann. Their next-door neighbours were her son-in-law Thomas McCoy and her daughter, Bridget Kearns.

When she passed away, her death record indicates she was

living on George Street in Westport, on Lot 2. This would be just down the street from where Patrick McCann later built his house, the house where Ford McCann was born and where my father also entered this world.

Bernard Kearns

Another member of this generation would have been Bernard Kearns, who appears in the St. Edward's church register as having been interred on April 13, 1877, at the age of 84, in the presence of Michael Kearns. He would have been born in 1793, if the numbers are correct. Perhaps he was a younger brother of Owen.

William Kearns

According to the Land Copy Book for North Crosby, Concession 1, Lot 19, at the end of Byrnes Road behind Owen Kearns, was Crown Reserve land that was granted to the surveyor Adiel Sherwood in 1808. Sherwood sold it to a man named William Kearns in March, 1832. Nearly 30 years later, William Kearns sold it to Michael Kearns in September 1861.

No other records have been currently found for this William Kearns, whose arrival in the area some time before 1832 must have predated almost everyone else we've looked at in this family history.

Patrick Kearns

The census of 1848 also reveals a Patrick Cairns living on Lot 17 of Concession 7, which is down the far end of Parish Road and across Mountain Road, now County Road 36 to Bolingbroke. There were six in this household, all Catholics, including five born in Ireland and one in Upper Canada. Patrick Kearns would have been the single male over 60; most likely he was a widower. Also with him were a boy 18 to 21, a boy 14 to 18, a boy and a girl between 5 and 14, and a boy under 5 years of age. He occupied all 200 acres of this lot, and farmed according to the local pattern with a few acres of wheat, oats, rye and potatoes.

This is the only solid record we have for Patrick, who would have been of the same generation as Owen and Bernard, if we can trust the 1848 census and assume that the male over 60 years of age in this household is Patrick.

Michael Kearns

The name Michael Kearns appears frequently in various records of the period. Apparently there were three men in the area, but none of them appears with enough regularity from decade to decade for us to differentiate between them.

The 1848 census includes Michael Kearns on Lot 21 of Concession 2, right between Arthur McCann's former residence (Lot 22) and that of Owen Kearns (20). The enumerator has listed one married male aged 60 or over and one single female over 45, two single males 40 to 59, and a married female between 14 and 44 with small children.

The enumerator usually listed the eldest person as the head of the household, from which we might infer that this Michael Kearns was age 60 or older, meaning he was born somewhere in the late 1780s. A contemporary of Owen Kearns and Arthur McCann, then.

The question arises, though—were there *two* elderly Michael Kearnses?

One was born in Ireland around 1802. The St. Edward's

registry records his interment on March 16, 1891 at the age of 89. Present at his burial was the aforementioned James Ryan.[180]

Another was the late husband of Mary Kearns, who passed away in 1875 at the age of 70; predeceased by her late husband Michael Kearns. Sixteen years before the other Michael was interred.

Michael Kearns was an active churchgoer and a frequent sponsor of baptisms. For example, he stepped forward when Mary Ann McCardle, daughter of Michael McCardle and Mary McCann, was baptized in 1848. Likewise when Betsy McCann and Peter Carberry's son Peter was baptized in 1856, and when Matthew McCoy, son of Thomas McCoy and Bridget Kearns (daughter of Owen Kearns and the other Ann Quinn), was baptized in 1866. Not to mention many others for couples not related to our family.

Was it the same Michael Kearns every time, or different men? Impossible to tell.

One other Michael Kearns turns up in the records who bears mention. A resident of North Burgess Township, he was born in Ireland in 1832 to John Kearns and Mary Larkin of County Armagh, making him a contemporary of Michael J. McCann. On November 26, 1850, he married Susan McCracken, daughter of Michael McCracken and Ellen Needham, at St. John's church in Perth. After appearing in the 1871 census for North Burgess, listed with their nine children, Michael and Susan immigrated to the United States in 1878, settling in Walsh County, North Dakota.

It's said they hosted masses and other church events in their log cabin until St. Patrick's Church was built in Minto. (The church was deconsecrated in 1959, and the building was hauled off to nearby Lankin for use as a reception hall. [181] Yes, yes, mission creep.)

Whether this Michael Kearns and his father John were connected in any way to Anne Kearns is unknown.

In fact, without the precious marriage record of Michael J. McCann and Anne Kearns in 1851 or 1852, we will never know for sure which one was Anne's father.

Anne the Matriarch

Anne Kearns was born in May 1834 in Ireland. She was illiterate, but all of her children attended school and learned to read and write.[182] An accomplishment, to be sure.

On January 10, 1853, her first child, Arthur F. McCann, was born. Sponsors of the baptism were Michael's sister Mary and her brother-in-law Michael McCardle. The rest of her family followed, in order:

- John A. McCann, born August 26, 1854;
- Mary McCann Ryan, born March 22, 1856;
- Patrick McCann, born January 10, 1858;
- Anastasia McCann, born January 20, 1860;
- Cecilia McCann, born January 10, 1862;
- Thomas J. McCann, born April 19, 1864;
- Michael McCann, born August 14, 1866;
- Michael McCann the second, born June 4, 1869;
- Rose McCann Leahy, born December 1, 1871;
- William E. McCann, born February 6, 1874; and,
- Margaret Jewel McCann, born January 1, 1877.

These children all have their separate biographical sections below.

After giving birth to 11 sons and daughters, Anne passed away on September 12, 1878.

She was buried in St. Edward's Cemetery. Her headstone reads:

> Pray for
> The soul of
> Ann Kearns
> Wife of
> Michael McCann
> Westport.
> Died Sept. 12, 1878
> Aged 44 yrs
> & 5 Mo's
>
> May her soul rest in Peace.
> Amen.

In death's cold arms lies sleeping here
A tender parent, a companion dear:
In love she lived, in peace she died,
Her life was asked, but was denied.

Chapter Eleven

The Children of Michael J. and Anne

Arthur F. McCann

Arthur F. McCann was the oldest child of Michael and Anne, born on January 10, 1853. His baptism was sponsored by his Aunt Mary and Uncle Michael McCardle. In keeping with Irish tradition, Michael named his first-born son after his father.

The Ontario census for 1871 tells us that Arthur, who would be 18 on his next birthday, had finished school and was working as a raftsman. This job would have seen him in the middle of the thriving lumber and logging business that had fuelled the growth of Westport for several decades. Several years later he married Margaret Leonard and they had a daughter, Ida Maud, who was born on March 17, 1874. Soon after came a son, Michael John, who was born on August 5, 1875, and another daughter, Annie, who was born about 1879.

Also born to Arthur and Margaret was a daughter, Matilda. Unfortunately she died as a young girl and was buried on August 17, 1879 at the age of five. Another daughter, Caroline, died on March 14, 1883, at the age of 12 months.

In 1887 Arthur and Margaret were building a house in Westport. The *Perth Courier* noted in their April 15, 1887, issue that it was being finished by "Mr. Speagle." Arthur had no doubt kept the business in the family by hiring his cousin Catherine McCardle's husband, James Speagle, or their son Casper J., who would have been 22 at the time and just embarking on his contracting career, the 11 churches and other assorted monuments to posterity still in his future. The *Courier* dutifully followed up on September 7, 1888, reporting that "Arthur McCann will shortly move to a new home on Spring Street."

Even more interesting is the news in the September 21, 1888, issue announcing that "Messrs. J.H. Whelan and A.F. McCann of Westport have started a covered stage line between that village and the Kingston and Pembroke Railway to connect daily with the Rideau Canal Steamer and Brockville and Westport Railway, fast time, promised."

John H. Whelan was a local Westport merchant who was born in 1843 and who died January 5, 1906. His father was Walter Whelan, the long-time postmaster, merchant and township clerk who was born in 1801 in County Wicklow, Ireland, and died in 1868. J.H. was himself very prominent in the village, and served as Reeve in 1872 to 1875 and again in 1879.

Arthur F. must have found that his father's entrepreneurial spirit had rubbed off on him, and it would be very interesting to know how the venture would have fared. Transportation must have been a particular interest for Arthur, beginning with his early experiences on the Rideau Canal system as a raftsman. He must have convinced Whelan, who was 10 years older, to finance his idea as a partner.

Unfortunately, Arthur F. died on April 28, 1890 at the age of 37, only two years after this project was begun. Margaret Leonard survived him by 20 years and died in 1910.

His tombstone reads:

> Arthur F. McCann
> d. Apr. 28, 1890
> Margaret McCann
> His wife
> d. July 19, 1910
> also their children
> Maud & Caroline
> Anne McCann
> Died Apr. 30, 1959
> Requiescat in pace

Fig. 21 The Raftsman

Fig. 22 John A. McCann and family

JOHN A. MCCANN

John Augustine McCann was born on August 26, 1854, and may have been named after his Uncle John, who had died the same year. His baptism on September 3 of that year was sponsored by George Coburn, the brother of his Aunt Sarah, John's widow.

As described earlier, the McCann family would have been quite familiar with the O'Brien family who lived behind them on Main Street. Although they would have been business rivals in the early days of Michael's career, Michael and John O'Brien may have shared a friendship that extended to his widow and children after John's death in 1862. Young John A. was eight at the time, and he may have only been peripherally aware of Margaret Anne, John's daughter, who was about five when her father died.

Despite a difference in age of three years, they became friends. So much so, that they married on June 13, 1875, when John A. was 20. John's younger brother Patrick proudly stood as a witness alongside Ellen Kelly, daughter of Peter Kelly the carriage maker, who lived around the corner at Main and Spring Streets and perhaps was Margaret O'Brien's best friend.

As a boy, John A. would have done well at school. Well enough, in fact, that he decided to become a teacher after graduation. By 1881 he was teaching in the separate school in Westport, and may have secured a position the following year in Pembroke. An item in the July 21, 1882, issue of the *Perth Courier* noted that "Mr. John A. McCann, late teacher in the Pembroke Separate School and Mr. William A. Smith, teacher, North Burgess, have recently graduated at the Ottawa Normal

School." Normal school being the term used for a teachers' college.

It would seem that his career took him at that point to Ottawa on a permanent basis. By then he and Margaret Anne had a daughter, Mary Gertrude, born June 2, 1877, and a son, John E. McCann, born on April 17, 1882.

Sadly, tragedy visited this family only three years later. Margaret Anne passed away on April 16, 1885, in Ottawa while giving birth to a son, Arthur McCann. She was only 28 years old. Unfortunately, the infant was not healthy after his birth, and must have been left in the family's care back home after Margaret Anne's funeral. Only three months later in Westport, on August 19, 1885, little Arthur also passed away.[183]

John A. carried on with his career in Ottawa. In 1888 he had risen from teaching to become the inspector of English classes for the Ottawa Separate School Board. He was living at 13 Nepean Street in downtown Ottawa at that time. However, he left that position in 1890 and joined the federal public service. He was appointed to the position of 3rd Class Clerk with the Department of Militia and Defence, now known as the Department of National Defence, on July 1, 1890. He remained in this position for a number of years, and by 1900 was earning a salary of $1,000 a year as one of only five such clerks in the Ministry. Only one other 3rd Class Clerk, William Davidson, was making an equivalent salary with four years' seniority over John, and another of their colleagues, Charles Panet, was making $150 less although he had six months' seniority over John.[184]

John A. eventually remarried. His second wife was Catherine Walsh, the daughter of William Walsh and Anne Tolty, and they were married on June 17 1891, in Ottawa They would have three children together, Catherine Constance Margaret McCann, called Margaret, born on January 5, 1893; Edith May Christina McCann, born July 9, 1899; and Hugh Michael Joseph McCann, born May 25, 1903, whom everyone called "Pat."

During these years John lived in a number of places in Ottawa, including 176 Nepean Street, 870 Maria Street and 589 Gilmour Street.[185]

In the 1901 census for Ottawa's Wellington district, the household of John A. and Catherine includes Mary Gertrude (23 years old); John E. (18); and Margaret (8), all children of Margaret O'Brien; and Edith (born July 9, 1899, 1 year and 10 months old), his daughter with Catherine.

Mary Gertrude married John McBride in Ottawa a year later, and two years later, Pat was born.

In the 1931 census for Ottawa, John Augusta and Catherine were 77 and 71, respectively, and still living with "Pat," single at age 28, and Margaret Catherine Constance, also single at 38. Their residence was 491 Gilmour Street. Both Pat and Margaret were working as clerks in the federal government while John, of course, was retired.

Pat eventually married Rose Leblanc, who was 13 years younger. He died in 1974, and Rose survived him until 2002. They're buried in Notre-Dâme Cemetery in Ottawa.

Margaret passed away on August 22, 1948, at the age of 55. Her parents were both deceased, and she was living at 32 Glen Avenue in Ottawa. She was still single. She'd struggled for several years with ovarian cancer, having had two surgeries, one in 1946 and another the day before she died.[186] She's also buried in Notre-Dâme Cemetery.

Of all his children, John A's daughter Edith has perhaps

Fig. 23 Edith McCann Bollini

the most interesting story. As he was an important member of the civil service at the time, John A. would have had an ongoing exposure to events taking place in the nation's capital. At one such event, it would seem, Edith met the Consul General to Canada from Argentina, Senor Don Adolfo Alfredo Bollini, the son of Alejandro Bollini and Celia Cordero.

Adolfo's father, also known as Alessandro Bollini, was also a career consul general from Argentina. The son of Francisco Bollini, Alejandro had postings in places such as Budapest, Hungary, and Adolfo would have grown up in the privileged and worldly environment of a diplomat and his family.

Edith married Adolfo on February 12, 1929, in Montreal. The following year they moved to Manhattan, New York, where they were enumerated in the 1930 census along with their infant son, Juan (John) Kevin Bollini,[187] who was born on April 17, 1929 (don't do the arithmetic). Their next son, Alejandro Adolfo, was born in June, 1930, in Ottawa. According to U.S. immigration records, he had fair hair and blue eyes. Edith and Adolfo also had a son named Alberto (Noel), born in 1936, who had similar colouring.

After postings in Manhattan and elsewhere, Adolfo was named Consul for the Republic of Argentina to the United Kingdom, at Liverpool for the County of Lancashire, in 1939.[188] While Argentina remained neutral during World War II, they had close ties to Germany that must have made Adolfo's job rather difficult.

Unfortunately, Edith passed away during this posting while at the nearby seaside town of Hoylake on July 15, 1940. A month later, the Battle of Britain began as Germany commenced their punishing air raids over England, including Liverpool and nearby

Hoylake. Her son John Kevin was 11 at the time, Alejandro was 10, and Alberto was four.

Edith's remains were returned to Ottawa, and she was interred in Notre-Dâme Cemetery.

After her death, Adolfo and the children left Europe, travelling from Foynes, Ireland, to New York in 1942, a dangerous crossing during the height of the Battle of the Atlantic in which the Germans had deployed countless U-boats to prey on Allied shipping. They arrived safely, and continued on with their lives.

John A. McCann died in Ottawa on November 27, 1939, at the age of 85. He was buried in Notre-Dâme Cemetery, alongside his wife, Catherine Walsh, who died on August 8, 1936.

Mary McCann

Mary McCann was born on March 22, 1856, the third child of Michael J. and Anne, and the first daughter. She was likely named for Michael's sister, Mary McCann McCardle. She was 22 years old when her mother, Anne Kearns, died.

She married James Philip Ryan, a farmer from North Burgess, and the 1891 census shows them living in North Crosby with their daughter Johanna Ryan (born October 23, 1882), their son Edward John Ryan (born March 20, 1885), their daughter Anna Ryan (born October 2, 1887), and their son Michael Ryan (born January 5, 1890). Also living with them at the time of the census, as mentioned before, was the widow Ann Quinn Kearns, who was 86 and would presumably have been Mary's grandmother.

James Ryan died on April 22, 1893, at the age of 42. The cause of death was listed on the death certificate as cirrhosis of the liver, usually an indication of severe alcoholism.

Mary was in Westport when the census was conducted in 1901. Head of the household, she still had Johanna (18), Edward (15), Ann (13), and Michael Joseph Ryan (11) living with her.

However, in 1905 she took her children across the border into the United States, and she was present in the 1910 census for Wayne County, Michigan, Detroit City, District 80, Ward 6. Again listed as head of the household, she was 52 and not working. Her daughter Johanna was 27 and employed as a telegraph agent in a telegraph office; her son Edward was 24 and worked as an express clerk for an express business; Ann was 22 and employed as a bookkeeper in a Five-and-Ten store; Michael J. was 21 and employed as an assistant shipping clerk for a cigar business (something about that name and cigars!). She also had two lodgers to help pay the bills.

She appears in the records back home much later, when the obituary of Bridget Donnelly McCann, her stepmother, mentions that "Mrs. J.P. Ryan, Detroit" was among those who travelled to Smiths Falls for the funeral on November 5, 1921.

Mary McCann Ryan passed away in Detroit on October 18, 1937, at the age of 81. Her death record, issued by the Michigan Department of Health, listed the cause of death as bronchial pneumonia. She was buried in the Mt. Olivet cemetery in Detroit.

Patrick McCann

The next child born to Michael J. and Anne was Patrick, their third son. As he is a main character in our story and a direct descendant from Arthur McCann to me, his tale will be told in detail in the following chapter.

Anastasia McCann

The second daughter of Michael J. and Anne was Anastasia, born on January 20, 1860. She was raised in town, where her father had built a very successful shoemaking business and the family kept a few animals penned in the yard in back. She was 18 when her mother died, and would have taken on much of the responsibility for looking after her six younger brothers and sisters, including the infant Margaret.

In the fall of 1879 she became ill. At first it would have seemed like a nagging chest cold with an annoying cough and blood-streaked congestion. Over the winter it got worse, with night sweats, shortness of breath, and weakness, and she was soon diagnosed with tuberculosis, referred to then as consumption.[189]

Six months after the appearance of symptoms she passed away on April 15, 1880, at the age of 20. Her father must have been heartbroken, as he chose to name his future daughter with Bridget Donnelly Anastasia in her honour.

She was buried in St. Edward's cemetery. Her inscription reads:

> Pray for
> The soul of
> Anastasia,
> Daughter of
> Michael &
> Ann McCann
> Westport.
> Died Apr. 15, 1880
> Aged 20 y'rs
> & 3 Mo's

May her soul rest in Peace.
Amen.

Weep not for me, my parents dear
I am not dead, but sleeping here
I was not yours but God's alone
He loved me best and took me home.

CECELIA

Cecelia McCann was born on January 10, 1862, and she was baptized in St. Edward's church by Father Foley on February 1. She appears in her father's household in the 1871 and 1881 censuses.

Cecelia likely married Peter O'Neil between 1881 and 1883. Unfortunately, during this time it would seem she began her own two-year battle with tuberculosis that finally saw her pass away on February 7, 1884, at the age of 22. She's buried in St. Edward's cemetery, but her headstone is one of those vandalized in the 1970s and subsequently piled at the back of the graveyard. Thankfully, the priest at the time, Reverend Heywood, transcribed what fragments he could, so that we could have some evidence of her passing.[190]

THOMAS JAMES MCCANN

One of the better known names in Westport from our family was probably "T.J. McCann." Thomas James McCann was born on April 29, 1864. He was the fourth boy in the family, and had three older sisters ahead of him as well.

On January 7, 1894, he married Annie O'Regan, the daughter

of Henry O'Regan and Annie Locke. The wedding took place at St. Lawrence Church in Gloucester, now a suburb of Ottawa.

As the century drew to a close, T.J. and Annie continued to live in Ottawa while he worked as a travelling salesman for a local company that made leather goods. For at least two years, from 1899 to 1901, he and the family resided at 108 College Avenue.[191] By 1908, however, he had moved back to Westport and was living on George Street in the house next door to his late brother Patrick's widow and children. This would have been his sister Mary's house, in which she lived with her husband James Ryan and their grandmother, Ann Quinn Kearns, until James died and Mary immigrated to Detroit.

Given that his father, Michael J., was now quite elderly, T.J. perhaps returned to Westport to assist him with the boot and shoe portion of the business. According to the 1911 census, taken not long after Michael J. had died, T.J. was still a commercial traveller selling boots, so he must have taken on the responsibility of moving his father's remaining stock, earning $1,000 a year (much more than any other head of household enumerated on that page).

T.J. and Annie raised a large family. Their eldest was Irene M. McCann, born on October 8, 1894; she passed away on August 31, 1941, at the age of 46. Next came Arthur McCann, who was born in 1897 and died in 1915 at the age of 18; Patrick McCann, who was born in 1918 and died in infancy that same year; John Francis McCann, who was a New Year's baby born January 1, 1899; Phyllis M. McCann, who was born on December 1, 1900; Henry M. (Harry) McCann, born in April 1904; Anna Marie McCann, born May 28, 1908; Thomas Joseph McCann Junior, who was born on January 12, 1906, and died July 19,

1978; Maria McCann, born in May 1908; Kathleen Rita McCann, born December 10, 1910; and an unnamed baby, stillborn, on February 6, 1918.

T.J. moved the family to Smiths Falls on June 24, 1918. They moved by boat, bringing with them two cows, hens, and all their belongings. They rented the house in Westport to a Rev. Gratton.[192]

T.J.'s son John Francis McCann was living in Ottawa, the city of his birth, in 1918 when he joined the army that October. According to the attestation paper that he completed when applying for enlistment in the Canadian Overseas Expeditionary Force, his address was 449 Gladstone Avenue, he was single and employed as a chauffeur, and he'd been a member of the militia for over a year. The physician who examined John noted on the form that he was 5 feet 7 inches tall, had "moderate flat feet" and a "rapid heart." He was accepted into the army in December of that year.

On October 29, 1919, John Francis married Marie Juliette Laura Hebert, daughter of Patrick Hebert and Sophia Chevrier. He married a second time on July 20, 1933, his second wife being named Kathleen Little, daughter of Joseph Little and Bridget Ford. While the marriage license notes that Kathleen, who was 28, was single, it states for John Francis: "wife left my domicile over nine years ago and I have no knowledge of her whereabouts since that date."

John Francis McCann died on August 15, 1960, and is buried in Notre-Dâme cemetery.

Thomas J. McCann passed away on March 24, 1935, at the age of 70, after a six-month battle with stomach cancer. At the time of his death, T.J. was the owner and operator of the

Alhambra Hotel on George Street. It later became known as the Westport Inn, and was torn down in the 1980s.

He was buried in St. Edward's cemetery in a plot that is dedicated to T.J. and his family. It would have started with the burial of sons Arthur and Patrick in 1915 and 1918 and at some point was enhanced with a concrete border around the family plots as others were laid to rest.

Annie O'Regan passed away on May 4, 1940. She was staying in Montreal with one of her daughters when she suffered a heart attack. Her obituary described her as "well known and highly esteemed throughout this community and her passing removed not only a good citizen but a lady who was beloved by all for her many fine qualities."[193]

She's also buried in St. Edward's cemetery with T.J., Arthur, Patrick, Irene, and T.J. Junior.

MICHAEL JR. THE FIRST

Michael Junior, son of Michael J. and Anne Kearns, was born on August 16, 1866. Unfortunately, he died on March 29, 1869, at the age of two years, seven months. He was buried in St. Edward's Cemetery, and his interment was witnessed by Michael Kearns and Patrick Ryan.

MICHAEL JR. THE SECOND

Michael A. McCann Junior, the second so-named son of Michael J. and Anne, was born on June 4, 1869, a scant nine weeks after the death of their two-year-old Michael. He would have been named in honour of his older brother.

He was nine years old when his mother died, and only about

11 when his father married Bridget Donnelly in 1880. These events would have been very difficult for the boy to handle.

In the 1891 census he was 22 and still living in his father's household while apprenticing as a shoemaker.

On June 4, 1895, he married Mary Ellen (Nell) Martin. He was living in Ottawa at the time and working as a commercial traveller like his brother T.J., perhaps selling his father's boots and shoes.

Nell was born on November 24, 1862, the daughter of Owen Martin, who was born in Ireland in about 1832 and was the son of Thomas and Ellen (Nelly) Martin. In 1851 the Martin farm was located on Conc. 3, Lot 22, not all that far from where Arthur McCann had originally settled ten years before, and close to the farms of Owen Kearns and Michael Kearns. By 1871, however, Owen Martin was living in Westport and operating a potash manufacturing business. Nell's mother was Elizabeth McCardle, who was born in Ireland in 1845.

The census of 1901 shows Michael A. and Nell living in the home of Nell's mother on Bedford Street. By 1911, however, when the next census was taken, Michael and Nell had gone their separate ways. Nell remained with her mother, but Michael returned to Ottawa, where he was living when they married.

In 1931, he was living in apartment 101 at 126 Albert Street in downtown Ottawa and working for the government as a clothing inspector, earning $1,925 a year. A good salary for the time.

As for Nell, the 1921 census gives her occupation as a dressmaker, and by 1931 her mother had passed away and Nell was living alone on Spring Street, still self-employed as a dressmaker. She was also a diarist, and a portion of her journals was informally printed by the Rideau District Museum as part of their fundraising efforts. She recorded many of the events that occurred in the village, such as marriages and deaths, but not much of a personal nature.

Michael A. McCann passed away on November 23, 1938, at the age of 69. He'd been battling prostate cancer, for which he'd had an operation in March of 1837. He was still living in the Albert Street apartment building in Ottawa at the time and, sadly, the death certificate lists him as single.

He was buried in St. Edward's cemetery in a plot included in the family group of his older brother, T.J.

Rose Anna McCann

Rose Anna McCann, known as "Rosey," was born on November 5, 1871. She was likely named after her father's sister, Roseanna. Rose was about seven years old when her mother died, and about nine when her father married Bridget Donnelly, a few months after the death of Rose's sister Ana-stasia. She was about 10 years old when her first half-sister Anna was born, about 13 when Teresa arrived, and about 17 when the family was completed with the arrival of Anastasia Magdeline, Bridget Donnelly's third and final child.

At the age of 20 she was still living at home, but seven years later, in 1898, she was down in Ogdensburg, New York, where she married William H. Leahy (Lahey) on October 5 of that year.

Her first child, Mary Helen Leahy, was born in Ogdensburg on February 23, 1900, and her second, William Harold Leahy, Jr., was also born there on October 6, 1903.

Unfortunately, Will passed away on February 28, 1904, at the age of 34. He was buried in St. Mary's cemetery in Ogdensburg.[194]

As for daughter Mary Helen, she travelled from her home at 330 Booth St., Ogdensburg, on December 15, 1919, to marry Joseph François Deschènes, son of François Deschènes and Mary Joly, at Notre-Dâme Cathedral in Ottawa. She was 20 and working as a typist, while Joseph was 24 and a "telephone man" who was originally from Arnprior.

She passed away from tuberculosis on October 21, 1946, after a long stay at the Royal Ottawa sanitarium, and she was buried in the Notre-Dâme cemetery in Ottawa.

Rosey's son, William Leahy Jr., was living in Morrisburg, Ontario, and working as a chauffeur and bus driver when he married a local woman, Sarah Isabel Lapierre, daughter of Harry and Dora Lapierre, on October 6, 1930. Known as Sadie, she was a Protestant, and the marriage may have created a few ripples in the family at the time.

Their children included W.J. Edward Leahy (1931-1991), who's buried in the Capital Memorial Gardens cemetery in Ottawa; Richard D.R. Leahy (January 12, 1933-December 4, 1987); and Ronald Harold Leahy, who was born February 1, 1934, and passed away on April 11, 2011, in Smiths Falls.

William Jr. and Sadie were living in Ottawa at 442 Cambridge St. in Ottawa in 1944 when William received a draft registration card from the United States government. He was working as a chauffeur for Colonial Coach Lines at the time, and it must have come as a bit of a shock to the 41-year-old bus driver.

On July 18, 1963, Rosey's son William Jr. passed away while living at 72 Arlington Ave. in Ottawa. His funeral mass was held at St. Patrick's Cathedral in the city, and he was buried in St. Mary's cemetery in Morrisburg.

As for Rosey, she had been staying with her sister Mary McCann Ryan at 1531 Eighth Street in Detroit in 1932 when she was hospitalized for an enlarged liver and severe anemia, likely the result of alcohol use disorder. She passed away on November 24 of that year, and her body was returned to Westport for burial in St. Edward's cemetery, in the family plot of her brother T.J. Present at the graveside were her nephews T.J. Jr. and Ford McCann, son of Patrick. My grandfather.

WILLIAM E. McCANN

William Edward McCann was born on February 6, 1874, the second-youngest of Michael J. and Anne Kearns' children. He was only four years old when his mother died, and six when his older sister Anastasia passed away from tuberculosis. Hopefully, the arrival in the house of his step-mother Bridget Donnelly that fall helped to restore the sense of security and stability that a young boy would need at that age.

On January 22, 1901, William E. married Sarah McCabe, the daughter of Michael McCabe and Sarah Donnelly of Perth. William's Uncle James Speagle witnessed the marriage at St. John the Baptist Church in Perth, along with Margaret McCabe. Sarah McCabe was born on September 28, 1873.

In 1901 they lived at 36 Spring Street in Westport, perhaps in the house built by Casper Speagle for Will's oldest brother Arthur F. more than 12 years ago. He was employed as church sexton by Father William Walsh, the priest of St. Edward's Church at that time. His duties included general maintenance work, digging graves, ringing the church bells, and other related tasks.

Will and Sarah had three children: Sarah Cecelia McCann (born December 19, 1902); Michael Clarence McCann (born September 19, 1904); and William Thomas McCann (born September 10, 1906).

Will would have gotten his start in house painting by working for his older brother, Patrick, but he soon started his own painting and decorating business in town, likely taking on many of his brother's clients after Patrick passed away in 1907. A special issue of the *Westport Mirror* published on April 8, 1909, features a very flattering puff piece that advertised William's services.

Later in 1909, Will, Sarah and the three children joined Sarah's family in Detroit, Michigan. Her brother Arthur McCabe had emigrated in 1907, and it appears that Will and Sarah brought their 68-year-old father Michael McCabe down to live with them. They were enumerated in the April 1910 U.S.

W. E. McCANN.
Painter and Decorator.

The subject of our sketch is one of the best known painters and decorators in the county. Mr. McCann has been engaged in the painting, decorating and paper-hanging business all his life and is considered an expert in his line. He served a thorough apprenticeship and has always kept abreast of the times, adopting new ideas that seemed practical and of benefit to the business and discarding those that were obsolete and out-of-date. In placing orders for house painting, graining or paperhanging, we feel justified in saying that it will be properly done if W. E. McCann has the contract. His prices all guaranteed.

Fig. 24 William E. McCann

census with McCabe and his family and, interestingly, Will's occupation is listed as a carpenter in a brewery.[195]

Will's father, Michael J. McCann, passed away that December. Perhaps that was a factor in the family returning to Westport by 1915. A census of school children conducted in Westport includes three children of William E. McCann: William McCann, age 8; Clarence McCann, age 10; and Secilia (Cecelia) McCann, aged 12.[196]

The following year they were in Ottawa, living at 117 Queen Street West, and Will had travelled to Montreal to enlist in the army, swearing an oath of allegiance to King George V while agreeing "to serve in the Canadian Over-Seas Expeditionary Force for the term of one year. . . during the war now existing between Great Britain and Germany."[197]

He reenlisted in Ottawa a year later, and for a third time in 1919. He served with the Canadian Railway Troops for a ten-month stretch during this period. The CRT was a corps responsible for the construction and maintenance of a light rail infrastructure behind the front lines to transport supplies and ordnance to British and Canadian troops. The CRT played an important role in the 1917 offensive in large part because of their expertise in railway construction and operation. The corps was disbanded in 1920.[198] On his 1917 form, Will declared his current trade as being railroad construction: perhaps he was talking a good game to get himself included in one of these units without having the appropriate experience.

An added bonus for us on these military attestation forms Will signed are the results of his physical examinations. His height was measured at 5 feet, 6-1/2 inches, he weighed 124 lbs., his hair was brown and his eyes were blue. He suffered from arthritis in his shoulder, which resulted in his discharge in 1918, his vision was 20-30 in both eyes, and his hearing was normal. During this time his addresses in Ottawa were 359 Nelson Avenue, 109 Queen Street West, 177 Queen Street West, and 37 Eccles Street.

Sarah McCabe passed away on June 8, 1924, in the Pontiac State Hospital, Pontiac, Michigan, after a battle with pulmonary tuberculosis. She'd been staying in Detroit when she fell ill.

William E. remarried on February 8, 1937, exchanging vows with Anne Violet Mitchell Burgess, a 31-year-old widow apparently from Herman, New York.

Something of a mystery woman, according to various genealogical sources, she may have been married twice before, once to a James Ellis (who died in 1927), and to Harry Burgess (deceased in 1930). Her place of birth was variously listed on documents as "River Desair"; Brandon, Manitoba; Maniwaki, Quebec; and the aforementioned Herman. She passed away on February 15, 1964, at the stated age of 66, and was buried in the Beechwood National Military Cemetery, likely in deference to William E.'s military service.

On March 21, 1981, I sat down with my grandmother, Ida Allore McCann, for a chat about our family history. This conversation took place in her apartment on Princess Street in Kingston, Ontario, while I was completing my graduate degree at Queen's University. When she married my grandfather Ford McCann in 1920, she moved into the McCann house on George Street that had been built by my great-grandfather Patrick and was still the home of his widow, Maria Hagan McCann.

My grandparents lived there for a number of years, raising a brood of kids that included my father, and my grandmother had plenty of opportunities to hear the stories and gossip about the McCanns, Hagans, and so forth.

Of Will McCann, she told me that she knew him, but didn't know what he did for a living. It was her opinion that he was "probably the black sheep of the family."

I've always wondered what Will had done to earn that dubious distinction, but after having done my research for this family history, I have a theory. The marriage record for Will and Anne V. lists her as an Anglican, which would have been rather scandalous back then.

Not to mention that it was her third marriage, and her husbands seemed to have a knack for departing this realm not all that long after tying the knot with her.

As for William, he also gave his religion as Anglican, which would have been the icing on the cake for the McCanns. However, he managed to outlast Anne V. by five years, passing away on May 13, 1969, at the age of 95. Apparently he'd reconciled with the Church, as a funeral mass was held for him in the chapel at the Rideau Veterans' Home, and he was interred in Notre-Dâme Cemetery in Ottawa.

Reflecting the pride of a military veteran, a member of the Canadian Ordnance Corps (COC) and the Canadian Expeditionary Force (CEF) in World War I, his headstone reads:

William E. McCann
Private
COC CEF
13 May 1969
Age 95

Margaret McCann

Margaret Jewel McCann was born on January 1, 1877. She was the final child born to Anne Kearns and Michael J. McCann before Anne's death a year and a half later.

When the census of 1891 was conducted, "Maggie" was 14 years old. Her half-sisters Anna Bernadetta, Teresa Elizabeth, and Anastasia Magdeline, the children of Bridget Donnelly, were eight, six, and three respectively.

On January 11, 1900, Maggie married Byron Stanley Klock in Ogdensburg, New York, where her sister Rosey had married Will Leahy two years earlier. Klock was local talent who was born on May 10, 1881. When they were enumerated in June of that year for the 1900 U.S. census, they were living in the household of Herbert Hunt and his family. Margaret was employed as a waitress, and Klock was working as a streetcar conductor.

This marriage didn't last long. In January 1906 Klock filed for divorce and was granted an interlocutory decree in court, represented by his lawyer. Maggie did not appear.[199]

On September 3, 1913, still using the Klock surname, Margaret married Charles Aloysius Rawlinson in San Francisco, California. On the affidavit they signed for their marriage licence, both declared that it was their second marriage, but Margaret listed herself as a widow, although we know Klock was still alive. Rawlinson was originally from New York state and worked as a telegrapher at the Western Union telegraph company.[200]

In the 1920 U.S. census, they were enumerated in District 20, Precinct 50 of San Francisco, California. Interestingly, living with them at the time were Margaret's half-sister Anastasia McCann Flynn, husband John J. Flynn, and their two children,

John Jr., just over two years old, and William, who was eleven months old.

Margaret passed away in San Francisco on January 27, 1929. She died at her home in the St. Dominic Apartments, 830-33rd Avenue. Cause of death was uterine cancer. A requiem high mass was celebrated for her at St. Thomas Church, and she was interred in Holy Cross cemetery.[201]

Fig. 25 Michael J., Bridget, and Daughters

Chapter Twelve

Bridget Donnelly and Her Children

As mentioned earlier, Michael J. went through a two-year period where he was the sole parent of a large household of growing children. As it happened, he became close to another strongly devout parishioner, Bridget Donnelly, the daughter of Arthur Donnelly and Anne Kelly. Five months after Anastasia's death, and two years after Anne passed away, he married Bridget in September 1880. The children would have seen her before at mass and other church functions, but they may not have paid very much attention until now. Who was this new step-mother who had entered their lives?

The Donnelly Family

The Donnellys had been established in North Burgess Township for a very long time. Owen Donnelly was a contemporary of Arthur McCann, born about 1768 in County Armagh.[202] He and his wife Margaret McCracken immigrated to Burgess some time before 1834.

Bridget's father Arthur Donnelly was born about 1802 in Armagh, Ireland. He married Ann Kelly (1812-1860), also born in Ireland, and their eldest child, Mary, was born in Upper Canada in about 1834, giving us the approximate timeline for the family's arrival. Other children included Margaret, Michael, Catherine, Ellen, Susannah, Bridget, Sarah, Teresa and Arthur.

In 1851 Arthur Donnelly's farm was located on the south quarter portion of Lot 14, Concession 8, in North Burgess, which is found today on Powers Road just past the intersection with Black Lake Road, a stone's throw from Stanleyville. He was farming 50 acres, 15 acres of which were under crops and another 15 devoted to pasture. His neighbours on that lot included Owen McGough, who was farming 50 acres on the east corner portion of the lot, and Rudolph Bachman, who owned 50 acres on the southwest quarter portion. McGough had been in North Burgess since about 1843, but Rudolph Bachman predated them all. Like Casper Speagle, Bachman was another veteran of the De Watteville regiment who was born in Switzerland and received his land in 1816.

Bridget was born on January 16, 1847. As a girl she was known as Biddy, which was a common familiar short form of her name at that time.[203] She remained single until the age of 33, when she married Michael J. at St. Edward's church on September 20, 1880.

Moving into the home on Church Street in Westport, she became step-mother to a family of growing children. Michael's three eldest, Arthur F., John A., and Mary were married and in their own homes, but Patrick was a 23-year-old young man who was still a year away from his own marriage. There were two teenagers—Cecilia, who was 18, and Thomas, who was 17. As well, there were four youngsters to win over: Michael, who was 12; Rose, who was 10; William, who was 7; and Margaret, who was 4.

Bridget would have understood what they were feeling.

When she was 13 years old her own mother had died, and she likely felt an affinity first of all with Michael and Rose, who were close to that age. Arthur Donnelly had waited eight years to remarry, to Catherine Morgan, and at that point Bridget was 21. She would understand the sense of responsibility that Cecelia, as the oldest girl remaining in the household, might have been feeling.

The following spring Bridget was expecting a child, and Anna Bernadetta was born on September 14, 1881. Almost three years afterwards came Teresa Elizabeth followed by Anastasia Magdeline four years later.

By 1901 the children of Anne Kearns had all married and left home. Michael was 70 and Bridget was 54, and they lived with their three daughters, lovely young ladies who were the pride of their parents. The photograph in Figure 25 is a portrait that is dominated by the girls. Their self-confidence and closeness to each other are evident in their posture and expressions.

We also see that Bridget wore a dark right lens in her glasses. Anecdotal evidence suggests that she fell into the fireplace when she was a child and lost the eye. She wore the dark lens to cover it up.[204]

As mentioned above, Bridget operated the family grocery store in Westport around the turn of the century. She remained for a time in Westport after Michael's death in December of 1910. By the time of the census that was conducted in the spring of 1911, she was living alone on Church Street. She may have gravitated toward baked goods, as the census mentions that she was supplementing her income through "baking" in the shop. Eventually she moved to Smiths Falls to live with her daughter Teresa and her son-in-law Tom Egan. She remained there until her death on November 3, 1921. Her funeral was held in St. Francis de Sales church in Smiths Falls and she was buried in the St. John the Baptist Cemetery in Perth.

Her headstone reads:
> Bridget Donnelly, 1848 - 1921, wife of Michael McCann.
> Thomas V. Egan, 1878 - 1855.
> His wife, Teresa McCann, 1884 – 1974

ANNA BERNADETTA MCCANN

Anna Bernadetta McCann was born in Westport on September 12, 1881, the first of Michael J. McCann's three daughters with Bridget Donnelly.

On September 12, 1904, Anna married Thomas Henry Sylvah, an iron moulder in an iron factory, who was the son of Francis Sylvah and Julia Dunn.

Fig. 26 Anna Bernadetta

The grandfather of Thomas Sylvah, Jean-François Sylvain (1789-1876), was originally from Saint-Michel-de-Bellechasse, a quiet little village on the upper St. Lawrence River above Quebec City. He was the son of Paul-Antoine Sylvain of Bellechase (1764-1845) and Marie-Anne Brousseau (1766-1825). The Sylvain family had lived in Quebec for four generations, going back to 1670 when Sylvain Veau emigrated from the Centre-Val de Loire area in France.[205]

Jean-François moved his family to Ontario and settled in the township of North Gower, south of Ottawa, where they were enumerated in the census of 1851. Jean-François's age was recorded as 64 and his wife Catherine's as 58. Francis, their son, was 11.

Twenty years later, in 1871, Jean-François and Catherine were living alone in their home in North Gower township. Francis had married Julia Dunn, an Irish immigrant, and the son of Francis and Julia, Thomas Henry Silvah, was born February 17, 1874.

Anna Bernadetta McCann and Thomas Henry Sylvah lived at 15 Aberdeen Avenue in Smiths Falls and raised five children, including Mary Julia, Aquaviva, Claude, Arthur, and Martina.

Mary Julia Sylvah, the oldest, was born on September 10, 1905, in Westport. An employee of Bell Canada, she died on January 8, 1979, and was buried in St. John's Cemetery, Perth.

Aquaviva Beatrice Sylvah was born August 27, 1907. She married John Cregg in New York City on May 8, 1933, and she passed away from complications of heart disease at the age of 80 on November 25, 1983, at Newport News, Virginia. She'd been living in Charlottesville, where she had worked as the secretary of the president of the University of Virginia before retirement. She was cremated.[206]

Claude Michael Sylvah was born on July 21,1 1911 in Smiths Falls. On June 15, 1942, still single, he enlisted in the Royal Canadian Air Force and became a flight gunner, flying missions in a Lancaster bomber over Belgium and France. Two years later, on May 9, 1944, he was killed in action while flying a mission over Haine St. Pierre, Belgium. The aircraft crashed at Gallaix and all members of the flight crew were killed. Claude is buried with his crewmates in the Municipal Cemetery, Chièvres, Belgium, grave number 33.

Thomas Arthur (Art) Sylvah was born on August 7, 1914, in Smiths Falls. He married Marie Halpin on April 18, 1949. Their son Mark Sylvah was born in Smiths Falls on June 12, 1954. Art passed away on May 11, 1985, and was buried in St. John's cemetery in Perth, Ontario.

The last of Anna Bernadetta's children was Anna Martina Sylvah, who was born on April 18, 1918. She married James Stanley Edwards in Smiths Falls on September 4, 1941. She passed away on March 16, 1976, in Oakville, Ontario, and was buried there in the Trafalgar Lawn Cemetery along with her husband, who died in 1993.

Anna Bernadetta passed away on November 24, 1924, and is buried in the St. John the Baptist cemetery in Perth.

Teresa Elizabeth McC'ann

Teresa Elizabeth McCann was born on January 18, 1884. She attended St. Edward's school in Westport, where her contemporaries included Frances McCann, her step niece. Known as Tessie, she married Thomas Vincent Egan (1878-1955), the son of John Egan and Mary Rice, on September 18, 1906, at the age of 21. The marriage took place in St. Edward's Church in Westport and was conducted by Father O'Rourke. Witnesses were William Egan for the groom and sister Anastasia Magdaline for Tessie.

Fig. 27 Teresa E. McCann

In her photograph (Figure 27), in which she would be about 20 years of age, Tessie looks at the camera with a directness that suggests she was a self-confident and bright young woman with a dynamic personality. Of the three girls in the family portrait, from which this photograph has been cropped, she is wearing the most jewelry. She has a cameo brooch at her neck, a locket on a pendant around her neck, another locket on the bracelet on her wrist, and a pocket watch pinned to the front of her dress.

Tessie and Tom Egan lived at 51 Mary Street in Smiths Falls. They went on to have four children: Mary Charlotte Egan (1908-1996); Margaret Egan (1922-2004); Maurice Egan (Morris) (1924-2021); and Teresa Egan (1926-2002).

In 1941, Mary Charlotte took vows to enter the Loretto Sisters, a Toronto branch of the Institute of the Blessed Virgin Mary, taking the name Sister Lidwina, the Dutch patron saint of chronic pain (and ice skating). She passed away on December 2, 1996, and was buried in the Mount Hope Catholic Cemetery in Toronto.

Tessie passed away in 1974 at the age of 89. Her requiem mass was celebrated at St. Francis de Sales Church in Smiths Falls, and she was buried in St. John's Cemetery in Perth.[207]

Anastasia Magdeline McCann

Anastasia Magdeline McCann was born on September 12, 1888, in Westport. After completing school she moved down to Watertown, New York, in order to attend the St. Joachim's School of Nursing. A graduate in the Class of 1908, she began a very successful career in the nursing profession that lasted right through to her retirement.

On June 5, 1916, she married John James Flynn of Watertown, the son of John Flynn and Catherine McCarrick.

Fig. 28 Anastasia Magdeline

The marriage took place at St. Francis de Sales Church in Smiths Falls, likely so that her mother Bridget, who was 69 years old, wouldn't have to travel.

Flynn was a confectionery wholesaler for the Clark-Flynn Candy Company in Watertown. At the time of his draft registration in 1918, they were living at 20 Cameron Place. When the 1920 U.S. census was conducted, as you may remember, they had travelled out to San Francisco, where they were enumerated in the household of Charles Rawlinson and Margaret Jewel McCann, Anastasia's half-sister, in January of that year.

Unfortunately, Flynn was quite unwell. Anastasia brought him back to Smiths Falls, but he passed away there on March 17, 1920, another victim of tuberculosis. He was buried in the Calvary Cemetery in Watertown.

Anastasia and John Flynn had two children. John James Flynn, Jr., known as Jack, was born on September 18, 1917, in Watertown. He married Annie Burns, the daughter of Thomas F. Burns, a yard conductor of steam trains, in Watertown on Feb. 14, 1942. (Apparently Burns was not related to members of the Stanleyville Byrne families we will examine later.)

At the time, Jack Flynn was working for the local office of New York Air Brake Co., a manufacturer of air brake control systems for the railroad industry. Trains were probably the connection in some way or another between the bride and the groom.

Later in the decade they lived in Chicago, Illinois, where their daughter Kathleen Flynn, was born in 1944. [208] Jack passed away in Sacramento, California, on December 21, 2014, at the age of 97, and his remains were laid to rest at the Calvary Catholic Cemetery and Mausoleum in Sacramento.[209]

William Joseph Flynn was born on February 2, 1919, in St. Petersburg, Florida. He attended college at Spring Hill College in Mobile, Alabama, and received his draft card at the age of 21. In 1944 he was an aviation cadet in the United States Army with the rank of lieutenant, based in Lincoln, Nebraska. While stationed here, he married Dorothy Parker, the daughter of Roland Parker, in December 1944. Dorothy had been living in Sacramento, and perhaps had met Will there, travelling to Lincoln to tie the knot with him.

Will Flynn was discharged from the U.S. Army with the rank of captain, and by 1950 was in Sacramento working as a lighting salesman doing business with the city utilities company. Enumerated that year with him and Dorothy were their daughter Patricia (1945-1987) and their son Justin (1946-2023). He passed away on January 17, 1984, in Sacramento and was buried in the San Francisco National Cemetery with Dorothy, who survived him by three years.

As for Anastasia Magdeline McCann, I mentioned earlier that she pursued a remarkable career in nursing during her lifetime. After graduating from St. Joachim's in 1908 she worked first as a private nurse before being hired by the Metropolitan Life Insurance company as a visiting nurse. After her husband died in 1920, she returned to St. Joachim's as an instructor. In 1938 she was appointed the principal of the nursing school, the hospital now being known as Mercy Hospital.[210]

By 1950 she had accepted a position in Sioux Falls, South Dakota, as superintendent of nursing at the local hospital, but by 1953 had returned to Watertown where she became assistant director of nursing education.

After retirement, she moved to Sacramento, California,

where her two sons were living. She passed away on August 16, 1978, at the age of 89. She's buried in the Flynn family plot at Calvary Cemetery in Watertown, New York.

Fig. 29 Anastasia McCann Flynn

Fig. 30 The McCann House, George St., Westport

Patrick and Maria McCann in front of their home.

Chapter Thirteen
Patrick McCann

When Patrick McCann was born on January 10, 1858, his father was in the process of establishing himself as a successful shoemaker in the village of Westport. Michael was a young ambitious man of twenty-eight, and Anne was twenty-four. Arthur F., their oldest, was celebrating his fifth birthday on the day that Patrick was born. John A., the next oldest, was three years old and Mary, his sister, was two years old. The fourth child and the third son, Patrick, who may have been named for an older brother of his father, was a welcome addition to a family that was just beginning to establish itself in the village.

Patrick as a Youth

As a boy growing up in the shop and upstairs rooms on Church Street, Patrick would have had his share of chores to look after. He likely helped around his father's shoe shop with odd jobs, and there were the animals kept in the back that would have required regular attention—sheep to tend, the cow to milk and the pig to feed. In the spring there were potatoes to plant in the garden, and in the fall Patrick likely helped to harvest the crop. Each January 10, when his birthday arrived, he shared his celebration with his big brother Arthur F. who, as we saw, was also born on that day.

Patrick's childhood was much different than that of his father. Where Michael J. had been uprooted as a youth and endured the hardships of the immigrant experience, including a long and arduous journey in the hold of a packet ship, the trek through the wilderness to a new home in the woods, harsh winters in a crude log shanty and bone-wearying summers helping his aged, struggling parents to clear the land and plant crops in rocky, infertile ground, Patrick had spent his childhood growing up in a comfortable frame structure in a thriving village with young parents who were confidently building a stable, secure home for their children. The chores that Michael expected his sons to carry out would have been nothing compared to what he had been required to do at their age. It was his legacy to his children that they would have an easier life than he had known, that their upbringing would provide greater opportunities than had been available for many of the boys Michael had known who had no choice but to stay on the land, much of which was not very good for farming, and scrabble as best they could to make ends meet.

What was Westport like when Patrick was a schoolboy?

As Neil A. Patterson[211] and others have noted, the village was a going concern in the 1860s and early 1870s. There were six general stores, including Patrick's father's; two grocery stores; three hotels; two sawmills and a shingle mill; two grist mills producing flour and feed; four blacksmiths; a carding and fulling mill; two cooperages for barrel making; two carriage manufacturers; a cabinet maker; an iron foundry; two harness shops; two lime kilns; one potash works; 18 weavers operating looms to make flannel and other cotton and wool fabrics; four tailors to make and sell clothing from this abundance of material; a tannery to process leather (for his father's boots and shoes!); a tin shop; and six boot and shoe businesses, including Patrick's father's establishment on Church Street.

In 1872, when Patrick was fourteen, his oldest brother Arthur F. held a job as a raftsman. Working under the direction of raft bosses, raftsmen guided the big logs down the river from the logging sites to the mills, a rather dangerous and spectacular job at times. To make it easier to move the logs along the water, they were bound together into informal rafts that young, daring men like Arthur would ride like rodeo performers.

As Léon A. Roubidoux notes, raftsmen were "hearty men, with plenty of nerve, they spoke a rough language and had ready fists."[212] Can't you imagine Patrick sitting on the step with his brother on a summer's evening, listening to Arthur's colourful stories of the river and his fellow raftsmen? Of course, they'd have to make sure their father wasn't in earshot, Michael being a strong Catholic who wouldn't approve of rough language and even rougher behaviour.

When Patrick was sixteen, Reeve William H. Fredenburgh bought the local sawmills owned by George Crawford. Adding them to three mills he'd also acquired from Robert Rorison, Fredenburgh established himself as an important lumber exporter while at the same time ensuring an endless supply of raw material for his furniture factory.

A year later, in 1875, Fredenburgh built his palatial home on the north corner of Bedford and Main Streets, just around the corner and down the street from the McCanns. I can imagine Patrick strolling over with his friends to check on its progress, his interest in houses and construction already growing. The house still stands today, now known as The Cove Country Inn.[213]

Arthur F. had already married Margaret Leonard and moved out to start his own family, and in June of 1875 older brother John A., the bookish one, married the young woman who lived behind them on Main Street, Margaret O'Brien. Suddenly, Patrick found that he was the oldest boy left in the house. With three brothers and four sisters remaining, only Mary was older. Between the two of them, they would have been responsible for helping their parents maintain the busy house and shop.

Patrick's sense of responsibility would have multiplied on that terrible day in September 1878 when his mother Anne passed away. With Mary soon married and gone, and his father coping with his grief while continuing to manage a thriving business, 20-year-old Patrick stood at the head of the household with his sister Anastasia, who was 18. Between them they knew they would have to take care of their six younger brothers and sisters and somehow cope with the loss of their mother.

For two years after the death of their mother and the departure of Mary, Patrick and Anastasia carried on as their father's support during what must have been a very difficult time. However, the family was dealt another blow in April 1880 with the death of Anastasia. She had taken ill the following autumn with what seemed like a cough and cold at the time. As the illness progressed, she lapsed into a constant fever with heavy night sweats, and spent a great deal of time in bed, weakened from weight loss and the constant coughing that soon showed blood. After her death the other children, particularly Cecelia who was the next oldest at 18, were then expected to step forward and assume their share of responsibility.

When we take a look at the census of 1881, we see check marks in the Occupation column suggesting that Patrick and his younger brother Thomas J., now 17, were working for their father. T.J. in particular seemed to have gravitated to the shop, listening to the customers that came in to chat with Michael and learning the ins and outs of the boot and shoe business. And although Patrick would have worked for his father out of a sense of obligation, it's a sure bet that his mind was often straying back to the newly built Fredenburgh house and the many other buildings and homes sprouting up in the village.

By now, Patrick had begun to show an active interest in Maria Hagan, the 24-year-old daughter of Hugh Hagan, a farmer living above Westport near Crosby Lake. Love blossumed, and they were married on October 29, 1881, by Father Stanton in St. Edward's Church. Brother T.J. was one of the witnesses.

Patrick then built the house on George Street that would see the birth of two subsequent generations of McCanns, including my grandfather, Ford, and my father, Hugh.

First, however, came their first three children: Monica Cecelia McCann in 1884; Frances Agnes McCann in 1886; and Cosmo Augustine McCann in 1888.

Meanwhile, Patrick started his own business as a house painter and quickly found success, turning that interest in buildings and homes into a lucrative profession. In 1888, for example, the *Perth Courier* noted in its issue of September 7 that "Thomas McRea's house is being painted by Patrick McCann."[214] Three years later, he was listed in the *Farmers and Business Directory* and *Ontario Gazetteer* as a painter in the village of Westport.[215]

At the same time, the family continued to grow. Mary Veronica McCann (Mazie) was born on July 16, 1890, followed by Adella Louise McCann on October 23, 1893 and Wilfrid Charles McCann on August 6, 1895.

Patrick was a member of the Catholic Mutual Business Association (CMBA), a fraternal society organized in Niagara

Fig. 31 Patrick McCann and Maria Hagan

Falls, New York in 1876 and had spread to Canada by 1880. Similar to other secret organizations such as the Oddfellows or the International Order of Foresters, the CMBA's chief function was to provide life insurance and sick benefits to members. It covered funeral expenses and might also provide widows and orphans with funds after a member's death. As with any other such order, the CMBA had ceremonies and meetings complete with passwords and other practices common to a secret organization. Its mandate also included counteracting or offsetting the efforts of other organizations such as the Orange Order, which existed to promote the interests of Protestants in the community. Patrick was able to establish and maintain business connections through the CMBA that helped his business to develop. At the same time, Maria belonged to the Catholic Women's League, a similar organization.[216]

Unfortunately the long finger of mortality reached out and touched Patrick at some point in 1903 when he fell ill with what was diagnosed as cancer. He fought a valiant battle against it for four years but finally succumbed on July 30, 1907 at the age of 49 years and seven months. The photograph of Patrick and Maria in Figure 31, taken about a month before his death, shows a man who is exhausted and drained from his long fight while Maria smiles bravely for the camera.

Patrick was buried in St. Edward's Cemetery. The funeral was conducted under the auspices of the CMBA, which would have paid the expenses on behalf of the family.

Fig. 32 Michael Hagan and Bridget Boyle

Chapter Fourteen
Maria Hagan

Maria Hagan was a Christmas baby, born on December 25, 1857, on the Hagan family farm located in the northern edge of North Crosby Township.

The story of her family begins for us in County Louth, which is, as we've seen before, located just across the line from Carrickasticken townland in Forkhill Parish, Armagh.

Maria Hagan's Family

While the Hagans and their assorted affiliated families are not direct descendants of Arthur McCann and Ann Quinn, which is of course the primary subject of this *Brief History*, they earned a connection to the family by marrying into it, just as the Kearns family, the Speagles, and the McCardles did. So, we should take a few moments to see what can be found out about them.

County Louth Hagans

Anecdotal information suggests that Maria's ancestors extended back to Henry Hagan, born in 1716 and a native of Ardee Catholic Parish, Dundalk.[217] One of Henry's offspring was Daniel Hagan, born in 1736. Among Daniel's children with his wife Elizabeth May was Daniel John Hagan, born in 1755.

Daniel John married Ann Marron, and their children included Patrick Hagan, born January 1776;[218] Mary Hagan, born April 1777;[219] Peggy (Margaret) Hagan, born October 1778;[220] Sara Hagan, born May 8, 1780;[221] Michael Hagan, born September 3, 1782;[222] John Hagan, born June 18, 1786;[223] and, Terence Hagan, born December 7, 1788.[224] These children were of the same generation as Arthur McCann and Ann Quinn.

Maria's grandfather was the aforementioned Michael Hagan. Michael married Bridget Boyle, also known as Biddy (a common nickname at the time). Anecdotal information suggests that Bridget came from Lurgankeel townland, in Faughart parish, which is immediately below Carrickasticken in Forkhill Parish, Armagh. The Hagans, meanwhile, lived farther south in Castletown townland, Ardee Catholic Parish, Louth.

Michael Hagan and his family had immigrated to North Crosby by 1848, when Michael appeared in the census for that year as a farmer on Lot 21 of Concession 6. The farm was situated up above Westport, just off Mountain Road and Big Crosby Lake Road. He had a family of six, five of whom were Irish-born while the sixth, a girl under 5 years old, was born in Canada. Of the rest, one was a married man in his 30s and one a single man in the same age bracket; one was a married man above the age of 60; and the other was a single female between the ages of 14 and 45.

The children of Michael Hagan and Biddy Boyle included Patrick Hagan (born in 1812); James Hagan (born April 30, 1819); Hugh Hagan (born in March 1821); and Alice Hagan (born in 1823).

In 1851, Michael Hagan and Bridget Boyle were living on their own next door to their son Hugh Hagan and his family. In 1866, however, Michael passed away and was buried on November 24 of that year in St. Edward's cemetery.

His son Patrick Hagan, Maria's uncle, had apparently lived an adventurous life before ending up in North Crosby with the rest of the family. In 1841, while they were still living in Ardee Parish, County Louth, Patrick is said to have abducted a woman, a crime for which he received a death sentence commuted to seven years' transportation to Australia.[225] It's possible that the ensuing trouble caused the rest of the family to immigrate to Canada thereafter.

Patrick married Bridget Mulholm, daughter of Daniel Mulholm and Bridget Burns, originally from Forkhill Parish, County Armagh, at St. Edward's church on April 26, 1855. In 1861 they were farming next door to Bridget's family, with a son, Michael Hagan, who was three years old. Patrick died on January 7, 1894, at the age of 81 after having been bedridden for two weeks. He was buried in St. Edward's cemetery, and it's worth our time to note that his monument, in addition to informing us that Patrick was "a native of the County Louth, Ireland," bears the following inscription:

> Tho' Neptune's Waves
> and Buzz have tossed
> me to and fro, Yet after
> All I came at last
> To harbour here below
> Good Christians all who
> Read the above pray for me.

A fitting epitaph for a well-travelled immigrant.

Alice Hagan, my great-grandmother Maria's aunt, was born in 1823 in Ardee Parish, County Louth. She would have been 19 or 20 years old when the family left Ireland around 1842, roughly the same time at which Arthur McCann and Ann

Quinn emigrated with their children.

On January 20, 1845, at the age of 22, Alice married Terrence McCann at St. John's church in Perth. Terrence was the son of Michael McCann and Jane Elizabeth (Betty or Jennie) Donnelly, originally from Mullaghbawn townland, Forkhill Parish, Armagh. This Michael McCann was the brother of Peter McCann, patriarch of the Foley Mountain McCanns, about whom we'll learn a bit more in the chapter "Other McCanns," along with more about Terrence and Alice.

James Hagan, another of my great-grandmother Maria's uncles, was born April 30, 1819. He married Bridget Ferrigan, the daughter of Stephen Ferrigan and Rose Duggan, and in the 1850s lived up on the mountain surrounded by relatives. Their children included Margaret Hagan (born 1849) and Michael Hagan (born 1850).

James Hagan was located on Lot 21 of Concession 6 and his occupation was listed as labourer. While he occupied one half of the lot, or 100 acres, none of it was under cultivation. His father, Michael Hagan, occupied the other half of the lot and was working 20 acres, 10 under crops and 10 as pasture. Three acres were devoted to oats, one acre to potatoes, and two acres to hay. Like every good Irishman, he produced maple syrup from some of those trees on the uncleared acreage, 100 lbs. worth, and he owned two sheep that yielded 100 lbs. of wool, a milking cow, a pig, and having produced 100 lbs. of pork, may have owned a second pig that didn't make it to enumeration day.

Given that Michael's age was listed as 72 at the time (69 might have been more accurate), it's a safe bet that James's labours were all on his father's behalf.

As I began to say, James Hagan had plenty of family around

him in the 1850s. His father-in-law, 70-year-old Stephen Ferrigan, lived on Lot 21 of Concession 5, which, if you looked at the map, would place both of them on Murphy Road, with James's brother-in-law John Ferrigan across the road on the other side.

Just a bit north of them, James's brother Hugh Hagan was farming on 100 acres next to Crosby Lake, on Lot 25 of Concession 5. As it happened, Hugh was my great-grandmother Maria Hagan's father, and so our focus on the Hagan clan will now settle down here for a bit.

Hugh Hagan, Mary Flanagan, and their children

Hugh was baptized on March 5, 1821, in Dundalk, County Louth.[226] After settling in Canada with his family, he married Mary Flanagan on August 17, 1845, at St. John's church in Perth. Mary was the daughter of the late Thomas Flanagan and Jane Ryan of County Laois, Ireland, known as Queen's County until 1922. It's located near the centre of the island, about 175 kilometres south of Dundalk.

Hugh and Mary built their shanty close to Crosby Lake, as we've noted, on a 100-acre parcel, 13 acres of which were in use in 1851: five in crops and eight in pasture. Hugh planted an acre of oats and another acre of potatoes, plus another two acres of wheat, and he kept one in hay. They dabbled in maple syrup, to the tune of 20 lbs. worth, and kept a milking cow and a pig. Hugh was only 30 years old at the time, and just getting started.

The enumerator for the 1851 census, Matthew Connor, included the marginal note seen previously on p.122, that was applicable to the farms of Michael Hagan, James Hagan, the Ferrigans, and Hugh Hagan as well:

> The whole of the land on this sheet is on what we call the Mountain. It has been valued by the assessors at from 1/3 to 2/6 per acre. At this season of the year it['s] difficult to value land, but if we may estimate it by the circumstances of the people and the general appearance of things, I would say the above is high enough. Much of the land which has been cleared is not cropped owing to its barrenness.[227]

At this point, having been married for just over five years, Hugh Hagan and Mary Flanagan had two children: Bridget Hagan, born February 22, 1845; and Patrick Hagan, born February 2, 1849.

By the time of the next census in 1861, their brood had increased accordingly: Stephen Hagan (born in 1852); James Hagan (Jim) (born March 24, 1853); Maria Hagan, my great-grandmother (born on Christmas Day in 1857); and Jane Alice Hagan (born in 1859).

The enumerator of this census also noted that young Patrick Hagan had died in 1859 as the result of a broken leg.[228]

By 1871, the family expanded to include: Hugh Joseph Hagan (born May 24, 1861);[229] and Theresa Hagan (born December 23, 1867).

As late as 1891, when Hugh was 70, he and Mary still had Jim, Stephen, and Hugh Joseph at home, ages 28, 26, and 24 respectively and all single, as well as Theresa, who was 20.

Where were the others?

Jane Alice Hagan married Thomas Gallagher, a carpenter from Hamilton, Ontario, on January 7, 1885, at St. Edward's church in Westport. Born on November 16, 1857, in Eagle Harbour, Michigan, Gallagher was the son of John Gallagher, a farmer who was born in Ireland, and Alice Flood. By 1891 Thomas and Jane Alice were living in Perth, and their children included Joseph Gallagher (born April 9, 1888) and Mary H. Gallagher (born January 28, 1890).

When the next census was taken in 1901 the family had moved to Hamilton. Two more children had come along: Veronica Gallagher (born December 24, 1891); and John Ambrose Gallagher (born November 25, 1896). Joseph Gallagher does not appear in this record.

Jane Alice passed away on April 22, 1919, in Cobourg, Ontario at the age of 60, after a 10-day battle with bronchitis. She was buried in Cobourg.

Thomas Gallagher remained in Cobourg, living with their son John A. Gallagher and his family, until his death on May 22, 1937. He was buried in St. Michael's cemetery in Cobourg.

As for Maria Hagan's parents, her father Hugh Hagan passed away in April 1894, and his remains were placed in the St. Edward's cemetery vault on the 10th day of the month. The cause of death was Bright's Disease, and he was 69 years old when he passed. Mary Flanagan died on September 13, 1908, while convalescing at her daughter's house on George Street in Westport.

Hugh Joseph Hagan

Hugh Joseph Hagan, Maria's younger brother, married Agnes Bennett on January 13, 1892, at St. Edward's church in Westport. The daughter of Henry Bennett and Mary Ryan of County Armagh, Agnes was born in December 1866. Their children, nieces and nephews of Maria, included: Henry Edmond Hagan (born March 1893); Emma Loretta Hagan (born June 1896); Bridget Emily Hagan (born June 8, 1896); Hugh John Hagan (born October 1897); William Alphonsus Hagan (born March 1901); Stanley Michael Hagan (born July 1903); Jerome Hagan (born October 1905); Joseph Hagan (born December 1906); and Margaret M. Hagan (born January 1911).

Fig. 33 Hugh Joseph Hagan

Hugh Joseph Hagan passed away on September 28, 1925, from heart disease. He was buried in St. Edward's cemetery.

In his last will and testament he left his farm on Lot 18 of Concession 4 to his wife, Alice, to pass on to their sons Jerome and Francis after her death; he left the south half of Lot 18 to his son John; he left his son Henry the north part of Lot 19 of Concession 2, 125 acres "known as the Richard Herlehy farm," on condition of a payment of $1,600 to the estate; and he left sons Alphonsus and Stanley the deeds to parts of Lots 22, 23, and 24 of Concession 4, and Lots 22 and 23 in Concession 3. He left his daughter Emma $400 and his daughter Mary $300 to be paid when she came of age.[230]

It's clear that Hugh Joseph had done a considerable job

consolidating Hagan farm holdings over the years.

As a personal note, I'd like to add the following. When I chatted with my grandmother in 1981 about our family history, she mentioned that my father, Hugh Joseph McCann, had been named after "Hughie Hagan." This made sense to me because when she married my grandfather, Ford, they lived in the house on George Street that still belonged to Maria Hagan. There were a few stories about Maria that I'll touch on below, but it seemed understandable that she would have exerted her considerable influence on my grandparents to name my father Hugh Joseph McCann.

All these years I thought my grandmother was referring to Maria's father. Now, after having done considerably more work on the Hagan side of the family, I'm pretty sure it was Maria's brother, Hugh Joseph, my dad was named after, as he'd died only six years before my father was born.

Jim Hagan

Next among Maria's siblings to discuss here is James Hagan. Jim, as you may recall, was born March 24, 1853. He's listed with his family in the censuses each decade up until his father's death. Thereafter, he remained with his mother Mary Flanagan in their log shanty on Lot 24 of Concession 5, located on Big Crosby Lake Road, until her death in 1908. He lived in the shanty, still working the farm, until illness finally caught up with him.

In the conversation with my grandmother in 1981 that I've previously mentioned, she spoke about Jim Hagan with some fondness. She gave me the photograph shown in Figure 34, in

Fig. 34 Jim Hagan and Granny Hagan

which Jim stands outside their log shanty while Granny Hagan, as Mary Flanagan was affectionately known in later years, grins from the doorway.[231] It would have been taken some time between 1901, when the census listed Jim and his mother living alone together, and 1908, when Mary passed away.

As we'll discuss in a little more detail below, Ford McCann and Ida Allore married in 1920 and lived in the house on George Street that Patrick McCann had built and that Maria Hagan still owned and occupied. For a three-year period, then, Ida was there at the house when Jim came calling on his sister.

Before Mary Flanagan, Maria and Jim's mother, passed away, Jim had brought Granny down from the shanty on the upper mountain to the George Street house, likely at Maria's insistence. After she died in 1908, Jim continued to walk down from the shanty on a regular basis to visit his sister.

Ida described Jim as a quiet, polite man. He spent the entire visit sitting at the kitchen table. He spoke only when spoken to, and when he did say something he was very long-winded about it. As a lifetime bachelor living all alone on his farm for the past two decades, he'd likely grown unused to conversation and had found silence comforting.

She described him as short and stout, with streaked reddish hair. When we look at the photograph he appears reasonably slim, but the stoutness was perhaps a symptom of enterocolitis, an inflammation of the intestines that can cause abdominal bloating and swelling. This is likely what Ida saw.

Jim died on August 28, 1923, at St. Francis Hospital in Smiths Falls, where he'd been admitted two weeks before when the condition became life-threatening. He was buried in St. Edward's cemetery in Westport.

Theresa Hagan and the Carty Family

Maria's younger sister Theresa Hagan, known as Tess, married Thomas Carty on February 2, 1868. Thomas was the son of Patrick Carty and Elizabeth (Bess) Ruth, the family having emigrated from Ballydonfin, Oylegate Parish, County Wexford, Ireland.

The patriarch of the clan arriving in Canada appears to have been Henry Carty, who was born in County Wexford about 1795. He settled in the township of Bastard[232] in Leeds County in the area of Philipsville. He was enumerated in the 1861 census with his wife Mary Bolton (age 70) and his sons John Carty (25) and Owen Carty (22). Elsewhere in the same township in 1861 was his son Patrick Carty (40) and his family.

In 1871, Henry Carty and Mary Bolton were living in the household of son Owen Carty, both listed as 80 years old. Henry passed away the following year, on September 21, 1872; on his headstone his age is given as 77 years. He was buried in the Holy Japanese Martyrs Catholic Cemetery[233] near Philipsville, where most of the family has been interred. Mary Bolton passed away nearly two years later, on March 21, 1874.

Patrick Carty lived on Concession 2, Lot 5, which is right on the Rideau Canal system where Upper Rideau Lake meets Big Rideau Lake. In fact, living next door on Concession 1, Lot 5, was Michael Mooney Sr., who was the lockmaster for what is now known as Narrows Lock 35.[234] Mooney Sr. was born around 1800 in Narraghmore Parish, County Kildare. His wife was Jane Cain, also from Narraghmore. Mooney was the lockmaster from 1856 to 1871.[235] He died on July 5, 1874, and was buried in the Holy Japanese Martyrs cemetery.

His son, Michael Mooney Jr., assumed the duties of lockmaster in 1871 shortly after his father's retirement and held the post until 1894, a run of 23 years. During that time, on February 27, 1876, he married Catherine Carty, the daughter of Patrick Carty and Bess Ruth, which is why we're discussing Mooneys at the present moment. Their son, Michael Edmund Mooney, became lockmaster in 1897 and remained in the position until 1946. Forty-nine years!

William Carty, son of Patrick and Bess, worked there as a lockman and enjoyed a brief spell as lockmaster in 1895 to 1896, perhaps in part because his wife was Jane Mooney, daughter of Michael Mooney Sr. and Jane Cain. Since the two families lived next door to each other, it's not surprising they became so closely knit.

Which brings us, after a bit of mission creep, back to Theresa Hagan, Maria's young sister, and her husband Thomas Carty. By 1911, when Theresa was 42, she and Thomas were operating a dairy farm on Lot 4 of Concession 2, immediately below the properties of Patrick Carty and Michael Edmund Mooney on the river. They had three children: Cecelia M. Mooney (born August 1901); Helen Mooney (born December 1903), who became a schoolteacher; and Evaristus Thomas Carty (born December 1907).

Evaristus, who was likely named after St. Evaristus, the fifth pope of the Catholic church, was 23 years old and still living at home in 1931. Surprisingly, the census for that year lists his occupation as "sailor." It's easy to imagine him hanging around the locks as a boy, bored with life on the farm, watching the boats come through, both commercial and pleasure craft, until he was able to get himself hired to work on one. It's a romantic

Fig. 35 Tom Carty

image, a young man sailing the Rideau Waterway and living a life of adventure, and one is tempted just to leave him there and carry on with the rest of our story.

But what's mission creep without a little more information? And in this case, as you'll see, I have a personal ulterior motive.

In the mid-1930s, Evaristus was a crew member on the *Brown Beaver*, a Great Lakes steamship owned by Upper Lakes Shipping of Toronto, and also on her sister ship, the *Grey Beaver*. While sailing on the latter, which steamed from Sorel, Quebec, and Toledo, Ohio, to Port Huron, Michigan, in June of 1935, Evaristus worked alongside his cousin, William James Carty, the son of James Carty and Mary McKain. Interestingly, the manifest includes the height and weight of each crew member, and we can see that Evaristus was a fairly large person for that time, measuring 5 feet, 11 inches and 197 lbs. William, on the other hand, was 5 feet, 7 inches and 160 lbs.

By 1939, however, it was time to settle down. Evaristus married Catherine Helena Hamilton, known as Helen, on June 14 of that year at St. Edward's church in Westport. A local, Helen was the daughter of John Hamilton and Catherine Cawley. Both bride and groom, according to their marriage certificate, were employed as clerks. It would seem that Evaristus had traded in steel deck plates, clouds of steam, and rolling waves for a desk and the bliss of holy matrimony.

To cut to the chase, among the children of Evaristus and Helen was Thomas Carty, who was born in Kingston on September 8, 1942. As a youth, Tom wasn't a particularly gifted student, but he loved hockey. Despite not playing until he was 12, which was a relatively late start for a Canadian kid, Tom ended up being drafted into the Ontario Hockey Association.

The OHA was at the top level of junior hockey leagues in Canada, and Tom moved off to Peterborough to play for the T.P.T. Petes.

He joined the team in 1959 when the head coach of the Petes was future NHL Hall-of-Famer Scotty Bowman. A left winger who measured 6 feet even and 168 lbs., Tom was named team captain in 1961.[236]

This is where I come in. In 1961 I was six years old, already a hockey fanatic and like every other kid in Peterborough a big fan of the Petes. I was taken to see a few of their games, and I came home raving to my dad about how much I liked the captain, Carty. He was my favourite player. Smiling, my dad explained that Tom Carty was related to us, that he was my dad's second cousin. You could have knocked me over with a feather. How proud did that make me feel?

To make a long story slightly less long, Tom went on to play professionally for the Omaha Knights in the Central Hockey League in the 1963-64 season, following Scotty Bowman, who briefly coached there on his way up the ladder to the Montreal Canadiens. Tom scored 18 goals and 24 assists that season, for 42 points, which was pretty good production for a first-year pro on a team that won the league championship.

The next year he was ordered to report to the Springfield Indians in the American Hockey League. Springfield was considered the armpit of pro hockey back then because the team was owned by Eddie Shore, known to be an absolute nightmare to play for. Future St. Louis Blues star Barclay Plager, a former teammate of Tom's at Peterborough, warned him about moving there, having played for Shore himself, and Tom decided to retire.

He obtained his teaching certificate from the Teachers' College in Peterborough and returned home to Kingston, where he taught high school for 34 years. As for hockey, he played five seasons with the Kingston Aces of the OHA Senior A hockey league between 1966-67 and 1972-73.

Tom Carty was not a descendant of Arthur McCann and Ann Quinn, it's true, but he is a distant relative of mine through the McCann family and one of my very first hockey idols. I've always wanted to learn the story of Tom Carty, how he fit into our family and where he went after leaving Peterborough, and now I have.

Okay, then. Where were we?

Maria Hagan: Wife, Mother, Grandmother

After Maria Hagan married Patrick McCann on October 29, 1881, and moved into their new house on George Street, the family began to grow. Monica Cecelia McCann was born in 1884 and Frances Agnes McCann followed in 1886. Cosmos Augustine McCann was born in 1887 and died in 1888, after which the arrival of Mary Veronica McCann in 1890, known to all as Mazie, would have been considered a blessing. Adella Louise McCann was born in 1893 and Wilford Charles McCann, known as Ford, was born in 1895.

When Patrick died in 1907, Maria was just short of her 50th birthday. Monica had been married to Francis McParland for two years, Frances was 21 years old, Mazie was 17 years old, Della was 13 years old, and Ford was eight. Patrick had been ill for the better part of the last four years, and his illness would have dominated the household. Suddenly it was over and the life of the family had to continue.

Echoing Patrick's membership in the CMBA, Maria was an active member of the Catholic Women's League (CWL). The time she spent involved in various activities on behalf of the CWL would have been a welcome diversion. This attachment was one manifestation of her strong religious devotion as a Catholic.

She was likewise dedicated in the raising of her children. It seems that music and religion both occupied places of special importance in the house on George Street as the children adjusted to the loss of their father and looked outward to their own futures. The beautiful piano seen at the corner of the photograph of Patrick and Maria in Figure 31 likely saw a great deal of service throughout the years. Monica was a well-known vocalist in Westport at the time of her marriage, Mazie played the piano and sang all her life, and Della also played piano. This musical talent likely came from Maria's influence.

As for the Catholic Church, Maria also would have impressed her strong religious devotion on her children. Both Mazie and Della entered religious service as nuns, joining the Sisters of Providence of St. Vincent de Paul in Kingston.

Once Ford had married and began to raise his family in the house on George Street, Maria ensured that her grandchildren likewise retained a constant awareness of their religious heritage and obligations.

My uncle Jack McCann told me in a conversation in 1981 that his grandmother was afraid of thunderstorms. He remembered Maria rousing the children from bed in the middle of the night during storms and gathering them together in the parlor to pray until it had passed.

On Monday, February 11, 1935, Maria was visiting a

neighbour who was ill when she fell down a cellar trap door that had been left open by accident. She must have sustained significant internal injuries from the fall, as she passed away nine days later, on Wednesday, February 20, 1935, while sitting in a chair talking to her family.

Her funeral mass, held at St. Edward's church, was officiated by Father McKiernan and was attended by her brothers-in-law John A. McCann and William E. McCann from Ottawa as well as Mazie, who was currently living in Arnprior, Frances, and Ford and his family. My father, who would have been three at the time, was probably there as well. Della, unfortunately, was ill in Perth and unable to attend. Maria was buried in St. Edward's cemetery.[237]

Fig. 36 Monica C. McCann and Francis McParland

Chapter Fifteen

The Children of Patrick and Maria

When Patrick McCann passed away in 1907, as we've seen, he left five children behind. What became of them?

Monica Cecelia McCann

The oldest of the children of Patrick and Maria, Monica Cecelia McCann was born on February 10, 1884. As a youth she was a prominent vocalist and a very active member of the church choir at St. Edward the Confessor Church. At the age of 21 years she married Francis John McParland (McParlan), of North Burgess at dawn on the first day of spring, June 21, 1905. Her sister Frances McCann was bridesmaid, and Daniel McParland, brother of Francis, was best man.

The McParlands were another of the Irish families that originated in Forkhill Parish and immigrated to North Burgess Township around 1840. Francis's grandfather, Patrick McParland, was born around 1783 in County Armagh and his wife, Annie McAleavey, was born around 1787, making them contemporaries of Arthur McCann and Ann Quinn.

They settled on Lot 8 of Concession 8 in North Burgess, Lanark County, not far from the hamlet of Stanleyville. In 1851 their children included Mary McParland (18 years old); Ann McParland (17); Bridget McParland (15); Patrick McParland Jr.

(8); and John (7).

Francis's father was John McParland, who was born in North Burgess on May 14, 1844.[238] John married Elizabeth (Lizzie) Troy, the daughter of Daniel Troy and Elizabeth Speagle, on April 2, 1883, at St. John's church in Perth. Francis was born on March 3, 1885. Their children included James McParland (born August 3, 1878); Francis; Philip Joseph McParland (born June 3, 1887); and Annie McParland (born July 8, 1890).

Monica Cecelia and Francis had eight children, including Augustus Raymond McParland (born April 11, 1906); Mary Elizabeth McParland (born December 1, 1909); Margaret McParland (born October 8, 1907); Monica Cecelia McParland (born July 22, 1911); Frances Ann McParland (born November 20, 1912); Joseph Daniel McParland (born March 1915); Philip James McParland (born August 11, 1916); and John McParland (born May 1918).

Sadly, Monica Cecelia McCann passed away at the age of 35 on August 19, 1919. The previous day, she'd had surgery at St. Francis Hospital to correct an abdominal obstruction, but unfortunately she did not survive. She was buried in St. John's cemetery in Perth.

Her obituary, which appeared in the *Courier*, was a heartfelt tribute to her short life, and bears repeating here:

> **McParlan.** It was with emotions of deepest sorrow that the people of Perth learned on Tuesday morning last, that Mrs. Francis McParlan had passed away at seven o'clock at St. Francis hospital, Smiths Falls. Her death, following an operation on the previous day, came as a shock to her many friends who had not

even learned of her recent illness. The late Mrs. McParlan was formerly Miss Monica McCann, of Westport. She was a graduate of St. Edward's Separate School of that place, and her amiable disposition accompanied by rare musical abilities made her a general favorite and deep sorrow is felt over her untimely death. On June 21, 1905, she became the happy bride of Francis McParlan, of Stanleyville. She came to Perth with her husband six years ago, and has since made a host of friends here. Naturally of a happy, cheerful character, and also deeply religious, she possessed to an eminent degree those traits which conduce to make a model Christian wife and mother. Her altogether too premature death at thirty-five years, may justly be considered an irretrievable loss and sincere sympathy goes out to the heart-broken young husband and eight little children who are left to mourn her loss, also her mother, Mrs. P.J. McCann of Westport, three sisters, Miss Frances, Westport; Rev. Sister M. Ethelreda and Sister McCann of the House of Providence, Kingston, and one brother, Ford, Westport. The funeral, the largest held in Perth for some time, took place to [sic] St. John's church, where High Requiem Mass was sung by Rev. Father Hogan. The love and respect shown the deceased was here so manifest that almost the entire congregation seemed unable to restrain their emotions at the sight of the little

> band following their mother to her last resting place and broke forth in heartfelt sobs. The pallbearers were Messrs. Hugh Hagan, Thos. Hogan, Daniel Lee, Frank Hutchinson, Jas. Gamble and John Kerr. We can only urge the sorrowing friends to now put in practice the noble resignation to God's will which ever characterized the deceased. Before the great white throne she will still love and guard her cherished friends until they join her in endless bliss which lot will surely be ours if we live as she has lived.—Con.[239]

Included in that "little band" following Monica to her grave were Raymond, 13; Mary Elizabeth, 12; Margaret, 9; Monica Cecelia, 8; Frances Ann, 6; Joseph Daniel, 4; Philip James, who'd just turned 3 the week before; and John, just over a year old and perhaps carried by his father. One can see how it must have been a sight to evoke a very deep sense of pathos.

Francis McParland continued to live in Perth, at 160 Gore Street, with the children. Their home was on the corner of Gore and Brock Streets, a block away from St. John's church. He worked as a shipping clerk in the local Wampole drug factory.

Unfortunately, on October 18, 1921, Mary Elizabeth passed away in St. Francis Hospital in Perth at the age of 12. She died after suffering for the past four years with a cerebral tumor that had been causing convulsions. She was buried in the St. John's cemetery in Perth.

In 1931, five of the children were still living at home with their father. Raymond had married Laura Oakes and moved out to start his own family; Mary Elizabeth had passed away; and

Margaret would go on to marry Patrick Murphy in Toronto the following year. In 1932, 13 years after Monica Cecelia's death, Francis remarried. Rose Ann Haughian was a widow seven years older who worked as a housekeeper (perhaps his). She died in 1957.

Francis McParland passed away on October 1, 1975 ,in Perth and was buried in St. John's cemetey.

Frances Agnes McCann

The second child of Patrick McCann and Maria Hagan, Frances Agnes McCann was born on July 10, 1886. As a young woman she worked as a teacher at St. Edward's Separate School in Westport.

On February 10, 1920, she married John Henry Bulger, a dairy farmer in the Bastard-Burgess South area of Leeds County, near Elgin. Bulger was the son of William Henry Bulger (1834-1916) and Ellen Baldwin (1836-1919).

Fig. 37 Frances Agnes

As late as 1931, which is the most current census presently available, Bulger and Frances Agnes were listed as living alone. Perhaps they remained childless throughout their marriage.

John Bulger died in 1967, and Frances passed away on July 3, 1973, just short of her 87th birthday. She is buried in St. Edward's Cemetery with her husband John and other members of the Bulger family.

Fig. 38 Johnny and Frances Bulger

COSMO AUGUSTINE MCCANN

Cosmo Augustine McCann, the third child born to Patrick and Maria, was born on January 6, 1888, and was baptised by Father Twohey on January 15 of that year. The baby died two weeks later.

MARY VERONICA (MAZIE) MCCANN

The fourth child of Patrick and Maria was Mary Veronica McCann, born on July 16, 1890. Known as Mazie, she followed in the footsteps of her older sister Frances and became a teacher at St. Edward's Separate School in Westport. However, where Frances left teaching to marry John Bulger and follow the life of a farmer's wife, Mazie chose a different path. She entered a life of religious devotion by joining the Sisters of Providence of St. Vincent de Paul based in Kingston, Ontario.

As a Sister of Providence, Mazie took the name Sister

Mary St. John Chrysostom, in honour of the Archbishop of Constantinople who lived from AD 347 to 407. St. John Chrysostom was famous for his eloquence, hence the name Chrysostom, which was given to him after his death and was

Fig. 39 Sister Mary St. John Chrysostom

derived from the Greek work *chrysostomos*, which means "golden-mouthed."[240]

The website of the Sisters of Providence posted a very nice obituary for Mazie, and the description of her life and career summarized below is paraphrased from there.[241]

"The influence of Catholic training at home and at school," as we've already seen with Maria Hagan as her mother, "was a factor under God in fostering vocations to the religious life in the two daughters who became Sisters of Providence."[242]

Mazie became a novice in 1917 and took her vows as a nun two years later. She then attended Ottawa Normal School, as the teachers' college was known at the time, and after obtaining her certificate taught Grade Eight and drama for the next 38 years, including at Arnprior, where she was living when her mother Maria died, and 15 years in Tweed, where she served as school principal.

She was not only a born teacher but a musician as well who loved to collect ethnic Irish music in addition to hymns and devotional music. She gave some of this music to my father, knowing he played the guitar and hoping he might be able to make use of it. Despite the fact that my father had left the Catholic church, Aunt Mazie loved him dearly and thoroughly enjoyed his visits.

After retiring from teaching, she moved to Kingston and served as the assistant to the Mother Superior at St. Mary's of the Lake Hospital, where she also filled in as switchboard operator and played the piano to entertain the patients.

In 1975, she had a heart attack and moved to the infirmary on the grounds of Heathfield, the former home of Sir John A. MacDonald, Canada's first prime minister. Located at Heathfield was the Providence Motherhouse, "the official home base" of the congregation,[243] and Sister Mary Chrysostom remained there for the next four years.

Ironically, the woman who had taken the name of the saint known as "golden-mouthed" began to develop throat problems that robbed her of her beautiful singing voice. The diagnosis was Paterson-Kelly Syndrome, characterized by severe anemia and an esophageal web that makes breathing, swallowing, and speaking difficult. She was admitted to St. Mary of the Lake Hospital on February 7, 1980.

She passed away on September 8, 1980, at the age of 90. As the Providence website notes, "Our Superior General, Sister Muriel, Sister Mary Clare, Superior of the hospital, and Sister Gracia Whalen were with her when she breathed her last at an early hour on Our Lady's Birthday."

Her funeral mass was celebrated two days later. I attended with my father, who was very saddened by the loss of a beloved aunt.

She was buried in St. Mary's Cemetery in Kingston.

Adella Louise McCann

The fifth child born to Patrick and Maria, Adella, known as Della, was born on October 23, 1893. She followed the example of her older sister Mazie and chose a life of religious devotion by joining the Sisters of Providence in Kingston on April 13, 1913. She adopted the name St. Mary Ethelreda in honour of St. Ethelreda, who lived about AD 630 to 679. St. Ethelreda was a noblewoman who gave up fine clothing and jewelry to work with the poor, and she is considered the patroness of those who suffer from throat or neck ailments.[244] Which is ironic, considering her sister's ultimate fate.

Once again, the website of the Sisters of Providence posted a very nice obituary for Della that may serve as a starting point for us.[245]

After professing her vows, Della went to the convent at Maryvale Abbey in Glen Nevis, Ontario, to continue her studies.[246] She then enrolled in Ottawa Normal School and, after earning her certificate, taught at several schools in the Diocese. At the time of her mother's death in 1935, she was teaching at St. John's Separate School in Perth. Unfortunately, she was not able to attend her mother's funeral due to illness.

While teaching, she also completed summer coursework at Queen's University to obtain her Bachelor of Arts degree, which she was awarded in April of 1936. She was then appointed to a teaching position at St. Francis Xavier Separate School in Brockville, Ontario.

This is the point at which amateur genealogy fails us, I confess. The Sisters of Providence tell us that five months after her appointment in Brockville, she took ill and passed away. Further research leads us to a Province of Ontario Certificate of Registration of Death that would seem to be hers.[247]

Although neatly typed rather than handwritten, as many of them were in 1936, this certificate poses a few problems. It states that she was in Brockville for six years before passing, which may not have been the case given the description of her career provided by the Sisters. It correctly gives Westport as her birthplace, but lists an incorrect birth date—August 24, 1894 rather than October 27, 1893—which we have found in the St. Edward's church register. Even more puzzling is that her parents are listed as John McCann and Margaret Leahey, rather than Patrick and Maria.

Clerical errors? A line was typed through the field where the informant's name would be listed, so the source of this information for the certificate may never be known.

All other details point to Della, though, including her profession, her adopted name and correct surname, and so on. The certificate also states that she underwent surgery for breast cancer in St. Vincent de Paul Hospital in Brockville but passed away the next day.

Della was buried in St. Mary's Cemetery in Kingston, Ontario.

WILFRED CHARLES (FORD) MCCANN

The sixth and final child born to Patrick and Maria was Wilfred McCann, known as Ford. As my grandfather, he becomes the focus of the next chapter.

Fig. 40 Ford and Mike McCann in Peterborough

Fig. 41 Ford McCann

Chapter Sixteen
Ford McCann

Technically, Wilfred Charles McCann was a 19th century man, having been born on August 6, 1896, but throughout his adult life he was the determining factor in the ultimate disposition of our family in the 20th century. He was the last McCann to have been head of the George Street household, and once he moved his family out, there was no turning back. His story is the end of the Westport chapter of our story.

Ford McCann, His Life

The only boy with four older sisters, his name was variously spelled as Wilfred, Wilfrid and Wilford in newspaper articles, obituaries, and the St. Edward the Confessor registry, but he was known to everyone as Ford.

Something to consider: Ford was born the year that Sir Wilfrid Laurier first became prime minister of Canada. The Liberal Party of Canada won the 1896 election largely because of what was known as "The Manitoba Schools Question," a controversy mishandled by the Conservatives in which Manitoba had eliminated funding for Catholic schools. When Laurier took office, he negotiated a settlement with the provincial government whereby they would provide denominational religious teaching as well as instruction in French.[248]

Aunt Mazie always delighted in asking my father if he supported the Liberals, knowing that he didn't, and pointing out to him that the Liberal Party was the family party. Given the strong feelings in the house on George Street when it came to Catholicism and teaching school, I suspect that Laurier was a fairly big hero when Ford was born. If I had to guess, I'd say his first name was inspired by the prime minister, although it ended up most commonly being spelled *Wilfred*.

Unfortunately, Ford lost his father only a week before his eleventh birthday. This loss must have had a profound effect on him, and there is little doubt that his older sisters and mother must have felt a strong need to look after him.

His Uncle T.J. returned to Westport and took over the house next door on George Street after the departure of his Aunt Mary McCann Ryan for Detroit. By all appearances, T.J. remained close to the family and would have done his best to provide Ford with a role model, no doubt.

His Uncle Will E. McCann was also still in town, and by 1909 had a flourishing interior decorating and house painting business that had taken up where Patrick had left off, but later that year he left with his family to take his wife, Ford's Aunt Sarah, down to Detroit along with her father so that he could be reunited with the rest of his family down there.

His Uncle Arthur F. McCann had already passed away, his Uncle John A. McCann had left Westport years ago to pursue his teaching and public service careers, and Uncle Mike was also in Ottawa working for the federal government. Uncle T.J. was it. (His mother's brothers were farmers up on the mountain, and likely had little time for a teenaged townie.)

All of which to say, it is quite probable that his primary influence during the formative years of his teens was his mother. We've seen how strong an influence Maria exerted on her three daughters, not only with respect to the Catholic faith but also through music, and Ford in his turn learned to play both the violin and the drums.

Ford attended St. Edward's Separate School where his older sisters Frances Agnes and Mazie were teachers, as the 1911 census shows us. Given the strictness with which schools were run at that time, Ford would have found himself in the unenviable position of receiving his schooling—and possibly his discipline—from teachers who also sat with him around the dinner table at home and likely supervised his homework in the evening.

In 1914, when he was 18 years old, he took the train on a solo trip down to Detroit to visit his Aunt Mary Ryan. You may recall that Mary's husband, James Ryan, had died of cirrhosis of the liver before Ford was born and that she'd immigrated to Detroit with her children in 1905, when Ford was about nine. Much later, Ford's Aunt Rosey was staying with Mary when she passed away from liver trouble, likely also as a result of alcoholism.

Nevertheless, Mary seemed to have stayed in touch with her family in Westport, and perhaps Ford was invited down for a visit after completing school.

The individual card manifest filled out for Ford at the Port of Detroit on his arrival has a few details about him that are of interest. First, it notes that he had $11 in his pocket to see him through the trip and that he'd paid for his ticket himself. It confirms that his objective was a visit with his Aunt Mary Ryan on Baker Street. It also tells us that he was 5'8", had brown hair and blue eyes, and that it was his intention to remain permanently in the United States![249]

Looking for a new beginning, far away from Westport?

Perhaps, but he likely found the big city of Detroit, which had a population of about half a million people in 1914, a little too different from the village, and eventually he returned.

On June 6, 1920, Father Michael O'Rourke of St. Edward's church signed Form 21 of the Registrar General of the Province of Ontario, a Certificate of Publication of Banns, announcing that Wilfrid Charles McCann and Ida Marcella Allore would marry. And so they did, eight days later, on June 14.

We'll look at Ida in some detail below. For the moment, we'll follow Ford's story.

So now that he was married, how did he intend to support his family?

In 1901, when Ford was five, there was a Chinese hand laundry on Main Street named Fong Lee Laundry. The individual enumerated under that name was 57 years old, had emigrated from China in 1892, and lived alone.

In 1910, the laundry was operating under the name Sing Lee Laundry,[250] and ten years later it was Wah Lee Laundry. The person enumerated in 1911 as running the laundry was 32, had arrived in Canada in 1910, and also lived alone.

The name Sing Lee will come up again in Ford's story, so a word of caution should be introduced here. Retired professor of psychology Dr. John Jung has written several books on the subject of Chinese hand laundries, including his memoir *Southern Fried Rice: Life in a Chinese Laundry in the Deep South* (2005) and *Chinese Laundries: Tickets to Survival on Gold Mountain* (2007). He also maintained an online blog on the subject, and in several posts lifted the veil on Chinese laundry names.

"Many customers of our laundry," he wrote, "mistakenly called my father, Frank Jung, 'Sam.' It was not unexpected that they thought he was 'Sam Lee' because our laundry, the only one in Macon, Georgia, between the late 1920s and mid-1950s was named, Sam Lee Laundry."[251]

When he did the research for *Southern Fried Rice*, he discovered that the most common names for Chinese hand laundries in Canada and the United States were Sing Lee Laundry and Sam Lee Laundry. They were not named for the laundrymen who operated them, but for concepts that were

> referring to wishful thinking and hopes that their laundries would be profitable and successful businesses. 'Lee' in any laundry name does not refer to a member of the Lee clan, but to the concept, li, meaning profit. Thus, Wing Lee means 'victorious profit' and Sam Lee means 'triple profits.'" Wah Lee means either "Brilliant Profits" or "China Profits."[252]

While we will never likely know the actual name of the men running the laundries in Westport when Ford was a youth, we can imagine that he may have picked up and dropped off items to be cleaned for his mother and sisters. It's also quite possible he hung around to watch what was going on, and the laundryman gave him part-time work. Whatever the case, Ford evidently developed a strong interest in the business.

In 1920 there must have been another change in the running of the laundry, and Ford saw an opportunity to go into business for himself. The wedding notice for Ford and Ida in 1920

Fig. 42 Ford McCann Advertising Postcard

described him as "a prosperous young business man [who] has recently opened a cleaning and pressing department of clothing." When we check the 1921 census, his occupation is listed as "Dry Cleaner & Presser."

Interestingly, his mother Maria is listed as a "laundress," suggesting that she assisted Ford with the business. Just as interesting is the fact that she is listed as Head of the household, rather than Ford. The place was still hers, and she was running the show. Also of note, Ida had already given birth to their first son, Charles.

The family grew through the 1920s. Charles Joseph McCann, known to the family as Chuck (born March 25, 1921), was joined by Monica Marcella McCann, whom everyone called Mona (born January 30, 1922); Patrick Henry McCann, known as Harry (born January 27, 1923); Mary McCann (born May 8, 1924); Wilfred Aloysius McCann, known as Wilf (born June 21, 1925); John Chrysostom McCann, known as Jack (born January 23, 1927); Anne Frances McCann (born August 30, 1928); and Rita Theresa McCann (born April 5, 1930).

As Neil A. Patterson writes, the Great Depression of the 1930s affected Westport just as seriously as any other community in Ontario. While unemployment was as high as 30 per cent in the province, Westport's council was applying for road repair grants to bring some sort of work to the village. Otherwise, people did what they could to get by. A man named Orville Forrester told Patterson that he picked dew worms and sold them for a penny each, and he recalled someone driving two cows into town and receiving only five dollars for the pair.[253]

Fig. 43 The McCann Family, ca. 1935

From left to right: Ford, Mary, Rita, Wilfred, Anne, Jack, Charlie, Harry with Hugh on his knee, Monica holding Veronica, Ida holding Mike, and Uncle T.J.

A Brief History

The photograph of the McCanns on George Street that was taken around September of 1934 (Fig. 43) shows us that the family had continued to grow during the decade of the Depression. In addition to Rita we can now see Hugh Joseph McCann on Harry's knee (born November 29, 1931); Veronica McCann (born January 12, 1933); and Michael Ignatius McCann (July 29, 1934) in his mother's arms, next to Uncle T.J. (Ford looks like Hugh did when he reached that age. Hugh used to roll up his sleeves the same way.)

Two years later, Patrick Joseph Gordon McCann arrived (born February 18, 1936), followed by Mary Ethelreda McCann (born May 19, 1938) and Ellen Catherine McCann (born November 1, 1939). Ford and Ida now could boast of a family of 14 children!

At some point during this time Ford was forced to close his cleaning business, as many of his customers would no longer have been able to afford his services. For a time he was a member of the Ontario Provincial Police, and the children were greatly entertained by the fact that he carried a gun and was involved in high adventures such as the confiscation of illegal beer and liquor.

My father Hugh recalled an instance when he was small when his mother and a few of the older children were gathered around a box in the back summer kitchen. Inside the box were a number of Ford's items that had been put away from his time in the OPP, including a clip-on holster for his gun and leather motorcycle leggings. The older boys were disappointed that the gun was not in the holster, and they carefully repacked the box as close to its original configuration as possible.

In February of 1935 Maria died, and so the house on

George Street passed into Ford's hands. It didn't last long, however. Some time between the winter of 1939-40, when Ellen was born, and 1943, Ford and Ida decided they could no longer make a go of it in Westport, and they gave up the house and moved to Kingston.

Margaret Rose McCann, known as Margie, was born in Kingston on September 8, 1943. Shortly thereafter, however, the family was struck by the untimely death of Monica in an automobile accident on August 13, 1944, at the age of 22. They were living at 665 Victoria Street at the time.

During the war, Charlie, Harry, and Wilf each served in the Canadian Armed Forces. Unfortunately, Wilf was wounded in action on April 11, 1945, and died in hospital that June. The family was living at 147 Brock Street in Kingston at the time, and they subsequently moved to 833 Princess Street.

That winter another heavy blow was struck when Veronica passed away. As a child, she'd suffered from a defective heart valve that would cause her to pass out if she became too excited or stressed.[254] She died two days before Christmas as a result of this ailment.

The following spring, Ida gave birth to Oliver Joseph McCann, known as Ollie, on April 29, 1946, in Kingston.

At this point, Ford entered a period of itinerancy, travelling from place to place and job to job, until his death in 1955. We've already seen reference to several different addresses in Kingston. He worked for Cleland and Flindall's dry cleaning in the city, and around 1947 he had started a new business on Clarence Street, but it would seem that conditions were not right for him to succeed this time on his own.

Ford and the family left Kingston and lived in the village

of Shannonville, Ontario. While there, he delivered milk for a Belleville-based dairy. His milk route extended east toward Napanee, and one of Ford's stops was at the farm of the Hull family at Point Anne (at this point Bobby and Dennis were boys younger than Hugh). He delivered as far as Marysville, a small community built around the St. Mary's Cement company. Ford's son Hugh often accompanied him on his route, and years afterwards vividly recalled waiting in the milk truck as Ford made his stops at innumerable cement buildings in Marysville. Even the houses were made of cement. Hugh remarked that of all the time he was there, he never saw a single soul. It would have been a typical factory town; everyone would have been at work. To my father, though, who was an introspective teenager at the time, it was like an existential wasteland, empty and depressing.

Shortly before they left this area Ford and Ida had their final child, Linda Marie McCann who was born on May 19, 1949.

At this point, the oldest children were no longer living in the household. Chuck, Mary, Harry, Jack, Anne, and Rita had married and started their own families, and Monica, Wilf, and Veronica had passed away. But there were still eight mouths to feed, including Pat, Mike, Hugh, Margie, Ethelreda, Ellen, Ollie, and baby Linda, and Ford decided to move from Shannonville to Peterborough, Ontario, in 1950.[255]

That year and in 1951, they lived at 238 Simcoe Street in the city, and Ford and Hugh worked at Grant's Cleaners at George Street, later to become Parker's Cleaners. A Sing Lee Laundry, by the way, was located at 232 Hunter Street West.

In 1952, Ford was absent from the Vernon's *Directory* for Peterborough, Hugh had gone to work for Canadian General

Electric, and Sing Lee Laundry had moved into their former address at 238 Simcoe Street. Make of that what you will.

By 1954, Ford and Ida had moved to a house on High Street, and before the end of the year, they moved the family back to Kingston. By this time, there were only three children still living at home with Ford and Ida—Margie, Ollie, and Linda. They took up residence at 545 Bagot Street.

Ford was not well, however, as he had begun to battle the cancer that would ultimately take his life. He was hospitalized in February 1955 and finally succumbed in the Hotel Dieu Hospital on April 7, 1955.

His funeral was held at St. Edward the Confessor Church in Westport. His pallbearers were Dr. Gordon Hamilton, Peter Donnelly, William Carty, W.K. Murphy, Henry McNally, and James Kane. He was buried in St. Edward's Cemetery in Westport. His simple headstone reads:

McCann
Ford 1896-1955

With the passing of Ford, the last link of the chain extending down from Arthur McCann and Ann Quinn to their descendants in Westport, Ontario, was broken. From this point forward, the family name moved in multiple directions, but such is the nature of families and offspring in the modern world. Which is why I hope this *Brief History* will serve as a useful touchstone for all of my relatives out there in the humanosphere.

Chapter Seventeen

Henry Allore

While my grandfather Ford passed away several months before I was born, I grew up knowing my grandmother, Ida Allore McCann, fairly well. As well as a kid could know a grandparent, I suppose you could say.

I loved and admired her quite a lot, and so I've decided to spend the next few chapters on her and her family—that is, the families that combined to bring her into this world.

Henry Allore's Family

Henry Allore, Ida's father, was born on March 29, 1868, in China Township, Michigan. His parents were Alexander Allore and Mary Jane Stephenson, both of that township, which is located near Marine City, Michigan, a town on the St. Clair River south of Sarnia, Ontario, and a few miles east of Detroit.

The area was originally settled by 16th century French coureurs de bois and missionaries. Subsequent French settlers cleared and cultivated the land in what was known as "ribbon farming," long, narrow strips of land with frontage on the river. The idea was to provide the settlers with access to the riverfront for shipping their produce, and also to ensure that their next-door neighbours were relatively close at hand.

After the Revolutionary War and Michigan's achievement of statehood in 1837, there was an influx of English- and German-

Fig. 44 Henry Allore

speaking settlers, but a French presence remained very strong in Detroit, especially in Grosse Pointe, and in counties to the north, including St. Clair.[256]

Several times, records connected to Alexander Allore and his family identify their residence as East China, which is on the shore of the St. Clair River above Marine City. Thus, it's quite possible that Alexander owned a portion of one of the original ribbon farms.[257]

Alexander Allore was born in New York state in September 1839; his father's name was Michael Allore, likely Michel. Both his parents were French Canadians, suggesting that they probably emigrated from Quebec into New York, and from New York to Michigan after Alexander was born.

Henry's mother, Mary Jane Stephenson, was born around 1847. She was the daughter of Edward Stephenson (1805-1887) and Jane Tate (1805-188). Her parents were from Pocklington, Yorkshire, England, where they married in 1825.[258] Edward's farm in China Township consisted in 1880 of 25 acres on which he grew oats and wheat and kept dairy cattle.

Alexander's farm was a modest 16 acres. He kept a few cows, sheep, chickens, and pigs. In 1880, he was 41 and Mary Jane was 33. They had five children: Mary Jane Allore (born September, 1862); Henry (born 1868); William Allore (born about 1872); Genieve "Jennie" Allore (born February 1873); and Alexander Allore, Jr. (born in April 1876).

Of Henry Allore's siblings, his sister Mary Jane married William Lang, an Irish immigrant who worked in Marine City as an engineer. Mary was working as a nurse. The marriage took place on New Year's Eve, 1900, in Marine City. Unfortunately, she died on January 9, 1904, as a result of hemorrhaging. She was 41 years old.

Henry's brother William had previously died of blood poisoning on May 13, 1890, in Marine City. He was only 18.

On February 15, 1897, Henry's sister Genieve, known as Jennie, married George Edward Stapley in Marine City. Stapley was a Canadian immigrant farming near Algonac, Michigan, a small city just down the river from East China. He was six years younger than Jennie.

In 1900, Stapley and Jennie were living with his mother, Nancy, in Clay Township, St. Clair, just across the river from Algonac. Ten years later, they were in their own place in Cottrellville Township, and Stapley was working as a packer in a salt works.

They had three children: James Stapley (born September 29, 1903); Mary T. (Tena?) Stapley (born around 1904); and Alvina Clara Stapley (born May 27, 1909).

George Edward Stapley died on April 28, 1924, of pneumonia in Marine City. Jennie was 41. Two years later, on April 24, 1926, she married 50-year-old William Delorge, also of French descent, in St. Clair City. When we peek at the 1940 census, they were still living together in Marine City, but Jennie passed away on June 16, 1941. Evidently she'd fallen and broken her hip in December of 1939, and complications from the injury eventually took her life.[259]

The last of Henry Allore's siblings to account for is Alexander Allore Jr., who was born in 1876. On August 21, 1895, in Marine City, Alex Jr. married Catherine (Katrina) Umlauf, the daughter of a Prussian immigrant, Paul Umlauf, and Mary Batchellor, daughter of Swiss immigrants John and Mary Batchellor.

Their children included Anastasia Allore (born February

1897); Harold Allore, known as Harry (January 1899); Raymond A. Allore (born in 1900); and Loretta Allore (born 1903).

Alexander Allore Junior died on October 19, 1940, in Royal Oak, Michigan, as a result of gangrenous diabetes.

Have we finally finished with Henry Allore's family so that we can get on with a description of his life?

No, not yet.

At some point around 1882, Alexander Senior remarried. I have to admit, after much hand-wringing, that I have not been able to find out what happened to Henry's mother, Mary Jane Stephenson. It's possible she died, or it's possible they divorced and she remarried. Every lead I followed, though, turned out to be the wrong person. It's one of those things that happens in genealogical research, I suppose. If you discover her in your own investigations, by all means write the information down in the margins here!

Alexander Sr. married a young woman named Caroline Lachpillar (or Lochbiller), known as Carrie. She lived on a farm very close to the Allores; her father was Joseph Lochbiller, a German immigrant. Born in 1861, she was about 20 when they were married, 22 years younger than Alexander.

Henry's first half-sibling, Joseph Allore, was born on November 8, 1883, in Marine City. By this time Alexander had left the farm and was working as a drayman in the city, a dray being a heavy cart without sides used to haul stuff around. A half-sister, Anna May Allore, was born April 19, 1886, after which came John Allore (born October 1887); another Genieve Allore (born April 1894); Edna Allore (born May 1899); and Andrew Allore (born in 1900).

Whether Henry Allore was at all close to his step-mother

and second family is not known, so for the sake of keeping this a *Brief History* we'll leave Carrie and her children to another day.

Henry Allore's First Marriage

When Henry Allore was 21 years old, he married Mary Byrne (or Burns) in Marine City on August 27, 1889.[260] Born in 1866, Mary was the daughter of Bernard Burns and Mary O'Hare of Perth, Ontario. At the time of his marriage, Henry was working as a drayman in Marine City, as his father had. (As for the spelling of her family name, it would seem that Byrne has been more common in North Burgess for Irish Catholics, while Burns is more common among Scottish immigrants and Americans. While the Michigan marriage record refers to her as Burns, I'll go with Byrne here, in keeping with the majority of Canadian records.)

One of the witnesses at the wedding was 20-year-old Annie McCoy, from up the river in Sarnia, Ontario. That name on this particular document is going to open up a can of worms for us that will take a bit of sorting out. First, though, we must look at the family Mary Byrne began with Henry Allore before her untimely death.

William Leo Allore

Mary gave birth to a son, William Leo Allore, on July 14, 1890, in Marine City. We'll take a few minutes to look at his life, as he was Ida Allore's half-brother and, as such, deserves our attention.

William Leo appeared in the 1901 census for Smiths Falls,

Ontario, with his father Henry Allore and his step-mother. At the age of 21, William married a woman named Annie Bissonette, 19, on March 21, 1912, in Smiths Falls. She was the daughter of John Bissonette and Alice Nolan. On March 16, 1914, Annie gave birth to Edmund Orville Allore, known as Orville.

On December 27, 1915, while working as a train brakeman, William Leo enlisted in the Canadian Expeditionary Force. He was a member of the 130th Battalion, Company A, which was based in Perth. According to his medical sheet, he was 5'7" and weighed 150 pounds. He had an appendicitis scar on his right side. A later medical form tells us he had brown eyes and fair hair.

Unfortunately, he didn't do very well as a soldier. While in basic training at Valcartier Camp, he was hospitalized on June 27, 1916, and treated for gonorrhea. He was released on July 24 and his training continued, but on September 22, a day before his battalion would sail to England, he deserted.[261]

The following June, he turned up in Farmington, Oakland County, Michigan, which is northwest of Detroit. He was working as a farm labourer for a man named Carl Utley. On June 5, 1917, two months after the United States entered World War I, he registered with the U.S. Armed Forces. He hedged on the form by saying he had no previous military service, not wanting to be tagged as a deserter, presumably.[262] Apparently it wasn't the army and war per se that he didn't like, just being in the Canadian army as opposed to the army of his homeland.

After being discharged from service in December 1918, William Leo moved to Cortland, New York. (In case you were wondering, yes, Cortland apples originated in the Cortland, New York area.) In September of 1919 he married a local woman,

Mabel Graham. During the 1920s, 1930s, and 1940s, he worked for the Cortland Corset Company as a corset cutter. The census of 1940 finds the couple living on a farm in Willet Township, but on April 27, 1942, at the age of 51, he registered again for military service in the U.S. Army. The form tells us that his fair hair was now gray and his weight had gone up to 180 pounds.[263]

On May 15, Mabel left him.

On July 8, he obtained a marriage licence in Susquehanna County, Pennsylvania, about an hour south of Cortland across the state line, to marry Dorothy Catherine Sweeney.[264] Twenty-nine and single, she was the daughter of Timothy Sweeney of the nearby village of Homer in Cortland County. They were married on the 16th by a justice of the peace right there in Susquehanna.

If, consumed with curiosity, we check out the census of 1940 for Homer, two years before the marriage, we find Dorothy still living at home with her parents at the age of 27. Sliding over the columns, we see that she was employed as a factory floor lady. At a corset factory.

A floor lady would be out on the production floor, involved with the assembly of the corsets, which I imagine would then be handed off to a corset cutter for completion. Or maybe the other way around. I don't know a lot about corsets. Anyway, it's pretty likely that William Leo and Dorothy had known each other for a while through work.

Setting aside how well they knew each other, and how it may or may not have affected his marriage to Mabel, the records tell us that for the rest of his life, William Leo remained with Dorothy. The 1960 directory for Cortland lists them living together in the household of William Leo's half-brother, Alphonsus Allore, for example.[265]

On December 26, 1975, William Leo Allore passed away[266] and was buried in St. Mary's Cemetery in Cortland. Dorothy lived until 1993 and was buried with him.

Orville Allore

Edmond Orville Allore was born on March 29, 1891, to Henry Allore and Mary Byrne Allore in Bay City, Michigan.[267] He died on February 24, 1893, in Bay City of a bowel inflammation.[268] He was not quite two years old.

As we saw above, his older brother William Leo Allore named his first son Edmond Orville Allore, born in Smiths Falls in 1914, after Edmond.

Mary Irene Allore

Mary Irene Allore was born in 1894 to Henry Allore and Mary Byrne Allore. She passed away on October 21, 1900, in Perth, Ontario, at the age of six after an unsuccessful battle with diphtheria, a severe throat infection for which a vaccine had been developed in Europe but was not yet widely available.

Her death came only a few months after her father married Annie McCoy. She was six years old.

Florence Allore

When you're performing genealogical research to the depth we've been reaching in this *Brief History*, you're bound to come across a few individuals who strike you as ineffably sad. There have been a few that I can think of, looking back through these pages, and Florence Allore, Ida's half-sister, is another.

Florence was born in May of 1897 in the United States and was brought to Canada by her parents when they moved to Stanleyville, Lanark County, in 1898.[269]

Mary Byrne Allore had not been well. In 1896 she developed an abscess of the liver, and it's likely that her pregnancy with Florence worsened the condition. Returning to Canada allowed her to be with her family while she struggled with it, but on September 11, 1899, she passed away in Stanleyville.

While her brother, William Leo Allore, was nine years old when his mother died, Florence was already living with her Grandmother Byrne, having been placed in her care at the age of six months. It would seem that her mother was not well enough to take proper care of a baby.

When Mary finally succumbed to her illness, Florence was two. She was being raised by her grandparents, Bernard Byrne, known as Barny, and Mary O'Hare. Barny passed away in 1908, and his bachelor son Bernard Jr. became head of the household, but Florence's grandmother Mary O'Hare remained in the home, still taking care of Florence.

On August 13, 1914, at 16 years of age, Florence married a local shoemaker, Thomas O'Neil. The son of Michael O'Neil and Sarah Byrne, Thomas was only 18. (By the way, Sarah was the daughter of Henry Byrne and Sarah Rossiter, according to her marriage record, and apparently not a direct relative.)

Because of her youth, and because no one currently knew where Henry Allore was, her Aunt Annie Byrne signed an affidavit that swore the following:

Perth. Ont. Aug. 13th. 1914.

> The paper writing here to annexed marked "A" is the consent to the said marriage. The address of the father of Florence O'Lore [sic] is unknown, & the mother is dead, & no guardian having been appointed the undersigned Annie Byrne is the Aunt of the said Florence O'Lore, & hereby gives her consent which is also the consent of the Grandmother of the said Florence O'Lore to the said marriage withwhom the said Florence O'Lore had her home since she was six months old.
>
> Annie Byrne[270]

Aunt Annie herself married shortly afterward. On October 26, 1914, Annie Evelyn Byrne, at the age of 30, married John Baptiste Vinette of Peterborough, Ontario, in Perth. Vinette was a trainman for CPR, and they raised their family in Toronto.

Unfortunately, marriage did not go well for Florence. She became pregnant, and on September 6, 1915, delivered a boy who was stillborn. The child was buried in St. Bridget's Cemetery in Stanleyville. Florence was only 17 years old.

On April 27, 1920, Thomas O'Neil obtained a divorce, apparently leaving the Catholic Church in order to do so, and he married Anne Marie DeBursey of Pembroke on January 25, 1923, in the Presbyterian church in Smiths Falls.

Left behind at the age of 22, no longer married, her protective

Aunt Annie off to start her own family, Florence Allore dropped from the grid. It's possible she went back to her grandmother's until Mary O'Hare Byrne's death in 1930. Perhaps she remarried. It remains a mystery for another day.

Having looked at Ida Allore's half-siblings to the extent possible, we should now return to her father for the rest of his story. (Annie McCoy's story will take a bit of telling, so we'll get to her in the next chapter.)

Henry Allore's Story

After the death of Mary Byrne, his first wife, Henry Allore married Annie McCoy on July 4, 1900. At the time, he was living in Perth and working as a carpenter.

As we've seen, although Henry had given his infant daughter Florence to his late wife's family to raise, he still had William Leo and Mary Irene with him. The latter, unfortunately, died of diphtheria that October.

A year later, as the 1901 census tells us, they were living in Smiths Falls with William Leo, who was 10 at the time. Henry was still doing carpentry work.

What the census doesn't tell us is that Annie gave birth to a daughter, Beatrice Anastasia Allore, on April 9, 1901. Sadly, the child died on October 3, at the age of six months, in Smiths Falls. The cause of death was acute diarrhea. [271]

Soon after, Henry, Annie, and William Leo Allore moved to a farm in the Stanleyville area, where Ida Marcella Allore was born on February 16, 1903; Alphonsus Henry Allore followed (born September 23, 1904); then Gladys Allore (born July 1906); and finally Edna Allore (born March 1908).

The 1911 census confirms Henry's farming endeavour. William Leo is still living with them and working as a mechanic at the age of 20. Also living with them was Annie's niece, Josephine Troy, and 17-year-old William Drew, a British home child who had come to Canada in 1907.

Why were the Byrnes unable to locate Henry in 1914, when Florence married Thomas O'Neil at the tender age of 16 and Annie Byrne was compelled to sign an affidavit giving her permission for the marriage to take place? There doesn't seem to be an available record between 1911 and 1917 to account for his whereabouts. It's likely he was either still on his farm at Stanleyville or down in Westport, and it's possible there'd been a falling out between him and his first wife's family.

By 1917 we find that Henry Allore had made a significant change of direction in his life. The family moved to Westport, and Henry took the bold step of purchasing the Windsor House Hotel at 11 Main Street.

Events leading up to the purchase of this hotel are somewhat interesting, so let's indulge ourselves for a few minutes.

The previous owner of the hotel, Richard D. Hogan, was originally from the Third Line of Bathurst Township in Lanark County. Hogan moved to Westport and took over the Windsor House in 1892, selling his Bathurst property in 1894. His first wife, Anastasia Whelan, was a daughter of Walter Whelan, the postmaster of Westport, and the sister of John H. Whelan, briefly Arthur F. McCann's partner in a stage line. After she passed away in October of 1901, Hogan married a woman whose first name was Teresa, and continued with the management of the Windsor House.

At some point thereafter Hogan and Teresa found them-

Fig. 45 The Windsor House Hotel

selves inundated by the McCoy family. Granted, we have not talked about the McCoys in any detail yet, but this little story is worth jumping the gun over.

When we check the census of 1901, taken just before Hogan's first wife's death, we see that three of Anastasia Whelan's stepchildren from her first marriage were living in the hotel with them. When we fast-forward to 1911, that lot was gone. In their place were the following relatives of Annie McCoy Allore: her Uncle John B. McCoy, 75, a permanent resident of the hotel who worked as the yardman; Mary Troy, Annie's sister, who had married the now-deceased Daniel Troy and was the hotel cook (her daughter Josephine was boarding with Annie and Henry); and Annie's unmarried sister Ellen McCoy, who also lived at Windsor House and worked in the dining room.

It's reasonable to assume, then, that Annie was a frequent visitor from the farm in Stanleyville to see her family at the hotel, and Henry likely accompanied her. The Hogans would have no choice but to become acquainted with the bunch of them, Henry included. And Henry would have gained an intimate knowledge of the hotel and its workings.

Here's how this all went down.

Patrick J. McParland was a man who loved to buy and sell hotels. An Irish immigrant who came to the area in the early 1880s, he married Margaret Stanley, daughter of Michael Stanley (the squire of Stanleyville), and began pursuing his interest in the hotel industry. He owned the Union Hotel in Perth for a while, and the Wardrobe Hotel in Westport.[272]

When Hogan died on December 19, 1918, he and McParland had already completed several financing deals for the Windsor House property, and ownership lay in McParland's hands. But when McParland's wife, Margaret Stanley, died, he apparently lost all heart and decided to return to Ireland.

He put up the Windsor House for sale at auction, and Henry Allore was the successful bidder. Ownership transferred to him on May 15, 1917, at a cost of $3,500.[273]

Moving ahead to 1921, Henry and his family were firmly ensconced in their new business. Listed as a hotelkeeper, he still had Alphonsus, Edna, and Gladys at home with him, along with two boarders, Howard B. Vincent, a schoolteacher, and Isabel Pollard, a housekeeper (perhaps theirs).

In March of 1923, however, a terrible fire broke out in the village that destroyed the hotel, the house next to it, and two houses across the road. An eyewitness reported that "the piano was saved from the flames [and] was rolled out the front door by helpful onlookers" but it "sustained damage when it crossed the road."[274] Which was probably the one paved with good intentions. Piano notwithstanding, Henry Allore's livelihood was wiped out that day, and on July 13, 1925, he and Annie sold the property to a man named John Leslie McEwen for $1,000.

On September 28, 1923, Henry and the family travelled from Westport to Watertown, New York, with the intention of resettling there. According to his primary inspection document, they took the passenger ferry S.S. Victory across the St. Lawrence River from Brockville to Morristown, New York, where they reported to U.S. Customs before continuing on to Watertown.

In his declaration, Henry gave his occupation as a hotelkeeper. He was carrying $600 with him, about $11,000 in today's Canadian dollars. Likely the family savings after the loss of the hotel. The document tells us he was 5'5"—another little guy!—and had grey hair.

Gladys and Edna, who were 17 and 16 respectively, gave their occupations as waitresses.[275]

Henry and the family remained in Watertown until 1925. He and Annie appeared in the Kimball's city directory in 1924 at 557 Pearl Street, a two-storey frame house that currently is home to the Pearl Street Pub, while Gladys and Edna had separate rooms at 555 Pearl.

In 1925 they lived at 707 Griffin Street, a storey-and-a-half house with a separate apartment in the back that Edna occupied. By this time, Gladys was married, and Edna was working as a telephone operator for the New York Telephone Company. More on the two sisters below, but we'll note that although Henry and Annie left the city by 1926, Edna remained alone for several years until her marriage there.[276]

By 1931, Henry and Annie were back on the farm in North Burgess. They were both in their early sixties now, and I can't imagine that Henry's farming efforts were very extensive. In a few years he retired, perhaps when he reached his 65th birthday in 1933, and he and Annie returned to Westport.

He died in the village on October 22, 1943, at the age of 75. The cause of death was a heart attack brought on by a blood clot in the heart caused by years of arteriosclerosis. He was buried in St. Edward's cemetery.

Chapter Eighteen
Annie McCoy

As promised, we now turn our attention to the second wife of Henry Allore, Annie McCoy, the mother of Ida Allore McCann.

Annie was born on February 20, 1869, the daughter of Thomas McCoy and Bridget Kearns, as we've seen.

One of the nagging questions that cropped up during this line of research was the following: How on earth did Henry, born and raised in St. Clair, Michigan, happen to marry *two* different women born and raised in North Burgess, Ontario, about 400 miles away? How did they meet, how did they get to know each other, and how did one follow the other as the mother of Henry's children?

Unsurprisingly, our best theory is a little bit complicated and will need some telling. This wouldn't be a *Brief History* if it were otherwise, would it?

The best place for us to start would be three sisters who each played a role in the families that ultimately brought Henry and Annie together.

The Three O'Hare Sisters

Francis O'Hare and Elizabeth Smythe, known as Eliza, were Irish immigrants from Killevy Parish, County Armagh, who married in 1841 or 1842.[277] They settled in North Crosby, Leeds County, on Lot 21 of Concession 1, on the upper mountain, right on the line with North Burgess. Next door to them was a man named John Smith, who might just have been Eliza's brother. In this neck of the woods we've also seen the homesteads of Owen Kearns, Michael Kearns, Matthew McCoy and Bernard Smith, likely another of Eliza's brothers.

In 1951, Francis O'Hare occupied 20 acres, 10 of which were in use: 3 acres in crops and seven in pasture. Not a significant operation, but then again, he'd likely arrived not long before. The agricultural schedule for the 1861 census is not available, but in the personal returns we see that Francis and Eliza have been counted as part of North Burgess Township, and their family has grown. The second and third sisters have now appeared in the record, but before I explain their importance, something significant must be mentioned.

Francis O'Hare and Eliza Smith moved from North Burgess out to Lambton County, Ontario. The 1871 census found them in Moore Township, close to the town of Corunna. This is the first time we've mentioned this place, but it won't be the last. And it's the place that's going to help us answer the question posed at the beginning of the chapter. Remember? How the heck did Henry Allore meet two young ladies from North Burgess, Ontario, and end up marrying both of them?

Here's the first clue: Moore Township and the town of Corunna are located on the eastern shore of the St. Clair River, directly across from St. Clair County, Michigan, with Stag Island and its ferry service available for river crossings. Within easy reach of Marine City, where Henry Allore and Mary Byrne were married.

Francis and Eliza were part of a little wave of migrants who relocated in this area, and this is how we'll use the three sisters to try to bring everything together.

The oldest, Martha O'Hare, married Michael McCoy on July 18, 1852. Michael was the son of Matthew McCoy and Alley Murphy, meaning he was our dear Annie McCoy's Uncle Mike McCoy. Michael and Martha moved out to Moore Township some time before the 1861 census, which finds them in a log shanty with three small children on the go.

Next was Catherine O'Hare, who was born in Killevy Parish, Ireland, on January 10, 1842.[278] On January 22, 1867, she married Thomas Byrne, the son of Michael Byrne and Bridget Lee, in Perth, Ontario. By 1871, Thomas, Catherine, and their young children were living in Moore Township, Lambton County, along with everyone else. Thomas, being our Mary Byrne's brother, was Annie McCoy's Uncle Thomas Byrne.

The third O'Hare sister was Mary. As we've seen, she married Bernard Byrne and was the mother of Mary Burns/Byrne, Henry Allore's first wife. Unlike everyone else and their dog Rufus, Barney Byrne and Mary O'Hare remained in North Burgess for the rest of their lives.

The most logical explanation, then, is that their daughter Mary Byrne and her cousin Annie McCoy travelled out to Moore Township together. They had their pick of relatives to visit, tied together by the O'Hare sisters, and they likely day-tripped across the river during their stay, where they met Henry.

However it happened, we know the end result was matrimony—twice.

Annie McCoy's Family

Let's dive into the history of the McCoy family. Heaven knows we've been circling around it in previous sections, but let's pull it all together here for the sake of neatness and tidiness.

Matthew McCoy, son of John McCoy, was born about 1794. He can be spotted in the 1821 census of Forkhill Parish, County Armagh, Ireland, in the household of his widowed mother in Latbirget Townland,[279] a long strip of land extending down through the middle of the parish from the northern edge to Maphoner Townland. He was 27 years old and still living in the household of his late father John McCoy along with his sister Sarah McCoy (born about 1792); his brother John McCoy (born about 1805); and sisters Catherine McCoy (born about 1804); Cecily McCoy (born about 1809); and Mary McCoy (born about 1811).

Matthew McCoy married Alice Murphy, known as Alley, and they started a family of their own while still in Forkhill. Their children included Mary McCoy (born about 1829); Michael McCoy (born about 1831); Thomas McCoy (born September 1832); John McCoy (born about 1835); Bridget McCoy (born about 1836); and Donald McCoy (born about 1838).

Matthew McCoy emigrated in 1847[280] along with so many others trying to escape the Famine. He squatted on Lot 18 of Concession 1, where he was enumerated in the census of 1848. This lot is up on the mountain, right at the end of Byrnes Road on the line between North Crosby and North Burgess Townships, where Scotch Line Road passes through. It's just a dogleg away from where Arthur McCann lived in the early 1840s.

This census shows no agricultural activity at all for Matthew, confirming he'd only just arrived, but in 1851 we see he was splitting the lot with James Ward, 100 acres each. He put 20 acres under cultivation, with 15 in crops and 5 under pasture. He grew two acres of wheat, an acre in peas, three in oats, two

Fig. 46 Thomas McCoy

in potatoes, and four in hay. I know that doesn't add up, but that's all the census tells us. Maybe he had the other three acres planted in rye, for you-know-what.

In addition to his crops, he owned an ox, two milking cows, five sheep, and a pig. He took 15 pounds of wool from his sheep, producing 12 yards of fulled cloth; he churned 50 pounds of butter; and again, like a good Irishman, boiled up 10 pounds of maple syrup.

A brief word on James Ward, Matthew McCoy's neighbour. The son of Michael Ward, James was from Maphoner Townland in Forkhill Parish.[281] Maphoner lies on the southern edge of Latbirget, so there's a possibility the McCoy and Ward families knew each other back home.

Ward travelled to Canada with many other immigrants on the ill-fated brig *Hannah* in April 1849. When it struck an iceberg and began to sink, Ward was reported to have jumped down onto the iceberg repeatedly to rescue stranded passengers, including a number of children.[282] Once settled in North Crosby, he likely found the harsh pioneer life on the upper mountain somehow less perilous than the voyage over.

As for Matthew McCoy, he passed away at the age of 80 on March 19, 1870, and was buried in St. Edward's cemetery.

We've already looked at Matthew's son Michael McCoy, who married one of the O'Hare sisters and moved out to Lot 18, Concession 11 of Moore Township, on the eastern shore of the St. Clair River.[283]

His son Thomas McCoy, who's of particular interest to us, of course, married Bridget Kearns on May 29, 1865, while his father Matthew was still alive to see it. We've already talked about Bridget being the daughter of Owen Kearns and Ann

Quinn Kearns, but what about their own family?

In 1851, Thomas McCoy was 19 and working on his father Matthew's farm. Twenty years later, Matthew had passed away, and Thomas was the head of the household on Lot 18 of Concession 1, right up there on the upper mountain with the Smiths, the Kearnses, the Hagans, and the other families we've mentioned. His son Matthew McCoy was 5, Michael McCoy was 4, Annie McCoy was 2, and baby Owen was eight months old.

His widowed mother Alley Murphy McCoy lived with them, as did his widowed sister Mary, who was 45, and his uncle James McCoy, 70, who was also a widower. The farm at Lot 18 had become a place of refuge for the McCoy clan as the advancing years robbed them of their independence.

As for their children, Thomas McCoy Jr. appears to have remained a bachelor all his life. Born on March 26, 1872, he lived in Kingston and passed away on December 4, 1862, at the age of 90. He was buried in St. Edward's cemetery in Westport.[284] Similarly, their daughter Ellen McCoy, who was born on July 4, 1879, remained unmarried after leaving home and lived in Kingston, where she passed away on January 31, 1968, also at the age of 90. She too was buried in St. Edward's cemetery.[285]

Their daughter Mary McCoy, born on February 17, 1874, married Daniel Joseph Troy, son of Francis Troy and Ann Murphy. He was a grandson of Daniel Troy (1813-1897) and Elizabeth Speagle (1816-1888), who was the daughter of Casper Speagle and Ann Byrne (see Mary McCann McCardle, above).

Among the children of Mary McCoy and Daniel Joseph Troy were Walter Francis Troy (1897-1994) and Mary Josephine Troy, who was born on April 16, 1899, and died during the Spanish Influenza epidemic in 1918. The Troys are buried in St. Bridget's cemetery in Stanleyville.

Annie McCoy's Children

As we saw previously, Annie's firstborn child was Beatrice Anastasia Allore, on April 9, 1901. Sadly, the child died on October 3, at the age of six months, in Smiths Falls.

Ida Marcella Allore was next, born in 1903, and we'll look at her life in the next chapter. The rest of the children, however, deserve a closer look in the following subsections.

Alphonsus Henry Allore

Born on September 23, 1904, Alphonsus Allore was a teenager when his father acquired the Windsor House Hotel and moved the family down to Westport. He was 19 years old when the family relocated to Watertown, New York. Evidently he decided to follow the example of his sisters and remain in the United States, finding his way to Detroit.

In 1927, at the age of 24, he was selling milk for a living when he married a woman named Gold Ardela Upthegrove, the daughter of Jacob Upthegrove and Cora Brown of Clare, Michigan. (Upthegrove is the Americanization of the Dutch surname Op de Graef.) Three years later, they were living with Gold's brother Ora, who was a factory driver, Ora's wife Carrie, and their daughter Sophie. Alphonsus and Gold had not yet had any children. On June 29, 1935, Gold was granted a divorce, having cited "extreme and repeated desertion and non-support." There were no children.[286]

Gold later remarried in Chicago, to a man named Harry Olson. Harry worked in Detroit and the couple retired to Gold's hometown, Clare, where she passed away in July of 1974 at the age of 71.[287]

Alphonsus Allore, meanwhile, relocated to New York state, where he married Anna Mary Hanlon in Syracuse on February 29, 1936. Anna Hanlon was born on March 21, 1911, the daughter of James Hanlon, a Stanleyville carpenter, and Elizabeth Haughian. By 1940 Alphonsus had moved back to Detroit, where he and Anna were raising two daughters, Joan Allore (1935-2007), who married Russell Teeter, and Mary Lou Allore (born 1936).

By 1941, Alphonsus had moved to McGraw, Cortland County, New York. In 1942, at the age of 37, he registered for military service, listing his address as 42 North Street, McGraw. His height was 5'8" and his weight was 150, his eyes were blue, his hair brown, and his complexion ruddy.

In 1944, however, he was still a civilian living in McGraw and working at the McGraw Box Company, a business that manufactured jewelry boxes, silverware chests, and other very nice-looking pieces that are now considered collectible. He worked there up to 1950, when the census for that year listed him as unemployed.

The census also shows that Anna Hanlon was employed as a machine operator in a corset factory. Next door, Mrs. Ruth Brown had the same job. At the Cortland Corset Company, no doubt, where Alphonsus' half-brother William Leo Allore had worked for many years.

By 1954, Alphonsus was working at Cogan's Shoe Store and the next year, the Endicott-Johnson Shoe Store in Cortland, while still living in McGraw. In 1960, we see that they had moved to 57 1/2 Lincoln Avenue in Cortland itself, making it easier for Alphonsus to get to work, where he was now an assistant manager. Anna was employed at the Cortland Memorial Hospital, and Mary Lou was nursing in Syracuse, which is only 33 miles to the north. Also living with them on Lincoln Avenue were Alphonsus' half-brother William Leo Allore and his wife Dorothy. William Leo was back working at Cortland Corset.[288]

Alphonsus Henry Allore passed away on March 24, 1968, at the age of 63. He was buried in Saint Mary's Cemetery in Cortland.

Gladys Allore

Gladys Bernadine Allore was born in 1906 in Stanleyville, as we've seen. She lived in the Windsor House Hotel from the age of 11 to 17 and accompanied the rest of the family when they relocated to Watertown, New York, in 1923.

The following year, on July 10, 1924, at the tender age of 18, she married George Albert Honeybell, 20, the son of James Honeybell and Mabel Grant of Watertown. George Honeybell worked as a house painter and chauffeur, and Gladys was a telephone operator.

Their son, James Henry Honeybell, was born on January 3, 1925. After his parents split, James lived with his father and grandmother Mabel Honeybell in Watertown until enlisting in the United States Army at the age of 18. Private First Class James H. Honeybell of the 7th Division Infantry was killed in action on November 20, 1944, at the age of 19. He's buried in the Epinal American Cemetery in Epinal, Departement des Vosges, Lorraine, France.

Their daughter, Mary Louise Honeybell, known as Mary

Lou, was born on May 25, 1933.

The marriage didn't last, unfortunately, and by 1940 Honeybell was living with his mother Mabel while Gladys had remarried, to a Watertown man named Edward T. Godkin, the son of Joseph Godkin and May Woodruff Godkin.

Honeybell, for his part, served four years in the U.S. Navy and moved to Nashville, Tennessee, where he worked as an interior decorator. He married a woman named Helene and died on February 2, 1953, when he put a gun in his mouth and pulled the trigger.[289]

Gladys Bernadine Allore died on October 15, 1971, and was buried in Brookside cemetery in Watertown, New York.

Edna Allore

Edna Annie Allore was born on March 13, 1908. She was nine years old when the family took over the Windsor House Hotel in Westport, and 16 when they relocated to Watertown, New York.

As mentioned, after Henry and Annie returned home, Edna remained behind. She rented a room on 61 Bronson Street in Watertown and worked as an operator at the New York Telephone Company. While her sister Gladys married soon after their parents left, Edna remained single for several years.

While working at New York Telephone, it's likely she became friends with another operator by the name of Catherine L. Gaffney, the daughter of John and Catherine Gaffney. John ran a service station at 840 Arsenal Street, and the family lived next door at 834.

There were a number of Gaffneys in town at that time,

including James J. Gaffney, who was likely related to John. James J. was the son of James A. Gaffney and Ellen Blanchfield of Osgoode Township, Ontario. James J. Gaffney was married to Nellie O'Connor, and in April 1880 the family emigrated from Ontario to Watertown, where they settled and eventually became American citizens.

It's probable that while Catherine L. Gaffney and Edna Allore worked together at New York Telephone, Catherine introduced Edna to her relative, Charles Rolland Gaffney. Charles was the son of James J. Gaffney, and Edna may have met him when at a social function attended by Edna and various assorted Gaffneys.

However it began, Edna and Charles married on February 6, 1928, in Watertown, at the age of 19 years. Charles was 24. In the early years, they lived with the Gaffneys. Edna's father-in-law was an auto body builder with a shop at 442 Cross Street, while Charles was a civil engineer working on the state highway system.

Edna remained at New York Telephone and soon rose to the position of supervisor. Meanwhile, on January 31, 1931, she gave birth to John Richard Gaffney, known as Dick, followed by Mary Ann Gaffney (born 1933), and David Rolland Gaffney (born February 8, 1936). After the death of James J. Gaffney, her father-in-law, they continued to live in the house at 432 Dimmick Street with Charles's mother, Nellie O'Connor Gaffney.

In 1942, Charles filled out his military registration card. The address remained 432 Dimmick, but he listed himself as unemployed. We can see on the card that, unlike many of the men we've profiled here who were small, Charles was a large man—6 feet 1 inch and 210 pounds. His hair was brown and his eyes were blue.

After Nellie passed away on April 16, 1944, they moved to a duplex at 113 East Flower Street, where they are found in the 1950 census. Son John Richard was 19 and working as a cashier at the A & P grocery store while Charles Rolland was 44 and a construction superintendent for a building contractor, and Edna, 39, continued on as a supervisor at New York Telephone.

Their daughter, Mary Ann Gaffney (Ida Allore's niece, remember) was not with them. She was a 17-year-old student nurse at Mercy Hospital,[290] formerly St. Joachim's, where we saw that Anastasia McCann Flynn had built a successful career in training and administration. (Anastasia was in Sioux Falls, South Dakota in 1950, but would soon return.) Afterward, Mary Ann earned a degree in Public Health from Catholic University in Washington, D.C., a private research university with close ties to the Church.

Enter Kishor C. Mehta.

Kishor emigrated from Ahmedabad, India, in 1954 in order to attend the University of Michigan. He completed a Bachelor of Science in civil engineering (BSCE) from the University of Michigan in 1957 and an MSCE in 1958. After graduation, he was hired by Merritt-Chapman & Scott, a former marine salvage company known as the "Black Horse of the Sea," to work as a project engineer on the Glen Canyon Dam project in Page, Arizona.[291]

Page was founded in 1957 as a housing community for the people working on the dam. A 25-bed hospital was built in 1958. Being a public health specialist, it's likely that Mary Ann Gaffney worked for the state department of health and oversaw the establishment of a nursing unit in the new hospital.

However it came about, they met in Page and married on December 27, 1960. They relocated to Austin, Texas, where Kishor worked as a teaching assistant at the University of Texas-Austin while he completed his Ph.D. in Civil Engineering, and Mary Ann worked as a public health nurse. After Kishor received his degree, they moved to Lubbock, Texas, when Kishor accepted a teaching position at Texas Tech University. They remained in Lubbock for the rest of Mary Ann's life.

She worked at Covenant Lakeside Hospital and Presbyterian Center Clinic. She volunteered for a stunning array of charities, and in 1979 was named Woman of the Year by the Lubbock chapter of the Association for Women in Communications. She and Kishor had four children: David Mehta, Jatin Mehta, Anna Mehta, and Raajan Mehta.

Mary Ann Gaffney, Ida Allore's niece, passed away on June 28, 2007, in Lubbock after a difficult battle with cancer.[292]

Ida's nephew, Dick Gaffney, worked for over 40 years as a telephone installer for New York Telephone, no doubt getting hired through his mother's influence (arm-twisting), and after he retired he formed his own company, "C & D Enterprises, selling and installing phone systems for over five years."[293] He married Linda Pipe and had three children. He passed away on April 23, 2022, and was buried in the Glenwood cemetery in Watertown.

Charles Rolland Gaffney died on August 21, 1979, and was buried in Glenwood cemetery as well.

Annie McCoy Passes Away

In 1951, Ida's mother Annie returned to Watertown, New

York, to live with her daughter Edna and son-in-law Charles Rolland Gaffney. In 1952, she fell and broke her hip. It was slow to heal and bothered her for the rest of her life. To add to her burden, she had gall bladder surgery in 1958.

She was hospitalized again in June of 1959 and passed away on August 4. Her remains were returned to Westport, and after a funeral mass she was buried in St. Edward's Cemetery.[294]

Fig. 47 Ida Allore, Confirmation Day

Chapter Nineteen

Ida Allore and her Children

We've reached the point now in our *Brief History* where we will be touching on descendants of Arthur McCann and Ann Quinn who are either still living or recently deceased. As I mentioned at the beginning, we live in an age where identity theft and the exploitation of personal information by unscrupulous individuals are real threats, so the less revealed here about my cousins and their children, the better.

To address this problem, I've added note pages at the back of the book. I encourage you to write down whatever information you wish about your own personal family line beyond the point in time that will be covered by this chapter. Best of luck!

We've also reached the point where I'm writing about people I knew and cared about when I was younger, and so some of the things I'll include will be subjective, personal notes. More along the lines of a memoir rather than genealogy. I don't apologize for this; it's just an explanation.

Ida's Story

Ida Marcella Allore was born on February 16. 1903, in Stanleyville, Ontario. Her parents, Henry Allore and Annie McCoy, had recently relocated from Smiths Falls out to their farm, and Ida had a rural upbringing in her early years. She was one and a half years old when her brother Alphonsus Henry Allore was born, three years old when sister Gladys Allore

Fig. 48 Ford and Ida McCann, Wedding Portrait

appeared, and five when Edna Allore was born.

The family moved down to Westport in 1917 when Henry acquired the Windsor House Hotel. Ida was 14 and no doubt helped her mother with the housekeeping chores that were suddenly thrust on them.

During this time she met Ford McCann, and on June 14, 1920, they were married by Father Michael O'Rourke in St. Edward's Church. Ida was 18 years old, and Ford was 24.

As mentioned, the couple lived in the house on George Street with Ford's mother Maria. Ida's first child, Charles McCann, was born on March 25, 1921. The children that followed will be spoken about in more detail below, but suffice it to say for now that by the time Maria Hagan passed away on February 20, 1935, she already had 11 grandchildren living in the house with her!

As we have seen, Ida gave birth to three more children—Patrick Joseph Gordon McCann on February 18, 1936, Ethelreda McCann on May 19, 1938, and Ellen Catherine McCann on November 1, 1939, after which the family left Westport. In Kingston, Ida gave birth to Margaret (Margie) McCann on September 8, 1943.

The following two years, however, brought heartache to Ida. Her oldest daughter, Monica Marcella, was killed in an automobile accident on August 13, 1944. Her son Wilf passed away the following year, on June 27, 1945, as a result of wounds suffered while serving overseas in World War II. Six months later, her daughter Veronica, known to have a heart defect, died two days before Christmas on December 23, 1945.

Since her role as mother to a large family of children was the dominating element of her life along with her Catholic faith,

Fig. 49 Ida McCann, as I knew her

these losses must have been crushing. She sought solace in God and carried on. The birth of Oliver Joseph McCann on April 29, 1946, whom she was carrying at the time of Veronica's death, gave her renewed hope.

Shortly thereafter, the family left Kingston and lived in a number of places, including Shannonville and Peterborough. Ida gave birth to her final child, Linda Marie McCann, in Belleville on May 19, 1949. After Peterborough the family returned to Kingston, where Ford passed away on April 7, 1955.

Living at the time at 545 Bagot Street, Ida was left with three children still at home—Margie, who was 11 years old, Ollie, who was almost nine, and Linda, who was not quite six.

Four months later her son Michael McCann, who was living near Peterborough, died of a brain tumor on August 18, 1955. Once more her faith was put to the test.

Ida later moved to Peterborough to be closer to her younger children who were living there, including Hugh, Ethel, and Ellen. In Peterborough she lived in an apartment in a tenement building attached to the North George Sundries at the corner of George and Dublin Streets, two blocks from where Hugh lived, and later lived around the corner from Hugh in a duplex on Waterford Street. At one point, Ethel occupied the other half of the house.

Once she had returned to Kingston and Margie, Ollie and Linda had all married and begun families of their own, Ida lived by herself in an apartment on Parkdale Avenue. Each summer during those years my family would spend about a week of my father's holidays visiting Kingston. We would stay with Ida in her apartment, my brother and I on a fold-out couch in the living room and my parents in the spare bedroom. My father Hugh treasured these times with his mother, as it was an opportunity for him to get to know her better. Being the middle child in a very large family meant that he would have spent almost no time at all alone with her, and Hugh shared his mother's belief that family was of supreme importance in one's life. These visits also provided an opportunity to visit with other family members. Ida enjoyed the odd game of four-handed euchre with Ethel, Anne, and my father. I learned the game from watching them play. After a few hands Ida's patience with cards would run out and she would recruit one of the others, perhaps Pat or Ellen or whoever else might be visiting, to take her place so that she could retire to her armchair with a cup of coffee and a cigarette to enjoy the company of her family.

It was her stated ambition to live to the age of 100, but unfortunately she fell a few years short. Ida passed away on August 26, 1998, three years to the day after the death of her son, Hugh. The Mass of Christian Burial was celebrated for her at St. Joseph's Catholic Church in Kingston and she was buried in St. Edward's Cemetery in Westport with her husband Ford. She left behind 45 grandchildren and 75 great-grandchildren.

Throughout her life she remained a faithful Catholic who treasured her family and prayed ceaselessly for them regardless of their successes or failures in life. It meant a great deal to me when she told me, while I was living in Kingston as a graduate student at Queen's University, that she included me in those nightly prayers.

She was particularly close to her daughter Ethel, whom she always called Ethelreda, and relied on her and her second husband Harley McIntosh, for assistance with appointments, getting groceries, and attending mass.

She could be reticent, private, and stubborn when she wanted to be, but she loved us all very, very much.

CHARLES MCCANN

Charles Joseph McCann was born on March 25, 1921, in Westport, Ontario. Charlie, called Chuck by his brothers and sisters, was the oldest of the children. He went to school in Westport. He was a veteran who served in the Canadian Armed Forces overseas during World War II. While overseas he met and married a woman named Winifred Arline. Their children included Anne, Brian and Bruce.

Fig. 50 Charlie McCann

Later in life, Chuck moved out west where he lived for a number of years in Salmon Arm, British Columbia. He also lived in Edmonton, where he was a sales representative for the Co-operative Trust Company of Canada.

Chuck passed away in Edmonton, Alberta, on November 26, 1981, at the age of 60. He was cremated.

MONICA MCCANN

Monica Marcella McCann was born on January 30, 1922. Known to the family as Mona, she was the oldest girl born to Ford and Ida McCann. Named for her Aunt Monica McCann McParland, she attended St. Edward's School in Westport and was about 18 when the family pulled up stakes and moved to Kingston.

She worked for Chown, Limited, a family hardware business in Kingston that had been in operation since 1845.[295] She lived at 665 Victoria Street with the family at the time.

Fig. 51 Mona and her Motorcycle

On August 13, 1944, when she was only 22, she was involved in a two-car accident on the airport road when an oncoming car crossed into the lane of the car in which she was a passenger. Mona was killed instantly.[296] She was buried in St. Edward's Cemetery in Westport.

Mona's studio portrait remained prominently displayed in Ida's living room throughout the years. I remember looking at it when we visited Ida in Kingston and wondering who she was. It was a tribute to how close Ida felt to her daughter, and how hard she took her loss.

Patrick Henry McCann

Patrick Henry McCann, known as Harry, was born on January 27, 1923, in Westport, Ontario. Named after his two grandfathers, he was the second-oldest of the sons of Ford and Ida McCann.

Harry was a veteran who served with the Canadian Armed Forces overseas during World War II. After the war, he took a job with the City of Kingston's Public Works Department and soon rose to the position of manager before his retirement.

Harry was married to Grace Lawrence and later married again to Ethel Thurlow Aitchison. He adopted Ethel's children, including Suzanne, John, Douglas, Barry and Edward Aitchison. Harry's family was of paramount importance to him, and he was very close to Ethel, his children and his grandchildren. He was a soft-spoken man with a wry wit and a good sense of humour who lived in a wartime bungalow on a quiet side street. When we visited him in the 1960s, we'd sit in his back yard on lawn chairs and I'd listen to the talk. The McCanns tended not to engage in a lot of conversation with the kids hanging around, so I never really talked to him much at all. Just listened. Memorized the sound of his throaty chuckle. There was a yellow plum tree in the yard, and when the fruit was ripe it was very sweet. Who the heck has a plum tree behind their house in the middle of the city? My dad was as fascinated by it as I was.

Fig. 52 Harry McCann

Harry passed away on March 20, 1996, after a long and difficult battle with cancer. He was buried in Glenhaven Memorial Gardens on Division Street in Kingston.

Mary McCann

Mary McCann was born on May 8, 1924, in Westport, Ontario. She was the second-oldest daughter born to Ford and Ida McCann. As a girl she attended St. Edward's School in Westport.

Mary met Anthony (Tony) Bantle while he was stationed in Kingston as a member of the Canadian Armed Forces, and they married on January 30, 1945. Tony was born and raised in Prince Albert, Saskatchewan, and after his discharge in 1946 they moved to his home town, later relocating to Drumheller, Alberta, where Tony worked as an automotive repair instructor at the Drumheller Institution, a medium-security prison run by Corrections Canada.

Fig. 53 Mary McCann

Mary and Tony would travel east to visit Ida in Kingston every now and again, and it was always an event. Ida would fuss about, wanting everything to be perfect. The various brothers and sisters would arrange to visit the apartment, and my dad would make a special effort to get down to Kingston while she was there. It was like a visit by Princess Margaret.

Mary behaved like the senior offspring that she was, reserved and full of good advice. It was great theatre, and I loved it. As with every other McCann, she never really spoke directly to me, and so we didn't develop a relationship to speak of, but again, I didn't mind. I loved listening to her talk to the family.

As for Tony, he barely spoke a word. Nice guy. Everyone really liked him.

Mary and Tony had three children: Philip Bantle, who died in a parachuting accident in 1972; Debra Bantle; and Sharon Bantle.

Mary passed away in Drumheller on April 12, 2001, after a brief fight against cancer.[297] She was buried in Drumheller cemetery.

WILF MCCANN

Wilfred Aloysius McCann was born on June 21, 1925, in Westport, Ontario. Named after his father, he was known as Wilf. Raised in the village, he was about 15 when the family moved to Kingston.

Wilf was 15 when he left school after completing Grade Eight, because he wanted to begin working for a living.[298] Evidently, he wasn't very good in school and was eager to get on with life.

He worked at odd jobs at 50 cents an hour until he was hired as a trucker's helper with the Canada Dry Company, where he worked for a year at a weekly wage of $18. He then landed a job with the Canada Shipbuilding Company as an

Fig. 54 Wilf McCann

electrician's helper. After eight months of this work, he decided to enlist in the Canadian Armed Forces.

He reported for his medical examination on January 20, 1944. He was measured at 5 feet 7 inches and 137 pounds, his eyes were blue and his hair brown, he had 20/20 vision, and his hearing was good. He'd suffered a bout of pneumonia in 1940 that kept him in hospital for six months but a chest x-ray showed no after-effects.

He reported for enlistment on February 17, 1944. In summary comments on his Personnel Selection Record, examiner Lieutenant J.N. Craig noted:

> He is of good average height, and some nervousness was evident, in the form of hand mannerisms.
>
> He has no particular hobbies, but enjoys reading detective, and romantic fiction. In sports hockey, and baseball are his activities.
>
> He is able to drive motor vehicles, and on occasion has driven a two ton truck.
>
> His Army attitude is good, and he has evinced a liking for the C.A.C. [Canadian Armoured Corps.]He seems particularly interested in either electrical work, or driving.[299]

(One of the documents in his file notes that he played a year of junior OHA hockey in Kingston, so his athleticism and interest in the sport were both evident.)

Wilf was taken on strength on March 2, 1944, and sent

to Newmarket, Ontario, to begin basic training. On April 12 examiner Captain D.J. Hynes wrote:

> McCann likes army life very well enjoys the training and is making average progress in training. He tries hard and is a good soldier. This man seems suitably allocated to C.A.C.

He then reported to Camp Borden, Ontario, for infantry training, and on June 1, 1944, examiner Captain H.J. Newman wrote in his file:

> Well built young soldier. Pleasant and affable in conversation. Is very interested in training as Driver i/c [internal combustion]. Has considerable experience in automotive work. Has driven a soft drink truck for a little over a year and has a very fair knowledge of automotive repairs. Should develop very satisfactorily in this type of training.
>
> Recommendation: Suitable for training as Driver i/c (Track).

Later in the month, Wilf completed a two-week course on operating a machine gun at the Canadian Machine Gun Training Centre and on August 16 passed a six-week driver training course at the Canadian Driver and Maintenance School in Woodstock, Ontario. He then received his Standing Orders as a qualified driver i/c, Class III (meaning he was qualified to drive heavy trucks and armoured cars).

Back at Camp Borden, examiner Captain W.G. Mann wrote on October 5:

> This soldier has satisfactorily completed Infantry Corps training and has qualified on Driving course at Woodstock. -Examination-and interview indicate suitability for overseas reinforcement.
>
> Recommendation: Infantry (MG) Dvr. i/c, Cl. III (W).[300]

Wilf flew to England on November 28, 1944, and engaged in further training, including a refresher firearms course, until he was flown to France on February 15, 1945, and was added to the list of reinforcements available to units in the field as a driver/mechanic.

He was just in time to participate in the Liberation of Europe.

Wilf was assigned to Company A of the Algonquin Regiment on March 4, 1945, as a reinforcement. Based in North Bay and Timmins, this infantry regiment has a history going back to 1900, and over the years was largely comprised of Indigenous recruits. As the war approached its end, they had participated in mop-up operations in France and Belgium, had played an important role in the liberation of The Netherlands, and in February 1945 they were right there in the mix when the Allies took the next big step, crossing the German border in what would be known as the Rhineland Campaign.

Catching up to the regiment on March 4, Wilf arrived the day after the Algonquin Regiment had participated in the capture of the Hochwald Gap, a forest passage west of the town of Xanten,

Germany. Between March 2nd to the 3rd, the Algonquins had sustained 87 casualties, and Wilf would have been joining a regiment exhausted from brutal combat in which progress was measured in hundreds of yards rather than miles.[301]

The Algonquin Regiment was an important component of what was known as Operation Blockbuster, the Canadian offensive underway west of the Rhine River. It began on February 4, 1945, and concluded March 23, and Wilf found himself right in the middle of it.

On March 7, the Algonquin Regiment advanced on the town of Veen, Germany, with the Lincoln and Welland Regiment on the right flank and the Algonquins on the left and in the centre, following the road between Sonsbeck and Veen, approaching from the west and northwest. At 1500 hours (3 PM) a command post was set up and at 1600 hours the attack began. By 1730 hours Company A had captured the crossroads southwest of the town and had cleared the buildings there, while Company B took another group of buildings, their positions supported by tanks. However, they'd suffered a casualty rate of 50 per cent.[302]

Company C joined B, but their casualties were also heavy, and the attack stalled. By the morning of March 8, it was raining. The Algonquins were pinned down by snipers and artillery shelling. Three ambulance drivers trying to evacuate casualties were shot by German snipers who ignored the Red Cross on their jeeps. Nevertheless, Company A still had 24 men, B had 35, and C had 33.[303]

On March 9, with the town still not yet taken, a new plan was devised whereby Company D of the Algonquins would join a force swinging around to attack Winnenthal, east of Veen. Meanwhile, "During the early morning hours Lt FR Caron was ordered to take command of 'A' Coy and to take forward 30 reinforcements who had just arrived in the theatre and none of whom had ever seen battle before."[304] Wilf would have been among this number.

At 8:30 in the morning, infantry and "crocodiles" (flame throwers) began the attack, capturing buildings that had pinned them down, and by 10 o'clock they'd succeeded in finally taking control of the town.

Wilf had had his first taste of battle.

As Operation Blockbuster reached its conclusion, the Algonquins rolled out as part of a pincer movement to clear out German forces in the northeast. It was largely mop-up duty, as the back of the German army had been broken and the end of the war was near.

Between March 13 and March 30, 1945, Wilf travelled with the regiment to the town of Gemonde, Netherlands. They were moving through an area where the Netherlands jutted east into Germany, and so over the next month they crossed in and out of both countries as they rolled forward.

After Gemonde it was Cleve, on the German side, where they crossed the Rhine River on the last day of the month.[305]

April 1 was Easter Sunday. It was raining, and the Algonquins were stationary southeast of Cleve, waiting for orders. The rain continued into the next day, and as they finally moved forward, "the men were surprised that we had crossed the border back into HOLLAND again."[306] They took up a defensive position at Barchem, Netherlands, before moving ahead once again.

On April 5, they were ordered to proceed to Almelo, Netherlands, where they would relieve the Argyll and Sutherland Highlanders, a Canadian unit fighting with them as part of the northeastern pincer movement. As the Algonquin War Diary records it,

> the unit rode into ALMELO at about 1100 hrs and were heartily welcomed by the cheering populace of this town of some 35,000 people, most of whom lined the streets to watch our triumphal entry.[307]

The regiment remained at Almelo through to April 9. Overnight and through the morning of the 9th, which was cool and foggy, Company A had held a bridgehead forward near Wierden, and during the day word was received that the Germans had withdrawn from there, so Wilf and the Algonquins moved out that afternoon.

The next day they were ordered to proceed to the town of Beckhusen, on the German side of the border. While other companies were sent off on various missions, Company A was ordered to remain in place rather than proceed to Breddenburg, the next objective. Because of this decision, the Germans were able to take advantage and occupy the town.

April 11 was a bright, warm, sunny day. At 10 o'clock, Company A, under the command of Major R.B. Stock, attacked the town,

> where they ran into a bloody battle against fanatical resistance. By 1400 hrs the battle was over with following results: Enemy captured 54. Killed 32, accounting for the entire coy holding that area. Own cas: Alq R, 3 killed 8 wounded.[308]

Wilf was among one of the eight wounded men, dropped by

bullets that struck his right abdomen and right chest.

His comrades in the Algonquin Regiment would carry on the battle without him.

Wilf was immediately moved from the Algonquin roster to the "X-3" wounded list and evacuated from the field by a 15 Canadian Field Ambulance team, which was attached to the 4 Canadian Armoured Division that had been accompanying the Algonquins during this final campaign. The field ambulance transported him to 6 Canadian Field Dressing Station, where his wounds received follow-up attention. On the 19th, eight days after having been shot, he was transported to the 2 Canadian Casualty Clearing Station at Heerenberg, the Netherlands, and evacuated to England.

At home, on April 16, his mother Ida had received one of those dreaded telegrams:

> SINCERELY REGRET INFORM YOU C52935 PRIVATE WILFRED ALOYSIUS MCCANN HAS BEEN OFFICIALLY REPORTED SERIOUSLY WOUNDED IN ACTION ELEVENTH APRIL 1945 NATURE OF WOUNDS NOT YET AVAILABLE STOP.[309]

One can only imagine how terrifying it was for Ida, holding this piece of paper in her hand, trying to accept such awful news about her third-oldest son.

On the 20th, she received a follow-up telegram telling her that the nature of wounds was in fact a bullet wound "RIGHT THORAC ABDOMEN STOP." One can only imagine how difficult it must have been for Ida to cope with this horrible turn of events.

On April 28, Wilf was admitted to No. 2 Canadian General Hospital in Cuckfield, U.K.,[310] a village north of Brighton on the coast of the English Channel. His wounds were found to include a gunshot wound that penetrated his right chest, a gunshot wound that penetrated his right abdomen, haemothorax on the right side, meaning internal bleeding, and a fracture of the ninth right rib.[311]

As April turned to May, Wilf's recovery proceeded. On May 1, Ida received the following telegram:

> PLEASED TO INFORM YOU C52935 PRIVATE WILFRED ALOYSIUS MCCANN IS OFFICIALLY REPORTED MAKING SATISFACTORY PROGRESS AND REMOVED FROM SERIOUSLY ILL LIST TWENTYEIGHTH APRIL 1945.[312]

Ida must have been enormously relieved. And it was official!

While he was in hospital, Wilf learned that the German armies had surrendered on May 8, 1945, only 27 days after he was wounded. If only they could have given up, he must have thought, before we reached Beckhusen.

Wilf remained in hospital until May 29, when he was transferred to a convalescence facility under the auspices of No. 1 Canadian Repatriation Depot in the Thursley-Bramshott area. That day, he wrote a letter to his mother that said in part:

> Just a few lines to let you know everything is going fine. I left the

> hospital to-day and now I'm in a convalescence hosp., but it is different here, this is just a place where you do exercise to get back in shape. I'm feeling pretty good Mom, and there's no reason for you to worry over me, you see when I leave here I will either go to a holding unit or be sent back home, I'm hoping it's the latter.[313]

It seemed certain that Wilf was in the clear, on the road to recovery, and almost ready to come home.

On June 13, Capt. B.L. Button interviewed Wilf at 1 Canadian Repatriation Depot and wrote the following report:

> This rather quiet, pleasant young man has no rehabilitation problems as he intends to return to his former employment as driver for Canada Drug [sic] Co. in Kingston Ont.
>
> This man is single and has only a year in the army so his readjustment back to civilian life should be no problem. He was wounded in action in the stomach and this is remedial, according to his pulhems profile, should not affect his returning to his former job.[314]

Despite the optimism all around, unseen forces of destruction were working away inside Wilf's body. On June 25, 1945, he fell ill again and was re-admitted to hospital, this time in the Bramshott Military Hospital.

He was diagnosed with acute necrosis of the liver and infectious hepatitis. The bullet penetrating his abdomen must have nicked his liver, which sits on the right side just under the ribs, and progressive destruction of cells must have carried on unnoticed until it reached the point that the liver couldn't resist an attack by the hepatitis virus.

On June 26, poor unsuspecting Ida rode the rollercoaster once again:

> SINCERELY REGRET INFORM YOU C52935 PRIVATE WILFRED ALOYSIUS MCCANN IS OFFICIALLY REPORTED SERIOUSLY ILL TWENTY FIFTH JUNE 1945 BECOMING DANGEROUSLY ILL SAME DATE STOP.[315]

The following day, June 27, 1945, at 2158 hours (two minutes before 10 PM), Wilf passed away in Bramshott Hospital. It was six days after his 20th birthday.

Wilf was buried in the Brookwood Military Cemetery, Woking, Surrey, England, in "grave 3, row C, plot 59."[316]

In recognition of Wilf's sacrifice, Ida later received the Canadian Memorial Cross, awarded to wives and mothers of military personnel who died in service.

JACK MCCANN

John Chrysostom (Jack) McCann was born on January 23, 1927. While his father's uncle was also named John, Jack was likely named in honour of St. John Chrysostom and his Aunt Mazie, who took the name of this saint when she entered the Sisters of Providence of St. Vincent de Paul.

Jack married Clara Hutchins, known as Claire, on April 5,

1947. They had four children: Christopher McCann, Edward McCann, Debra (Debbie) McCann, and Jennifer McCann. Jack worked for a number of years at NYAB Vicom (New York Air Brake) as well as Dacon Corporation.

Perhaps my cousin Chris will forgive me for adding a few *brief* notes about him.

Chris was always interested in music and as a youth gravitated to the drums. He formed the rock band Bramble with Kingston musicians Michael Myers, Peter Hutchison, Gord Craig, Tim Mavety, Paul Shilton and Craig Perry. Bramble was largely a Chicago cover band with a brass section included. They were represented by the Bernie Dobbin Agency of Deseronto, Ontario, who also represented the Guess Who, Mashmakhan, the Five Man Electrical Band, and Lighthouse, among other notable Canadian bands of the time.

Fig. 55 Jack and Claire

Why I mention this is because Bramble played my high school graduation dance at Peterborough Collegiate and Vocational Institute in 1974. I was thrilled, not only because my cousin was up there doing Danny Seraphine, but also that they made Chicago, one of my favourite bands, sound so great.

Chris also played in a Kingston band called Two Minute Hate, the name coming from the novel *1984* by George Orwell. Also in the band were Brian Hinchey and Bill Joslin. Figure 56 was a promotional photo; Chris is the one in the middle.

Chris had already built up a certain level of local fame after a concert in the Kingston Memorial Centre on July 15, 1968, headlined by The Who.[317] It seemed that the famous British

Fig. 56 Two Minute Hate

rockers had been held up at the Detroit-Windsor border. Canada Customs imposed a security bond of $20,000 on their equipment and instruments, most of which had to be left behind when they couldn't afford the bond. They flew to Kingston in a small charter plane and, after arriving, immediately started hunting around for replacement instruments.

Given The Who's tendency to smash guitars and so on as part of their stage act, finding loaners wasn't easy. Keith Moon, their drummer, was referred to Chris as someone who might be willing to lend his kit for a good cause. Moon went to check them out and couldn't believe his eyes. Chris had invested his money in a double set of Rogers drums, which were top of the line and very expensive, and they also happened to be exactly the drums Moon had left behind on the other side of the border.

That night he put on a show that Chris watched with awe. Chris "remembers Moon doing moves that [I] can't do today, like bouncing a stick off a floor tom tom three metres into the air and catching it in perfect time to keep the beat."[318] Unfortunately, three songs into the performance, Moon drove the foot pedal of Chris's bass drum right through the face. However, when it was all over, Moon gladly paid Chris for the damage.

Later, Chris migrated to jazz. He became a professor of music at McGill University in Montreal, Quebec. He toured internationally and launched a recording career. His albums include "Bay D'Espoir," Rob Frayne/Chris McCann Quartet (1991, Unity); "Calypsony," Rob Frayne/Chris McCann (1989, Unity); "On This Night," Chris McCann (1994, Unity); and "Froggin' Around," Chris McCann-Billy Pierce Trio (1996, CIMP).

According to his daughter Debbie, Jack was also musically talented, having recorded the 1946 standard "The Old Lamplighter." He had a pleasant singing voice and the same throaty chuckle as his brothers and sisters. He was kind and soft-spoken, a good dresser, and someone I liked to be around.

John Chrysostom McCann passed away on July 3, 2011, and was buried in the Cataraqui Cemetery in Kingston, Ontario.

Anne McCann

Fig. 57 Anne and Jimmy

Anne Frances McCann was born on August 30, 1929. Anne was a common name in the family, but I expect she was likely named for her maternal grandmother Annie McCoy Allore and her Aunt Frances McCann.

Anne attended St. Edward's Separate School in Westport where she was a good student. My father recalled that the nuns who taught him at St. Edward's after she'd graduated often asked him why he wasn't as good a pupil as his sister Anne. She was a hard act to follow, it would seem.

Anne married James Brushett, a native of Newfoundland, on July 30, 1945. Jimmy was a pipe fitter by trade. Anne and Jimmy had one daughter, Diane Brushett.

Anne lived a quiet life in Kingston. We would always stop in to see her and Jimmy when we were on vacation in Kingston, not only because my father tried to see everyone in the family while he was there but also because Anne was his favourite. He loved her dearly.

Jimmy was an unrepentant Newfoundlander who liked to talk non-stop about his love of fishing. Anne and Jimmy rented a small house on Alfred Street, and he kept a fishing boat in the back yard. It might have been about 15 feet, wood and not fiberglass, and it had a small cabin up front. (Forgive me, I was a kid and no expert on boats.) It was Jimmy's ambition to fix it up and take it back home on a fishing trip. When he talked about it, Anne would look at my dad and smile.

I understood why my father treasured his sister Anne so much. She was like most of her siblings—kind, quick to laugh, a heavy smoker, and a mellow-hearted drinker. Also like the other McCanns, she rarely said a word to me, but once again it didn't matter. I liked being around her.

Anne passed away on October 31, 1983, at the age of 55 after a battle with cancer. She was buried in St. Mary's Cemetery in Kingston.

Rita McCann

Rita Theresa McCann was born on April 5, 1930. She was

the fourth daughter born to Ford and Ida McCann.

Rita married Howard Johnston, son of Joseph Johnston of Jones Falls, on March 13, 1947, a month short of her seventeenth birthday. For the young girl it was a case of "act in haste, repent at leisure."

Johnston worked as a manager with the Department of Sanitation in the City of Kingston Department of Public Works. I've made every attempt not to write negatively about the people in this *Brief History*, but I'm compelled to record that throughout their marriage he had a very negative effect on Rita's mental health.

Fig. 58 Rita McCann

At one point when they were having "marital difficulties," Rita came up to Peterborough to stay with us for a week. She bonded with my mother right away, and they spent afternoons sitting together on the couch, chattering away and watching television. Rita taught mom how to crochet. When she went back home, my mother was upset.

Rita had three children: Bonnie Johnston, Joe Johnston, and Bill Johnston. She passed away on February 21, 2011, at the age of 81 while in long-term care in Cobourg, Ontario. She was buried in the Glenburnie Cemetery in Glenburnie, Ontario.

Hugh McCann

While it may seem a difficult task to be the middle child in a field of seventeen, that's exactly what Hugh was. And since he's the final link in the chain extending down through the centuries from Arthur McCann and Ann Quinn to me, Hugh will be the subject of the final chapter in this *Brief History*, coming up next.

VERONICA MCCANN

Veronica McCann was born on January 12, 1933. Her brother Hugh recalled that she was "very tall for her age and very thin with a mop of thick, straight red hair. She had a lot of freckles on her face and arms. . . . Despite the reputation of red hair she was a very pleasant and mild-mannered person." Hugh explained that "We rarely or never called her Veronica, but her nickname Bungie," which was pronounced with a hard "g."[319]

She had a shy and sweet disposition that endeared her to Hugh and the rest of her family. Unfortunately, she suffered from a defective heart valve that would cause her to lose consciousness during moments of stress or excitement.

This heart problem tragically led to her death from heart failure at the age of 12, two days before Christmas on December 23, 1945. The family was living in Kingston at the time. She was buried in St. Edward's Cemetery in Westport next to her older sister Monica, who had been buried there the year before.

MICHAEL MCCANN

Michael Ignatius McCann was born on July 29, 1934, in Westport, Ontario. He was very close to his brothers Hugh and Pat, and they spent a great deal of time together as youngsters. They were a tough trio of boys who would not back down from a fight. As youths they'd trawl around the village, ready to scrap with any Protestant

Fig. 59 Mike

kids who'd offer to take them on. It was something that, in retrospect, Hugh wasn't very proud of. It wasn't in his nature to behave this way, but apparently Mike had a more assertive personality. Hugh admitted that despite the difference in their ages, Mike tended to be the leader and Hugh the follower.[320]

Mike married Elaine Strohm on November 14, 1952. They lived in Bridgenorth, just above Peterborough, where they had two children, Stephen McCann and Catherine McCann.

Hugh and Mike were very close. Hugh recalled later that "When Stephen was a baby Mike and I spent more time together than we did separately. We always had done. Where one of us was, the other was. In fact, Rene and I spent most of our honeymoon with him and his family."

When Mike fell ill it was Hugh who convinced him to go to the hospital for examination. Tests revealed a brain tumour, and Mike died on August 18, 1955. He was buried in St. Peter's Cemetery in Peterborough.

When I was born three months later, I was named after him.

Patrick McCann

Patrick Joseph Gordon (Pat) McCann was born on February 18, 1936 in Westport, Ontario. As mentioned above, he was part of the trio of McCann boys who stuck together in the village like peas in a pod.

Pat married Anthea Wilson on February 1, 1958. They had three children:

Fig. 60 Pat and Anthea

Shawn McCann, Catherine McCann and Karen McCann.

Shawn followed a career in law enforcement, and was a police officer with the Peel Regional Police Department until his recent retirement. His assignments included the Special Weapons and Tactical (SWAT) team and homicide investigation.

Pat worked for the Pubic Works Department in Kingston. As a graduate student attending Queen's University in Kingston, I lived in a one-bedroom apartment on Nelson Street, and Pat rode the truck that picked up on that street. When I did not have classes in the morning I always tried to be at the window to wave to him when he went by.

I always had a standing invitation to supper every Thursday night, which I took him up on. Pat probably told my dad he'd keep an eye on me, since it was my first time away from home. My favourite meal, I must admit, was Aunt Anthea's bouillabaisse, which Pat and I devoured like hungry animals.

It was a very nice opportunity to get to know them better. Little things, like Pat telling me once that he couldn't sleep at night unless his feet were sticking out from underneath the covers! The things we remember long afterwards, for no particular reason. Things that make us human, and make us family.

Pat later rose to the position of Garbage Co-ordinator with the City of Kingston and also was a foreman with Public Works before his retirement.

He had a lively sense of humour and a kind, generous temperament. He and Anthea were terrific dancers, and I loved watching them when they took the dance floor at wedding receptions and other family events to show off their jitterbug moves.

He was also very focused and serious-minded when it came to his family. He spent time after his retirement researching his family history, and visited Westport to gather information, take photographs, and visit friends. Many of the photos included in this family history were gathered by Pat and included in his family history album.

Pat passed away on September 30, 2001, at the age of 66. He was buried in St. Mary's Cemetery in Kingston.

Mary Ethelreda McCann

Mary Ethelreda McCann was born on May 19, 1939, in Westport, Ontario. She was named in honour of her Aunt Della McCann, who took the name Sister Mary Ethelreda when she joined the Sisters of Providence of St. Vincent de Paul.

Ethel married Stanley (Pete) Ketcheson on July 24, 1954. Pete worked at Nashua Paper in Peterborough. They had four children: Tony Ketcheson, Debbie Ketcheson, Sandra Ketcheson, and Ken Ketcheson.

Fig. 61 Ethel McCann

Ethel worked for a while with Hugh at Peterborough Cardboard, and she lived in the other half of the duplex on Waterford Street, around the corner from us, next to Ida and Oliver. She later moved to Kingston and married Harley McIntosh, a mail carrier for Canada Post.

I've mentioned that while I was a graduate student in Kingston, living on Nelson Street, that my Uncle Pat rode the truck that picked up our garbage. At the same time, Harley was the mailman who delivered on that street. A kind and positive-minded person, he enjoyed leaving notes with my mail wishing me a good day. For a young man on his first adventure away from home, it was a fine comfort to have these two uncles keeping an eye on me.

I hope Tony won't mind if I mention that for the past several years he's been doing very important Good Samaritan work distributing food, water, and warm clothing to street people in Kingston. A model for the rest of us to follow![321]

Ethel was very close to her mother, and spent much of her time with Ida, accompanying her to appointments, taking her to mass and keeping her company. She and Harley shared Ida's devotion to their Catholic beliefs, which was a very positive thing for Ida.

Ethel passed away on October 18, 1993, at the age of 55 after a battle with cancer. She was buried in St. Mary's Cemetery in Kingston.

Ellen McCann

Ellen Catherine McCann was born on November 1, 1939, in Westport, Ontario. She was the last of the children of Ford and Ida to be born in the village.

She married Joseph (Joe) Carr and had six sons, including Paul Carr, Ron Carr, Terry Carr, John Carr, Dan Carr and Michael Carr. She also had three daughters: Anne Carr, Joanne Carr, and Rose Marie Carr, who died in

Fig. 62 Ellen McCann

infancy.

She was a devoted mother who cared very much for her children. In her later years, when she was married to Phil O'Connor in the Spencerville area, she hosted what she liked to call her "Spring Fling," just before Lent. She, Linda, and others would cook up a feast and everyone would gather for a meal to end all meals. I was invited, and I think I only missed it once. She was very kind to me and, unlike other McCanns, liked talking to me, which I appreciated.

Ellen passed away on January 6, 2017, in Brockville General Hospital at the age of 78. She was buried in the Oakland Cemetery in Brockville, Ontario.

Margaret McCann

Margaret Rose McCann was born on September 8, 1943, in Kingston, Ontario. She married Len Stephens, a member of the Canadian Armed Forces, and had a daughter Holly Ann Stephens.

When Margie left Kingston, she lived in an upstairs apartment in Peterborough on George Street, part of a tenement building that included the North George Sundries on the corner of George and Dublin Streets. Two blocks away from where we lived on Dublin, and three blocks away from Ida and Ollie, around the corner.

Fig. 63 Margie McCann

We'd occasionally have a family gathering up in her apartment. It was the only time I spent around her. Despite having split with Len, she always seemed to be in good spirits.

She loved to laugh, that same deep chuckle the others had, and she was very fond of my dad. She wore her reddish-brown hair long, her cheeks were plump and dimpled, and she was freckled the same way that Hugh described Veronica, above. I liked her very much.

Margie later moved to Calgary, Alberta, where she married Ken Davidson. Their children included Charity Davidson, Joslyn Davidson, , Kevin Davidson, and Hyrum Davidson.

Margie passed away on April 5, 2007, at the age of 63 after a battle with lung disease. She was buried in Queen's Park Cemetery in Calgary, Alberta.

OLIVER MCCANN

Oliver Joseph McCann was born on April 29, 1946, in Kingston, Ontario. He was the youngest of the sons born to Ford and Ida McCann, and was the only boy not born in the house on George Street in Westport.

Ollie did well in school, and followed in the family tradition established by his great uncle John A. McCann and his aunts Frances and Mazie by becoming a teacher. Ollie taught at St. Anne's Separate School in Peterborough for a number of years before retirement.

Fig. 64 Ollie McCann

I remember hearing that his older brothers, Charlie and Harry in particular, tried to talk him into becoming a priest. Certainly he was a devout Catholic, like his mother, and he had the intellectual gifts to dedicate himself to a life-long study of theology, but he resisted the pressure and married Sharon Kennedy on August 5, 1977.

They had three children: Matthew McCann, Sarah McCann, and Tina McCann.

In his younger days, Ollie was musically inclined and a good vocalist who followed the folk scene of the 1960s very closely. He loved the music of the Kingston Trio; Peter, Paul and Mary; Melanie; Donovan; and Bob Dylan. After I received a copy of *The Songs of Paul Simon* for Christmas one year, he and I sat together many times to sing while Hugh accompanied us on his guitar. I loved those sessions, and so did Ollie, because he kept coming back for more.

In keeping with his interest in theology, he read widely on the subject and was particularly attracted to the works of Thomas Merton, the Trappist monk who promoted interfaith ideas meant to draw Catholicism and Protestantism closer together. In this spirit, he loaned Hugh a number of Merton's books to read, including his autobiography *The Seven Storey Mountain* (1948), perhaps hoping it would help my dad, who'd left the Catholic Church, to find his way to a reconciliation of sorts. They spent a lot of time together chatting on the subject.

Ollie obtained his Bachelor of Arts degree from Trent University in Peterborough as a mature student while teaching full-time during the day. He and I shared courses in John Milton and 18th century poetry while I was an undergraduate at Trent in the late 1970s. When I graduated, Ollie gave me copies of the works of Northrup Frye as a congratulatory gift that I still cherish today.

Oliver Joseph McCann passed away on September 17, 2007.

He was buried in Highland Park Cemetery in Peterborough, Ontario.

LINDA MCCANN

Linda Marie McCann was born on May 19, 1949, in Belleville, Ontario. She was the last child born to Ford and Ida.

When Linda was a teenager, she was walking along River Road South in Peterborough when she was struck from behind by a car. The car dragged her for several meters underneath it before the driver realized what had happened and stopped. Linda was hospitalized with serious abrasions that required extensive skin grafts. She bore the scars from that accident for the rest of her life.

Fig. 65 Linda McCann

Linda married Jerry Barber of Smiths Falls, a former member of the Canadian Navy who was a male nurse. Linda and Jerry had two children, Kurtis Barber and Melanie Barber. Linda worked as a health care provider and hair stylist over the years. Jerry was a good-natured guy who got along well with most people and didn't mind running up to the nearby tennis court with me to play a few matches.

Linda passed away in Brockville General Hospital on March 21, 2016. She was buried in the Oakland cemetery in Brockville, Ontario.

Fig. 66 Hugh McCann

Chapter Twenty

Hugh McCann

We've finally reached the last link in the long chain that connects Arthur McCann and Ann Quinn to me, one of their many, many descendants. Since this is *my* family history, at the end of the day, I've decided to end it by telling the story of my father, Hugh McCann.

Hugh was an ordinary man, with minimal formal education and not much to call his own. He never owned a house. He spent his life working in unskilled labour jobs where the pay was crap and recognition was nil. If you Google him, you won't get a hit. No one else will ever tell his story, so I will.

Hugh Joseph McCann was born on November 23, 1931, in Westport, Ontario. He was the middle child of seventeen, which meant he was sort of buried in the crowd when it came to getting attention.

Typical of this obscurity and its lack of communication is the fact that he always understood his birthday to have been November 29. Late in his life Ida corrected him, explaining that he was *christened* on the 29th. Since that was my birthday, he'd gone through life thinking that his first-born son had been a birthday gift. He was very upset to learn that this was not the case.

Just as upsetting was the late news that his middle name was supposed to be Dominic, not Joseph. He'd been told he was named after Hugh Joseph Hagan, so it was natural for him

Fig. 67 Duke

to believe this was his middle name. Sure enough, though, his baptismal record shows "Hugh Domnick," a name he'd never heard before. I don't know why he was allowed to go through life using the wrong middle name, but I do know once he finally learned of the mistake, it made him grind his teeth even more than he already did.

(I should mention here that Hugh's nickname in the family was "Duke." They all called him that, except for Ida, who always stuck to "Hugh".)

As I said, he was very close to his brothers Mike and Pat. They spent most of their time together, mooching around the village like little hellraisers. I'm sure, in retrospect, it was pretty harmless stuff. They weren't juvenile delinquents, after all. Just three brothers at loose ends.

Hugh attended grade school at St. Edward's Separate School in Westport, where the nuns apparently weren't very impressed with his intellectual skills. As I wrote earlier, they would often ask him in frustration why he couldn't be as good a pupil as his older sister Anne.

He was about twelve years old when the family moved to Kingston. He had fond memories of this time, when he haunted the local theatre to watch the matinees, taking in as many western serials as he could catch. His favourite stars were Johnny Mack Brown, Bob Steele, Randolph Scott, William Boyd, and others of that generation.

He often said later in life that if he could be any age again, he'd be twelve.

However, he also remembered that they were lean times. World War II was underway, and his older brothers were in Europe. Charlie and Harry returned, but Wilf did not.

Fig. 68 Ford and Hugh in Peterborough, ca. 1953

Ford was working for the Aluminum Company of Canada, later known as Alcan, which was manufacturing product in support of the war effort, and wages would have been minimal at best.

Hugh remembered being hungry all the time. When Harry returned and rejoined the work force, Hugh would get up early in the morning and eat the lunch that Ida had prepared for Harry to take to work. "He never said a word about it," Hugh recalled. "I don't know what he did to feed himself during the day."

Once they moved to Belleville in 1949 and Hugh's youngest sister Linda was born, Ford worked as a milk man on a rural route that took him all around the countryside. Hugh accompanied him as a sort of driver's helper but spent most of the time waiting in the truck for Ford to complete his deliveries.

The following year, they moved to Peterborough and Hugh left his childhood behind for good, entering the workforce in order to earn money in support of the family. That year and the next he worked at Grant's Cleaners on George Street, later to become Parker's Cleaners.

While the McCann family lived on Simcoe Street, Hugh became familiar with the Brook family that lived around the corner on Aylmer Street. He became friends with Janet Irene Brook, the only daughter of Harry and Jane Elizabeth Brook. In 1953, at the age of 21, Hugh was hired by the Canadian General Electric Company (CGE) with the assistance of Mrs. Brook, who wrote a letter of recommendation to the manager, an acquaintance of the Brook family. The job involved working on the grit blast, which was used to clean and sand manufactured parts. It paid well, averaging just under $60 a week, but it was dirty, tiring work that took its toll. Hugh saw the doctor several times to have grit removed from his eyes, which left small yellow scars on the whites of his eyes that were visible for the rest of his life.

On pay day when he emerged with his hard-earned pay packet, Ford would be waiting for him on the sidewalk. Hugh gave him his earnings to help pay for the family expenses. It bothered Hugh that his dad was there without fail with his hand out, but he understood the necessity.

When I graduated from high school and enrolled at Trent University, I received a series of student loans to pay for tuition, books, and other expenses. Because I was eighteen, I was certainly old enough to begin paying for my room and board, but Hugh vehemently refused to take a dime from me. He told me the story of his dad and his pay packet, and he insisted I spend my money on my education. And on books. He loved books, and was pleased I could haunt the remainders bin at the university bookstore and cherry-pick all kinds of odd and interesting stuff. (I remember a beautiful translation of *Orlando Furioso*, the Italian epic poem by Ariosto, that I looked at and put back. To this day, fifty years later, I still wish I'd bought that book. It was only a few bucks.)

Hugh was laid off from CGE and found work again in 1954 at Parker's Cleaners, then at Burtol Cleaners on Charlotte Street. He was also recalled by the CGE for a 22-week period.

During that year his friendship with Janet Brook, who was known as Rene (pronounced *Reen*, not *Ren-aye*), blossomed into romance and they were married on June 28, 1954, in St. John's Anglican Church on Brock Street.

As Rene was a Protestant, the marriage was not very well received by Ford, but Ida intervened and ensured that Hugh's family supported him in his decision.

At the same time, Rene's brothers weren't too wild about the idea of their little sister marrying an Irish Catholic. By this time, Mrs. Brook had passed away. Rene and Mr. Brook were living in a house at 99 Princess Street, and when Hugh and Rene were married they lived there. The house was owned by Noe Duranceau, who operated a music store on Hunter Street. We'll mention Mr. Duranceau again in a little while.

While Ford was always waiting for Hugh on pay day, their relationship otherwise was not close. Hugh remembered an occasion during these times when he was walking down the street one day and saw his father approaching on the sidewalk on the other side. He knew his father could see him, but he walked on past without acknowledging his son. Hugh told me that story to emphasize how much he'd wanted his father to love and value him, and that it had never happened. He would always, he promised me, be the father he'd wanted to have himself.

In 1955, work was again difficult to find. Hugh was employed for six weeks at Burtol Cleaners, one week at Silverwood Dairies, two weeks at the Simpson-Sears Company, and 18 weeks at the Canadian Nashua Paper Company. Hugh was a hard-working and determined young man who would take any job in order to earn money for his family, but work was hard to come by and he spent almost half the year unemployed.

In addition, Hugh suffered two severe losses in 1955. The family had returned to Kingston, leaving Hugh behind in Peterborough with his bride, but in April Ford died. Four months later, in August, Hugh's brother Mike died from a brain tumour.

Hugh was devastated. He closely questioned the priest

for an explanation of God's reason for allowing such things to happen and was not happy with the responses that he received. His relationship with the Catholic Church, which had been strained before, was irreparably damaged. After Mike's funeral he turned away from the Church and never took communion again as a Catholic.

When I was born at the end of such a difficult year, he felt

Fig. 69 Father and Son

he could turn the page and build a life for himself, his wife, and his new son.

In 1956, Hugh was forced to continue taking work wherever it could be found. He was employed by Trent Valley Bakeries for four weeks, by Nashua Paper for 29 weeks, and by the CGE for five weeks. Toward the end of the year, the family moved from the house on Princess Street. Mr. Brook went to live with his son Harry, while Hugh, Rene, and I moved into an upstairs apartment at 123 Brock Street, at the corner of Brock and Water Streets. The rent for this apartment was $55 a month.

I don't remember much about the inside of the place, but outside we were right across the street from Victoria Park. Located down the hill from the county court house, with Central Public School a block away on the other side, it was like paradise for a little toddler such as myself. It had a large fountain in the middle that had stone turtles all around it. The turtles fascinated me, as did the vast expanse of green grass. It may be what influenced me to want to live in a rural environment once I grew up.

Hugh loved music, and he began to teach himself how to play the guitar. I remember family coming to the apartment for singalongs, everyone belting out their favourite country and western songs at the tops of their lungs, fuelled by rye and Cokes, the family drink, and a lot of cigarettes. I will forever have in my mind the image of Hugh sitting on a kitchen chair in the cramped living room, squinting against the smoke from the cigarette in his mouth, strumming his guitar, thoroughly enjoying himself.

Hugh soon decided he wanted to take lessons to learn to play it properly. He became a pupil of Geoffrey Townsend, who had studied under the great guitar maestro Andrés Segovia. Townsend lived in Toronto, so once a week Hugh and a friend would drive there for their lessons.

He knew he couldn't practise properly on his banged-up old Stella Harmony from Simpsons-Sears, so he talked to Noe Duranceau, who'd rented him the house on Princess Street. Mr. Duranceau also owned buildings on the south side of Hunter Street, and ran the Orpheus Music Store from there. He sold sheet music, instruments, and other musical paraphernalia.

Hugh bought a concert guitar manufactured in Spain by Vincente Tatay of Valencia, a sweet-sounding instrument that I still have. It was like a dream come true. Mr. Duranceau also likely recommended him to Geoffrey Townsend for his lessons.

The Orpheus Music Store was a hole in the wall at 231 Hunter Street, wide enough for racks of music in the middle,

Fig. 70 Hugh and his Tatay

instruments hanging on the walls and suspended from the ceiling, and very little else. The Star Laundry was on one side and Sandy's Cigar Store was down at the corner. Mr. Duranceau was a pipe smoker, and he likely bought his tobacco from Sandy. When you walked in, the pungent odour of stale smoke was the first thing you noticed, something to which Mr. Duranceau had likely gone nose blind long ago.

To see the man himself, it was necessary to walk all the way down through the centre aisle through a forest of sheet music, folios, and books, to a big oak desk at the back, where you'd find the man puffing up a cloud and chatting pleasantly with a friend. Hugh bought his sheet music here at the beginning, and when I was taking music lessons myself as a teenager my music teacher sent me here as well. Often what I needed was in a pile on the floor, but Mr. Duranceau knew where to find it. He'd point, and I'd search.

The Orpheus was a Mecca in Peterborough for everyone who was serious about music, and it opened up a new world for Hugh. Mr. Duranceau was a talker, and Hugh was a listener. It inspired in him a new love of classical music, and he worked hard to develop a technical foundation in his guitar playing. When Townsend died unexpectedly, Hugh was very upset. Another death that blocked his path toward the future.

All of this while Hugh continued to earn a weekly wage in unskilled labour. One day, he was operating a machine at the Nashua Paper plant when it jammed. Hugh's partner shut the machine off and Hugh proceeded to clear the blockage. Through a miscommunication his partner turned the machine back on before Hugh had finished. His right hand was caught between the rollers of the machine and the tips of his three middle fingers were crushed. The ring finger was also split a centimetre or two toward the middle knuckle. Surgery repaired the damage, but he was left with stubs on the ends of these three fingers. His right hand was his fingering hand on the guitar, as he played left-handed, and so he discovered that once the fingers had healed and he could resume playing he had lost a measure of dexterity, that fraction that would forever make the difference between being good and being really good.

Never one to quit, he persevered and once calluses had formed over his fingertips he carried on as though nothing had happened. Throughout his life he learned many of the classical standards, such as Segovia's transcriptions of Bach, pieces by Robert de Visée, Fernando Sor, and Gaspar Sanz. He practised every day. He played upstairs in his bedroom, and I loved to stretch out on the bed and listen. Of course, being me, I couldn't keep my mouth shut. When he'd struggle with the fingering of a particular passage, I'd hum how it was supposed to go. He was a patient man by nature, but I swear this drove him nuts and I eventually learned just to shut up and let him get there without the unwanted help.

Hugh and Rene remained in the apartment at 123 Brock Street for about two years before moving. The traffic on Water Street was, of course, very busy and Rene worried constantly that I would be hit by a car. I was a very active kid and my mother took to putting me on a leather harness when we went outside for fresh air and exercise. We often went across the street into Victoria Park, as I said, so that I could play at some distance from the traffic. I remember watching the children playing in the park at recess from Central Public School on Murray Street and wanting very much to go to school with them myself.

When I was three, Rene became pregnant again and they decided they needed a better place to live. We moved into one half of a duplex at 102 Dublin Street where we would remain for the next 15 years. This house, on the bank of Otonabee River within walking distance of downtown Peterborough, had once been a rooming house for loggers who worked for a mill not far away. It was big, old and drafty with bats and squirrels in the attic and river rats in the basement. It had been owned for many years by the King family, and Hugh rented it from a King daughter who was the wife of Homer Borland of Toronto. We loved it, and never wanted to leave.

Although I will say I'm still afraid of bats because of that place. There were cold mornings when I'd wake up, open my eyes, and see a bat hanging on the wall a foot or two from my head, it having crawled down from the attic to get warm. Mom, on the other hand, was constantly freaked out by the sound of squirrels running back and forth up there, *tikka-tikka-tikka-tikka*, doing whatever bizarre things squirrels do in unused attics.

Hugh's first job in the morning was to go down and light the fire. The day couldn't start until he tended to that old furnace in the basement, which must have been installed during the Boer War. We had two bins each with a window facing the driveway; one for coal and one for wood. Hugh would make the calls, and guys would come around with their trucks. They opened the appropriate window, stuck a chute inside, and delivered the means for us to avoid freezing in the winter. When the Borlands finally replaced that beast with a modernistic gas furnace, we thought we'd time-travelled to some futuristic paradise. Rene was a little worried about the gas blowing us to Kingdom Come, but I liked sleeping in a warmer bedroom than before, so I didn't care.

It was that time, the late fifties and early sixties, when things were different. The streets were cleared of snow by horses drawing big-bladed ploughs. A milkman delivered our milk and orange juice. A guy drove around in an old truck selling fresh produce off the tail-gate; the local school janitor sold us cow manure for the garden out of his truck; and an elderly Italian man came around in summer with a push cart selling fresh popcorn to the kids. It was *really* good popcorn. We played street hockey in front of the house all winter and ball hockey all summer.

Hugh worked in a number of places during this time, including Twin Cleaners, Orr's Grocery Store, and the Peterborough Civic Hospital, where he was employed for several years as an orderly. This job did not pay especially well. For example, in 1961 he earned $3,173 from Civic Hospital, or about $61 a week, and with a family to care for it was barely enough to get by.

Just the same, this job gave Hugh an opportunity to show the qualities that defined him as a person and endeared him to everyone that knew him.

As a hospital orderly, a position that has been eliminated in many hospitals today due to budget constraints, Hugh was called upon to provide assistance to patients in situations where a nurse was either unavailable, required help, or would not normally perform a particular task. This assistance might include helping a patient out of bed to visit the washroom, rolling a patient over while a nurse carried out one of her functions, restraining a patient who was agitated or out of control, or even removing deceased patients from their rooms.

In the well-defined hierarchy of a hospital, the orderly occupied the lowest rung but was often the common denominator, the go-between who could maintain communication and continuity of care between doctors, nurses and the patients. To be effective, an orderly needed to be concerned about the welfare of patients, be a good listener, be conscientious on the job, and maintain good relations with nurses who provided the next tier of care. Hugh was perfectly qualified for the job, as he had an extremely high level of empathy for other people, he was very meticulous and conscientious when doing his job, and he communicated with others very well. The patients and nurses loved him.

There were a few difficulties with the job, however. Hugh was occasionally required to work the midnight shift, which meant that he had to sleep during the day. This was a supreme challenge for him and the two small boys who were required to tiptoe around so as not to disturb him. In addition, he was occasionally required to work shifts in the Hutchison Wing of the hospital, which was the location of the psychiatric ward. Hugh found these shifts extremely upsetting. When he was told he was going to be permanently assigned to the "Hutch Wing," he decided to look for another job.

In 1967 after much family discussion he reluctantly left the Civic Hospital and took a job with the Peterboro Card and Paper Works, later known as Peterborough Cardboard. He had learned about the opening from Harry Brook, Rene's oldest brother, who had worked there for many years. During his years at Peterborough Cardboard, Hugh was responsible for the operation and maintenance of several machines, including the embosser, the inker and the hated dryer.

Peterborough Cardboard was a typical small factory in that it was a family-owned business with plenty of internal politics. Hugh sometimes thought that the primary qualification for shop foreman was to be a butt-kisser to the owner and his two sons. In fact, at one point when the job was offered to him, Hugh reluctantly declined because he wanted to stay his own man. He could have used the bump in his wages, but not at the price he would have had to pay for it.

There were also a lot of internal jealousies and rivalries. Disagreements between two workers became clashes which became feuds. One guy fell into a conflict with Hugh and afterward refused to speak to him or acknowledge his presence for something like the next 15 years. This was extremely stressful for Hugh, who wanted to like people and be liked in return. It was so different from the work environment at the hospital. He was employed at Peterborough Cardboard from 1967 until 1994, when he became ill and took disability retirement.

While he took his job very seriously and suffered from a lot of work-related stress which brought on a chronic stiff neck and difficulty sleeping, Hugh always found solace in music.

When I began to take piano lessons as a young teenager, Hugh arranged through my music teacher, David Whyte, to buy an inexpensive upright piano from an associate of Whyte's, Ambrose Engli. Mr. Engli was a charming Swiss piano tuner and technician who, like Noe Duranceau, had dedicated his life to music. It was inevitable that Hugh and Ambrose would strike up a friendship, and eventually Hugh expressed an interest in learning about piano repair and maintenance. When Mr. Engli offered to teach Hugh and to take him on as an assistant, Hugh jumped at the chance. As a result, he became a part-time piano technician.

Our basement was transformed into a repair depot. Hugh set up a work bench and filled bins with springs, felts, pads, spare hammers and other paraphernalia of the trade. Piano actions, the removable internal mechanism that held all the hammers and other joints and parts, stood in specially-made blocks in two rows—one for incoming piano actions dropped off on a regular basis by Mr. Engli, and the other for outgoing actions that Hugh was finished refurbishing and were ready for pick-up. Mr. Engli was happy to reduce the amount of time that he had to spend performing mundane repairs, preferring the more artistic efforts involved in tuning. Hugh, for his part, was happy to have the additional income and to have responsibilities that kept him busy in the evenings. The work appealed to his meticulous and detail-oriented mind, and he took particular pride in finding creative approaches to especially challenging repair jobs. It also provided a useful outlet for the stress that he accumulated during the day.

Hugh still found time to practise the guitar. He had initially learned to play from Carl Fischer's *Langey-Carl Fischer Tutors for Guitar (Carcassi)*, which followed the very popular Carcassi Method. Over the years he built up a massive collection of printed music and recordings, which he catalogued in two volumes, one devoted to the printed music that he owned and the other to the recordings that he owned, each cross-referenced to the other. His interests initially centred on the standards popularized by Andrés Segovia and other maestros who recorded in the 1950s and 1960s, such as Fernando Sor, Robert de Visée, Gaspar Sanz, Luis Milan, and the music of Bach transcribed for the guitar by Segovia and others. His favourite performers were Segovia, Julian Bream, and the husband and wife duo of Alexandre Lagoya and Ida Presti. Hugh gravitated toward Bream because he felt that Bream played with more heart and spirit than Segovia, and he insisted that Ida Presti was a much superior guitarist to her husband and was one of the best players in the world. He was deeply disappointed when she passed away.

During the late 1960s and early 1970s Christopher Parkening burst upon the scene, and for a period of time he was the darling of our household, as "Parkening Plays Bach" found its way to the turntable over and over and over again, usually at my hands. His shining star was eventually superseded, however, by John Williams, in whom Hugh found a style of play more satisfying and a selection much more eclectic and intriguing.

The Canadian Liona Boyd, unfortunately, the self-styled "First Lady of the Guitar," did not receive a very warm reception in our house. Much more style than substance was the verdict. However, Hugh insisted that her recordings were important because her selections were off the beaten track and often provided him with his only recorded example of certain composers or certain pieces.

I swear, Hugh could see the bright side of a plague.

He always came back to Bream, though. I used to comment on the finger noise that was audible in Bream's recordings, the squeaking sound that Bream's fingers made as they moved back and forth on the fingerboard, and compared him unfavourably to Parkening, still the darling, whose fingering hand was silent. Hugh would shake his head at this, disagreeing. For him, the finger noise brought him closer to Bream and the performance. He explained that it was a human sound, the sound of a man making music straight from the heart. Segovia made no finger noise because he was a technical perfectionist to the extent of being almost machine-like. Segovia was a marvel, but he was perhaps too perfect. Bream, on the other hand, was Hugh's idol.

His admiration for Bream the guitarist soon extended to Bream the lutenist, and he began to collect Bream's recordings of lute music. His interest gravitated from the European masters to Renaissance and Elizabethan lute music, and Hugh began to teach himself to play this music transcribed for the guitar. His preferences included John Dowland, William Byrd, Jean-Baptiste Besard and Anthony Holborne.

Hugh's favourite, though, was an Italian composer. In his copy of *Nine Suites for the Guitar* by Lodovico Roncalli, Hugh wrote: "The music of Roncalli is probably my favourite. The key to its charm is in the playing of it to keep it light and graceful. Never hurry and never heavy."

In the margin next to the Corriente in the Suite in G Major he wrote: "The rhythm is easiest found by beating eighths instead of quarter notes; the over-rhythm of ¾ will still be heard once the off-beat rhythm is grasped." He also made a footnote for himself as a reminder that "Although throughout this book it appears to be calling for an E sharp it is actually the D being sharpened." The Gavotta in the Suite in E Minor he noted was "A beautiful piece, at its best when played with audible restraint. Rubato." He carefully cross-referenced most of the pieces in this book to favourite recordings, either to Konrad Ragossnig on "La Guitare Royale" or Ernesto Bitetti on "Four Centuries of the Guitar."

Hugh also enjoyed composing music. He filled notebooks with melodies that came to him at any hour of the day, and kept a paper and pencil in his pocket to jot down scraps of music that occurred to him while he worked. Often he could not wait to get in the door at the end of the day to rush to his guitar and work out the piece, carefully noting it down as he went. He loved to compose melodies for his grandchildren in particular.

I want to emphasize that Hugh taught himself almost everything he knew about music. While he began with formal lessons, they didn't last very long and provided him with only the initial foundation on which he would build his expertise over the years. While he often played with a friend who brought around a banjo for singing sessions, Hugh had no one with whom he could share his love of classical guitar music, and so he studied it himself. What he was able to accomplish all alone, without coaching or tutoring, with a maimed fingering hand, is remarkable.

We saw that Hugh had left behind his schoolboy days for good by 1950 when he entered the workforce, but the truth of the matter was that he only had a Grade Six education. He was a reader, though. I've always maintained that as an auto-didact who was never without a book at hand, he was more well-read than I was with my university degrees.

He read the works of Jean-Jacques Rousseau and Descartes. He read Swift, Dryden, Bunyan and Pope. He read Johnson and Boswell and devoured the diaries of Samuel Pepys, whose name he always pronounced correctly (unlike myself). He particularly enjoyed the diarists, and owned a copy of everything that Anaïs Nin ever wrote. He read a great deal about European history and was interested in Catherine the Great, the Medicis, and Louis XIV.

Oh, and being a working class man, he was fond of the books written by Eric Hoffer, the longshoreman philosopher.

He could discuss with animation everything that he read, but once again there were very few people who shared his interests with whom he could compare his ideas and impressions. For example, I was heavily into fiction, particularly American fiction, and it was an effort for me to read the kind of non-fiction he loved so much. He realized this right away and while he always made me aware of what he was reading, he never urged it on me. He was a very considerate man.

Inevitably what he did was discuss the interests of others with them. When Ollie loaned him books by Thomas Merton, he read them and was happy to talk about why they appealed to Ollie.

In the same way he occasionally read books that I was particularly interested in, and discussed them with me. When I think back, though, I realize that I did most of the talking and he did most of the listening, and I understand now that it was the same with others. While he would express his opinions and challenge ours, he was actually more interested in what these books told him about us as people than in what the books themselves said, as they usually lay outside his areas of interest. Hugh was such a patient and compassionate man that he would give up a great deal of his time for others in order to provide them with the feedback and sense of companionship that he himself often lacked.

In 1974, we were forced from our home on Dublin Street when the duplex was sold to two lawyers who purchased it as an investment. They raised the rent by more than 100%, knowing that Hugh couldn't afford it but knowing that someone else could. They told Hugh, without a trace of irony, that the Borlands had been very kind to him by charging less rent than the property was worth.

Fortunately, Hugh found another kind soul in the person of Esther Thornton, who lived a half-block away on Harvey Street and owned a house in East City that was currently vacant. She agreed to rent this house, at 748 Snelgrove Road, to Hugh for what the lawyers would disparagingly have termed a charitable amount, and so we moved that year.

During the next four years, from 1974 to 1978, I attended university in Peterborough as an undergraduate majoring in English literature. As I've mentioned, Hugh refused to take a dime in room and board, insisting he was investing in my future. As always, he was right.

His supreme patience also extended to my choice of working hours. As an undergraduate, I soon discovered that I wrote my best papers in the middle of the night when there were no distractions. Hugh told me later, much to my surprise and relief, that he actually found it comforting to awaken at three o'clock in the morning and hear the sound of my typewriter pounding away in my downstairs bedroom. Despite the fact that he had to get up at six o'clock to go to work, he instinctively supported me in what I did as only the best of fathers would.

When the essay was finished, usually around five o'clock or so, I'd fall asleep, exhausted. It was my mission, however, to get up and out of my bedroom, down the hall and into the bathroom before Hugh walked in the back door at noon for lunch. I was embarrassed that I was sleeping while he was working to support us all, and those times when I didn't quite make it to the bathroom before he came in, he would look at me without saying a word. I know now that he enjoyed the game as much as I dreaded it, but he would not let me off the hook that easily. My sense of guilt, he understood, was a motivator.

Another facet of Hugh's life that we should mention is his interest in religion. Although he left the Catholic Church after the death of his brother Mike, he didn't turn his back on God. To the contrary, he began a life-long search for God that was quintessentially Protestant in that it was a personal, individual quest for understanding. It was also true to Hugh's nature, as we have seen in every other aspect of his life. Whether by necessity or by choice, he inevitably made his own pathway toward his goals. This pathway led him to a particular group that seemed to share many of his beliefs.

While working at Nashua Paper, he met his banjo-playing friend who was also very interested in religion. For once, he'd discovered someone with whom he could discuss a subject of interest to him at his own level. Before long, he joined this small group that conducted Sunday worship in their homes and held regular Wednesday night Bible study sessions.

The group was loosely affiliated with the Christadelphian Church in England. They subscribed to a newsletter from this organization and corresponded with Christadelphians in the U.K. on a regular basis. They shared many beliefs and practices with this sect that are worth mentioning.

To begin with, they were strongly millenarian in their beliefs, in that they placed a very strong emphasis on the notion that Jesus would some day return to Earth and found a kingdom that would last for a thousand years. This belief was a key way to deal with the stress, pain and suffering of life—it was understood that Jesus would eventually return to make things right, and that all good people (not just good Catholics, or anyone else who believed in the Elect) would be resurrected to enjoy eternal life with Jesus.

Christadelphians also believed that there is no human soul that exists throughout eternity, but rather that Jesus, upon his return, will raise the dead who have, like himself, died a complete and human death.

By extension, Hugh's group also believed that there was

no literal Heaven and Hell. They felt that the translation of the Hebrew word *sheol*, the Judaic "abode of the dead" which was a dumping ground for bodies to be cremated, construed as Hell by Christianity, should more properly be understood as the grave. Rather than a communal place of death to which human souls went, they believed in a personal death that was complete and could only be undone by the intervention of Jesus.

Heaven, then, was not a literal place in the sky either, but could perhaps be better understood as comprising all of Creation. Christadelphians also rejected the concept of the Trinity, asserting that Jesus was fully mortal and that the Holy Spirit is merely an anthropomorphic personification of God's power. This belief tended to demystify Christianity and move it away from the Catholic assertion that God's will cannot be understood or appreciated. Hugh was strongly attracted to this "humanizing" approach to belief.

Christadelphians also conducted simple Sunday services in a manner that the group adopted. Hymns were sung to the accompaniment of organ music played on an old reel to reel tape recorder. Women were required to wear hats during the service. As there was no priest or minister, each adult was able to take a role in the service and could say whatever they wished at given points. One person was designated to lead the service each Sunday, and each male took a turn. They believed in personal baptism and occasionally practised full-body immersion.

The group differed from the Christadelphians in certain respects that were particularly important to Hugh. Christadelphians believed that the Bible is God's only message to humanity and that it is without error, except for errors in translation introduced by people. Hugh studied this aspect of the Bible in some depth, and went so far as to try to teach himself Hebrew in order to assess for himself the issues introduced by translation, such as with the word *sheol*. Although he had very little extra money to spend, he bought a number of books to assist him in this study, including *A Critical Lexicon and Concordance to the English and Greek New Testament* by Bullinger, *The Holy Scriptures of the Old Testament, Hebrew and English*, a Greek-English dictionary, various translations of the Old and New Testaments, and other books. Ultimately Hugh felt that the Christadelphian assertion that the Bible was error-free was subjective and limiting. He believed very much that God communicates to us in other ways in every moment of our lives. Again, he chose a very personal approach that resisted fundamentalism and authoritarianism and invited personal exploration and personal understanding.

Our family participated in the activities of this group for quite a few years. Eventually Hugh had certain disagreements with them that caused him to put some distance between himself and the others, but he continued to study and contemplate on his own. Through his influence I had also developed a strong interest in religion, and as a teenager I loved to discuss ideas with Hugh in great detail, trying to be someone he could talk to about a subject of great interest to him.

During the time we spent discussing religion, Hugh's attitude and approach were uniformly positive. He often said that religion for him as a child had been a negative experience and that he was determined that it not be so for me. His overriding message was that religion should be an expression of love for one another and for God. Once again, it was another manifestation of his way with people, his empathy for them, and his wish to love and be loved.

Hugh fell ill with what he thought was an autumn cold in 1993. His physician misdiagnosed it as bronchitis and told him to quit smoking. During the winter it became much worse, and follow-up consultations with the doctor were unsatisfying. He asked her for a chest x-ray but she repeated instead that he should simply quit smoking.

After the New Year, frustrated, he went to another doctor who immediately ordered an x-ray that discovered a tumor in his lung. He was diagnosed with adema carcinoma, which he explained to me on the telephone was the "Conan the Barbarian of cancers." If he'd been diagnosed earlier, when he first asked for a chest x-ray, there's a slim possibility that surgery might have saved his life. As it was, the cancer was too far gone to do anything about. He passed away on August 26, 1994, at the age of 62. He was buried in Little Lake Cemetery in Peterborough, Ontario.

Rest in peace, Dad.

Chapter Twenty-One
Other McCanns

Up to now, I've pretty much skirted the other McCann families who lived in North Crosby Township or farther afield in places like Bathurst, Burgess, Bedford, or Perth. It's been enough of a challenge to trace our direct ancestors and their hundreds of miscellaneous offshoots without explaining which McCanns don't fit into our *Brief History* master plan.

Until now.

When I wrote the first draft of this monster a couple of decades ago, I included a chapter briefly covering these other fine folks. After much dithering back and forth, I've decided to include that material here. Such as it is.

The Foley Mountain McCanns

Most notable among the other McCanns were the "Foley Mountain McCanns." This family emigrated from Mullaghbawn Townland, Forkhill Parish, County Armagh, and they settled on what is now known as the Parish Road on Foley Mountain, just north of the village of Westport.

The family consisted of Peter McCann, who was born about 1785, his wife Rose Murphy (born about 1791), Peter's father, Peter McCann Sr., who was born about 1750, and Peter Jr.'s five sons. These sons spread out along the Parish Road, spanning Concessions 5 and 6 on Lots 17 and 18, establishing farms next to each other.

Michael J. McCann

The eldest of the five sons was Michael McCann (1814-1898). He married Mary Ferrigan (1828-1914) and raised three sons, including James F. McCann (1846-1905), Peter McCann (born 1854) and John S. McCann. Michael's farm was located on Lot 18 of Concession 6.

The second son of Peter McCann Jr. and Rose Murphy was Thomas McCann (born about 1815). He married Catherine Ryan, the daughter of Andrew Ryan and Mary Loughran, in 1849. He had four sons, including Peter McCann (born about 1850, married Anne Byrne in 1874), Andrew McCann (born about 1851), Thomas (born about 1853), Michael (born about 1855), James (born about 1858), and Edward (born about 1868), along with four daughters, Rose, Mary, Catherine and Maggie. Thomas' farm was on Lot 19 of Concession 5 in 1861, then on Lot 18 of Concession 5 in 1871.

The third son of Peter McCann Jr. and Rose Murphy was Edward (Ned) McCann (1819-1896) who married Margaret Trainor (1827-1897), the daughter of Patrick Trainor and Nancy Atkinson. Ned raised eight sons: Thomas McCann(born 1846), Peter McCann (born 1848), John McCann (born 1850), Edward (born 1852), Patrick (born 1854), Hugh McCann (born 1856), Andrew McCann (1862-1917) and George McCann (born 1865). Edward's farm was on Lot 18 of Concession 6.

The fourth son of Peter McCann Jr. and Rose Murphy was Andrew McCann (1820-1896) who married Mary Donnelly (1821-1908) and had four sons, Peter McCann (born 1847), Andrew J. Thomas (1855-1902) who married Catherine Kelly, and James (born 1863). Andrew appears to be the only son who did not have a farm on Parish Road. In 1848 he lived on Lot 24 of Concession 6, and in 1851 he appears to be located on Lot 7 of

Concession 8, which is below Westport between 8th Line Road and Highway 42 on the way to Newboro. Andrew's son James Edward McCann, who married Edith Deming in Gananoque in 1887, became a blacksmith in Westport. His shop on Bedford Street is now the home of the Rideau District Museum. His son Deming McCann was a contemporary of Ford McCann.

The fifth son of Peter McCann Jr. and Rose Murphy was Peter McCann III, who was born about 1829 and married Elizabeth Burns. He had four sons, including Peter McCann IV (born about 1855), James McCann (born about 1857, married Anne Bennett in 1882), Thomas McCann (born about 1860), and Henry McCann (born about 1867), and one daughter, Catherine. Peter's farm was on Lot 18 of Concession 6.

Peter McCann Jr. donated a portion of his land for the construction of the first Roman Catholic church in the area in 1840. This log cabin was the home base for the mission overseen by Father Edward Vaughn, the founding missionary priest, for seven years. It also served as a school house for the Catholic children in the area.

In 1847, the St. Francis of Assisi Church was built in Bedford Township at the current site of the St. Edward's Cemetery, on the border between Bedford and North Crosby Townships. By this time, Father John Foley was the missionary priest, and he divided his time between the mountain church and St. Francis of Assisi. Unfortunately, this new church burned down almost immediately after it was built. Thankfully the log church remained while another church could be built at Bedford.

In 1852, however, the church property within the village of Westport was purchased and the first residence was built. Plans for the construction of a substantial church were then begun, and the cornerstone was laid in 1859. Construction of the granite church was completed in 1863 and the church, dedicated to St. Edward the Confessor, opened its doors thereafter.

Ultimately, the log church on the mountain also burned down, but a monument has been erected to mark its site, as seen in Figure 66. This photograph, taken about 1982, shows Hugh McCann, the author's father, standing with the monument at a time when the site was essentially an open field as it would have been when the log church still stood. Today the site is engulfed in trees and is accessible through a well-kept path and sanctuary. As for the Foley Mountain McCann brothers, they continued to be very active in church life after the construction of St. Edward the Confessor Church, serving on the church committee and maintaining a high profile in its business for decades.

As you can see, the Foley Mountain McCanns present quite a genealogical thicket, given all the crossover names from one generation to the next. Since this *Brief History* is long enough as it is, we'll leave this family to others with more of a vested interest to research on their own.

Thomas and Bridget McCann

Among the other McCanns in North Crosby Township during the middle 1800s was a couple that tantalized and thwarted. Thomas McCann (1798-February 10, 1864) was married to Bridget Kelly or Keilly (born about 1805). Thomas farmed on Concession 7, Lot 18, kitty-corner to the lot shared by Arthur McCann, John McCann and Michael Toole as early as 1848.

A brief word on the surname Kelly. It derived from the

Irish *Ó'Cadhla*, descendant of Cadhla, which means "beautiful" or "graceful." It was the name of an ancient Connaught family. Through the centuries it has been anglicized as Kiely, Keily, Killeen, Kealy, Keeley, Kelly, and so on.[322] As we saw much earlier with "Kierans," the surname of the mother of Michael Toole, it's difficult to say which variant connects to another, other than to say they would all come from a common source.

The children of Thomas and Bridget included Michael (Mick) McCann (born about 1836), Barny McCann (born about 1837), Ann McCann (born about 1840), Thomas McCann Jr. (born about 1841), Catherine (Kitty) McCann. (born about 1844) and Bridget McCann (born in 1847).

In August 1856, Ann McCann married George Coburn, the son of Thomas Coburn and Ann Lock. In the St. Edward's registry record of the marriage, Father Foley noted that Thomas McCann and Bridget Kelly were from Forkhill Parish. As were Arthur McCann and Ann Quinn, of course. And Thomas and Ann Coburn were the parents of Sarah Coburn, wife of Arthur's son John.

Ann's brother Mick McCann married a woman named Margaret Byrne, the daughter of Michael Byrne and Bridget Lee, on May 12, 1859, in Perth. If you remember our previous discussion of the Byrne family as they were connected to Henry Allore (come on, you can do it), Michael and Bridget were also the parents of Bernard Byrne, who married Mary O'Hare and was the father of Mary Byrne, Henry Allore's first wife. (There never seem to be many degrees of separation in this family history!)

Mick and Margaret had a daughter Bridget (born around 1860) and a son, Thomas (Jan. 1862–Feb. 14, 1863). This little boy was memorialized on the gravestone of his grandfather, Thomas.

It appears that Mick and his family immigrated to the United States some time before 1873, where Mick died on October 19, 1910, in Youngstown, Ohio. He was buried there in the Calvary Cemetery[323] along with his daughter Catherine McCann Moran, who died December 9, 1925; his son Bernard McCann, who died December 31, 1913; his daughter Ella McCann (1871-1924); his wife Margaret Byrne, who died on September 10, 1894); and his son William John McCann, born October 27, 1873, in Youngstown and died there on January 3, 1950. All of the family members were buried together in section 13 (D) of the cemetery.[324]

Thomas McCann passed away on February 10, 1864, at the age of 66 and was buried in St. Edward's cemetery.

For years while I researched this family, I nursed the theory that this Thomas was directly related to Arthur McCann, either as a young brother or a nephew. The closeness of their farms in North Crosby, the connections of both to Thomas Coburn, the fact that both were from Forkhill Parish, and the naming of Michael J.'s son Thomas J. all suggested they were family. Try as I might, though, I couldn't find the smoking gun. Can you? I hope so.

Edward and Mary McCann

To the west of North Crosby Township, in Bedford Township, was another McCann family about which little is known. Edward McCann (1803–1881) and his wife Mary Langan (born 1797) were from County Mayo, Ireland.[325] Farmers in the area not far from St. Edward's Cemetery, their children included Bridget McCann (1827–Feb. 14, 1849); Catherine McCann (1829–Dec. 2, 1859); Peter McCann (1830–Jan. 29, 1872) and Robert McCann (1842–June 7, 1861). They also had a son Patrick McCann (1835–Apr. 20, 1905) who married Catherine McCue (1850–1929). Edward and Mary lived on the farm with their son Patrick and his family into their 80s, and their family plots in St. Edward's Cemetery are right at the back along with those of our family. Edward died on July 5, 1881, at the age of 78.

SAM MCCANN THE CHEESEMAKER

Samuel McCann and his grandson of the same name were Protestants and so were not descendants of Arthur McCann and Ann Quinn, but just the same, the younger Sam's cheesemaking business was important enough during his lifetime that the family merits *brief* mention here.

Samuel McCann the elder was born on August 11, 1822, and he was one of the early settlers in the area, arriving in 1829 with his family. According to Neil A. Patterson, he emigrated from Belfast, Northern Ireland.[326] He married Sarah Steadman in 1848, and by 1861 he was on a 59-acre property on Lot 2 of Concession 1, in the southern end of North Crosby Township, down near the village of Newboro. He was growing wheat, peas, corn, and potatoes in modest amounts, but wasn't making cheese.

Fig. 71 Samuel T. McCann

Among the children of Samuel and Sarah McCann was Thomas McCann, who was born on August 11, 1850. Thomas married Emma (Emily) Jane Pyne, who was born in nearby Portland in 1854. Thomas farmed next to his parents' place, and among their children was Samuel Thomas McCann, whom we'll call Sam.

Samuel T. McCann was born on August 27, 1872. Neil A. Patterson tells us that as a young man Sam travelled down to Watertown, New York, to work. After saving his money, he returned home to buy the Centreville Cheese Factory, located in Lot 9 of Concession 9, on Centreville Road. This area is what's known as the Blair Settlement, south of Westport on the border of North Crosby and Bedford Townships. The factory soon became known as Blairs Cheese Factory.

On April 19, 1899, Sam married Christine Blair, the daughter of William Blair and Anna Forester. The Blairs lived on Lot 6 of Concession 8, on McAndrews Road between Bedford Mills and Westport. Their farm was right down the road from the cheese factory, and the newly-weds took up residence above the factory to begin raising their family. Their children included Lillian McCann (born June 1900), Anna Mildred McCann (1901-1970), Alma McCann (born October 1903), Rhea Belle McCann (July 1904-1970) and sons Arden McCann (November 1906-March 1920, age 14), Cecil MCann (born July 1907), Ronald McCann (d. October 1908, age three months). Donald McCann (d. November 1909, age 16 months), and Russel McCann (March 1910-July 1921, age 10).

However, it was cheesemaking that ran in his blood. Not content with a single factory, by 1911 Sam had added the Mountain View Cheese Factory in partnership with John Dyre.[327] By 1918 his holdings had expanded to include the successful Salem Cheese Factory in nearby Bedford Township,[328] followed by the Westport Cheese Factory[329] in 1928, the Ardmore Cheese Factory, and the Ontario Cheese Factory.

The Salem factory was the most successful in the area, shipping nearly 100,000 lbs. of cheese to wholesalers annually. They travelled in 40-pound round boxes and were shipped by rail in a specially refrigerated cheese boxcar every Friday.[330]

One could say that Sam McCann was definitely the Big Cheese in North Crosby Township. It's likely why the township named McCann Road after the family.

Sam T.'s grandfather, Samuel McCann, died on February 3, 1906, and his grandmother, Sarah Steadman, died eight months later. They were buried together in Saint Mary's Anglican Cemetery in Newboro, Ontario.

Sam T.'s father Thomas McCann died on March 23, 1939, at age 88 and was buried in the Newboro United Cemetery.

Samuel T. McCann died in 1966 and was buried in the Knox Presbyterian Cemetery in Westport with his family.

Patrick McCann and Anne Fitzgerald

The only information I've been able to gather about the origins of this couple is anecdotal, I'm afraid. The website from which I drew it has now been taken down, but I found in previous research that it was much quoted among the genealogical community, so it bears repeating here. For what it's worth.[331]

Patrick McCann was born around 1809 and may have been the son of Anthony McCann and Molly McDonald, likely from County Cork, Ireland. While still in Ireland, he married Anne Fitzpatrick, the daughter of John and Bridget Fitzpatrick of Laurel Hill, Errigal-Trough Parish, County Monaghan. Anne gave birth to John A. McCann in 1841 and Thomas McCann around 1843, before the family immigrated to Canada in 1846.[332]

They settled on Lot 5 of Concession 4, South Burgess Township, where by 1851 he had 30 acres of a 60-acre parcel under cultivation, with 20 in crops, including five in wheat, and the other 10 in pasture.

In addition to John A. and Thomas, their children born in Upper Canada included Margaret Anne McCann (born about 1848); Arthur McCann (born September 10, 1849-August 30, 1915); Sarah McCann (born about 1852); Mary McCann (born about 1854); James McCann (born about 1855); Joseph McCann (born about 1857); Elizabeth McCann (1859-1936); Lucy Luretta McCann (born 1862); and Hugh McCann (born about 1866).

Their oldest son, John A. McCann of Perth, catches our interest in particular.

As a young man, he moved into town and found work as a stonemason. On February 13, 1872, when he was about 31 years old, he married Mary Hourigan, the daughter of Michael Hourigan and Bridget Maloney. Originally from County Clare, Ireland, Hourigan had settled in Poonamalie, near Smiths Falls, and served as township councillor and reeve of Elmsley Township,[333] so it would have been a good marriage for John, politically speaking.

In 1889, when he was 48, he was appointed to a civil service position as a licence commissioner, part of the body responsible for issuing liquor licences in town. He resigned this position in order to accept an appointment as a licence inspector, auditing taverns and other public places where liquor was served, charging tavern keepers whenever violations were found.[334] It must have made him very popular in that sector of the town, at least with the temperance folks.

Of the children of John A. McCann of Perth and Mary Hourigan, one in particular bears notice here.

James Parnell McCann was born in Perth on March 29, 1887. Also known as James Joseph McCann, or J.J., he attended Queen's University in Kingston, Ontario, and the University of Chicago, earning an MD as a medical doctor.[335] He was a practising physician and surgeon in Renfrew, Ontario, and was also county coroner, until politics called him to public service.

In 1935, at the age of 48, he was elected to the House of Commons as Liberal Member of Parliament for the riding of Renfrew South. While in the process of putting together a cabinet for his newly elected government, Prime Minister William Lyon Mackenzie King received a telephone call from Cardinal O'Connor of the Roman Catholic Church, expressing a desire to see the Irish Catholic community appropriately represented. However, while Dr. McCann was the obvious candidate, King felt he lacked the necessary political experience and passed him over.

The general election of 1940 saw Dr. McCann returned to office. King's diary shows that Dr. McCann was given serious consideration as Minister of National Revenue, but was again not chosen.[336] Re-elected again in 1945, Dr. McCann finally received his much-coveted cabinet appointment when he was sworn in as a member of the Privy Council and Minister of National Revenue. Although Revenue traditionally is viewed as a lesser post, it gave King the English-speaking Irish Catholic he needed, and it gave Dr. McCann the prominence he desired.

H. Reginald Hardy reconstructed the appointment of

Dr. McCann in *Mackenzie King of Canada*:

> It is interesting to note just how King's mind worked in making some of his cabinet appointments. For instance, many people were quite surprised when he appointed Dr. J.J. McCann to the post of Minister of National Revenue. McCann had been prominently mentioned for the portfolio of National Health, but it seemed that a lawyer, or a man trained in economics, would have been the logical choice for the Revenue Department. Certainly it seemed rather strange that King should choose a medical man.
>
> But King knew what many others did not know, that McCann had been largely responsible for putting a well-known trust company back on its feet; that he had interested himself most successfully in a number of other business enterprises; and that he had a sound business sense.
>
> "Why do you want a man like me for the job?" McCann asked King when he was called over to the East Block to discuss the appointment. "I'm a doctor, not a lawyer or an economist."
>
> "Because I want a man with good common business sense who is capable of doing a tough job," said King. "I think you're that kind of a man."[337]

In October 1946, for example, he attended a dinner with Prime Minister King, the Ambassador from Brazil, the

Count and Countess de Menthon of the French Legation and representatives of the Ambassador from Greece, and a luncheon in honour of Cardinal McGuigan of Toronto that was also attended by the Prime Minister, the Chief Justice of the Supreme Court of Canada, the Governor General, the Mayor of Ottawa, Archbishop Vachon and the Ambassador from Peru.[338]

Not bad for the grandson of an Irish Catholic farmer from South Burgess.

After King retired and Louis St. Laurent had replaced him as leader of the Liberal Party and prime minister, Dr. McCann was once more re-elected in 1949. He was appointed Minister of Mines and Technical Surveys in addition to his National Revenue portfolio. In May of 1950 he led the delegation from the Canadian government that attended the Third Meeting of the World Health Organization held in Geneva, Switzerland. After being re-elected again in 1953, he served as Vice-Chairman of the Canadian delegation to the 10th General assembly of the United Nations in New York.

In 1957, however, after a scandal involving his connections to the Guaranty Trust Company, he lost his seat in the House of Commons after 22 years as the MP for Renfrew South.

Four years later, at the age of 74, the Honourable John Parnell McCann, MD, CM, LLD, passed away on April 11, 1961, and was buried in St. Francis Xavier cemetery in Renfrew, Ontario.

His father, John A. McCann of Perth, passed away on July 9, 1926, at the age of 86. His mother, Mary Hourigan, had previously died on March 14, 1901. They were both buried in St. John the Baptist cemetery in Perth, Ontario.

The patriarch, Patrick McCann, died on July 25, 1880, at

the age of 71. His wife, Anne Fitzpatrick, passed away on March 23, 1888. They were both buried in St. John the Baptist cemetery in Perth.

Post-Amble

I can't believe I've reached the end.

Not the end of the story, of course, because the descendants of Arthur McCann and Ann Quinn continue to be born, live their lives, and give birth to new generations. Just the end of my story. I've taken it as far as I can, and now I pass it over to you, my cousins, nieces and nephew, extended family, friends. Carry it forward into the future. Tell the story in your own way now.

You may notice that I didn't extend this *Brief History* with a chapter on Hugh McCann's wife, Janet Brook. In the original draft of this manuscript, which began in 2006, I devoted a fair bit of space to the Brook family, tracing their history just as I have that of the Hagans, McCardles, McCoys, and Kearnses (to name a few). In writing this revision now, I've made the executive decision to move that information into a chapbook of its own. Another project, for the near future, I hope.

This book, part Irish history, part family history, part Canadian history, and part memoir, is the most important thing I'll ever write. Although I love crime fiction and have written a couple of novels I'm particularly proud of—read *The Disappearances*! You won't be sorry!—I know this has a personal meaning to me that goes above and beyond.

I've written it my way, informally. For this I apologize to the professional academics, who will be horrified by my casual approach to end noting, for example. I've tried to document my information as well as I possibly could, but my scholarly days are far behind me, and what you see is what you get.

I also apologize to family members who may find this

whole thing a little muscle-bound in terms of begets and begats, references, and the like. I've tried whenever possible to tell stories that you'll find interesting or even amusing, but in most cases the book will best serve as a reference volume for our family history.

Some of those stories will stay with me for a long time. Take my Uncle Wilf McCann, son of Ford, for example. All I knew about him beforehand was a photograph in my grandmother's living room and a few pictures in a family album kindly photocopied for my use. To be able to use online resources to reconstruct his youth and track his final days in the Netherlands and Germany was mind-blowing. It brought him alive for me, if only for a short time.

Florence Allore, daughter of Henry Allore and Mary Byrne, was another. Given up by her father and taken in by her grandparents, Barny Byrne and Mary O'Hare, was a sad and touching thing to discover. Her miscarriage and failed marriage, followed by her disappearance from the grid, were heartbreaking. It felt as though I were reaching back through time and felt her fingers slip from my hand, forever.

I admit, too, it was pure self-indulgence to tell the stories of Tom Carty and my cousin Chris McCann, the musician and university professor. But we should never be too full of ourselves to admit to hero worship, should we?

In all, this has been an adventure for me that I'll always treasure.

I hope you'll get something out of it, too.

August 14, 2024
Oxford Station, Ontario

Acknowledgments

My research, needless to say, has been open-ended. A few decades ago I spent many hours in the National Archives and Library of Canada in Ottawa and the Leeds and Grenville Genealogical Society (LGGS) archives in Brockville, spinning microfilm reels and roaming the stacks for reference books. In addition, I enjoyed an afternoon viewing the parish registry at St. Edward the Confessor Church in Westport, thanks to the kindness and patience of the parish priest of the day, the late Reverend Father Ed Keyes.

I was also given complete access to the township archives in the Westport Public Library, now known as the Rideau Lakes Library. Genealogical records had just arrived in the building back then and were sitting in cardboard boxes down in the basement, waiting to be processed. I wish I'd written down the name of the librarian who allowed me to root through those boxes over the course of the afternoon that day, as I remain very grateful. It's my understanding that there's now a historical centre for Rideau Lakes Township, located in Delta, and I expect that the contents of those boxes have ended up there.

When I tackled the rewrite this summer, I relied heavily on the online genealogical sites familysearch.org, ancestry.com, and findagrave.com in particular. My objective was to find a primary source to document each piece of information used, be it census records in Canada and the United States, church registry entries, civil birth, marriage, and death records, and so on. Most of this stuff has been hoovered up by ancestry, so I had to break down and register for a free trial. Between them and the other two, though, I was able to find a ton of primary sources that have substantiated my work. And contributed to the mission creep I mentioned in the Preamble.

A word of caution, though. The family trees constructed by users of ancestry and familysearch in particular are not to be trusted. I found a few valuable connections I hadn't suspected, but I also found some egregious errors. Beware.

Thanks go out to Mary Porritt, my cousin Debbie Ferguson, and the late Kathy Flynn Simons for photographs that have been included in this *Brief History*—I'm very grateful.

Other photo credits: Fig. 1, Johan Temmink; Fig. 2, Christian Birkholtz (Pixabay); Fig. 35, courtesy The Original Hockey Hall of Fame, Kingston, Ontario; Fig. 41, courtesy Ellen McCann; Figs. 42, 43, 44, 50, 51, 52, 53, 54, courtesy Anthea McCann; Figs. 34, 38, 46, courtesy Ida Allore; all others are public domain.

I don't know what I would have done without the black binder of family history documents given to me by my cousin, John Carr. Thanks, John. It was a huge help in checking dates, names, and a lot of other stuff.

Finally, thanks as always to my life partner and best friend, Lynn Clark. This one was a real time-eater, wasn't it?

About The Author

Michael J. McCann lives and writes in Oxford Station, Ontario, Canada. A graduate of Trent University (Peterborough, ON) and Queen's University (Kingston, ON), he served as Production Editor of *Criminal Reports (Third Series)* and Law Reports Coordinator for Carswell Legal Publications (Western) before spending fifteen years at the Canada Border Services Agency as a project officer and national program manager. He's married to author Lynn L. Clark. They have one son.

Family Charts

McCann Family Line

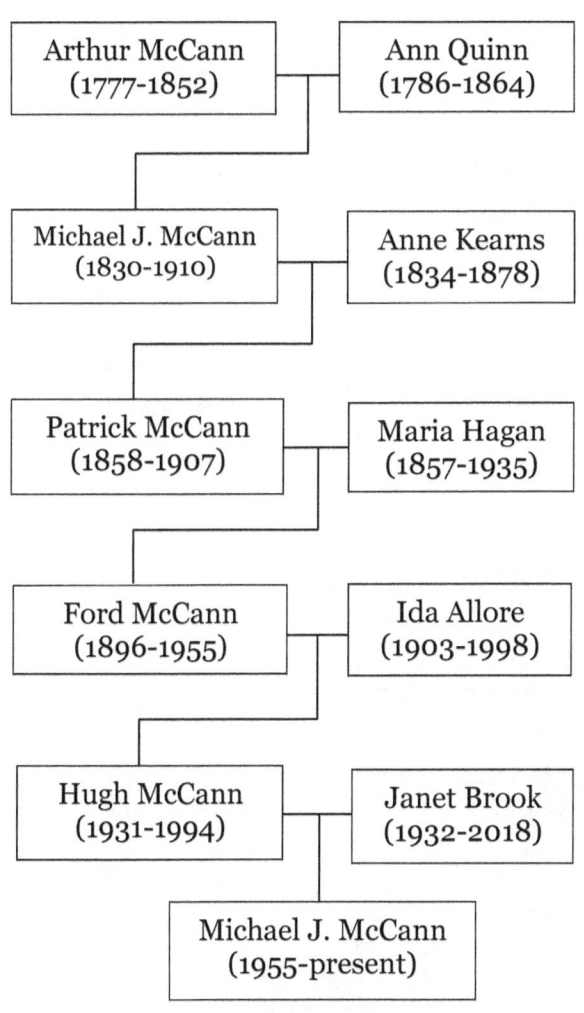

Family Charts

Allore Family Line

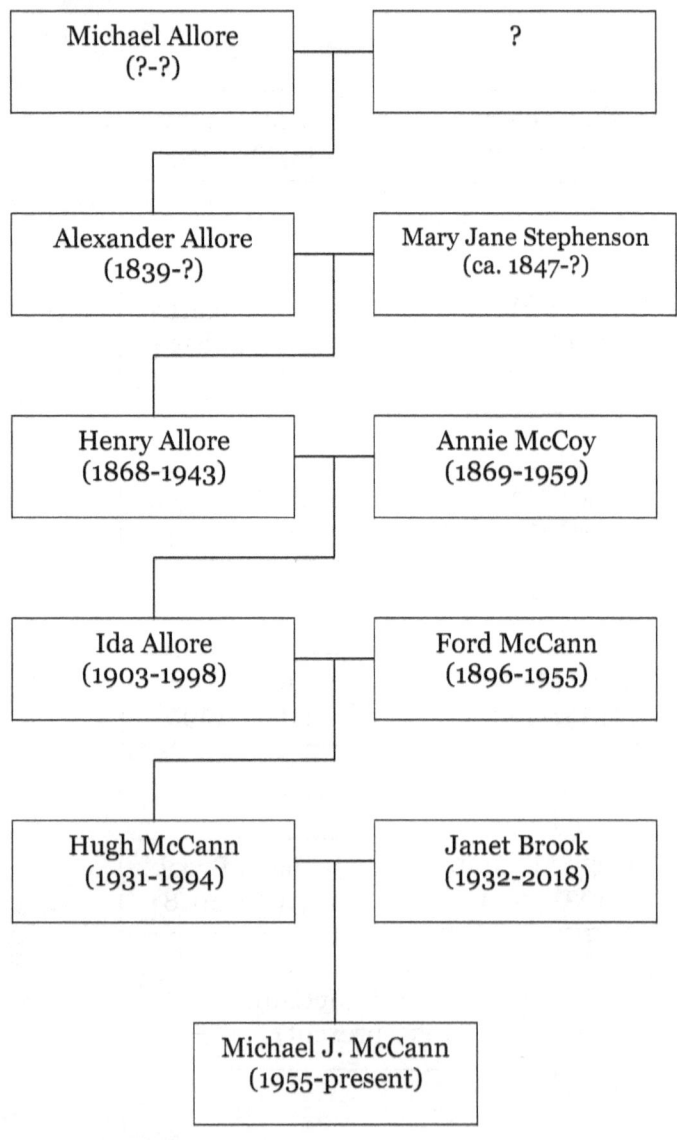

Family Charts

Hagan Family Line

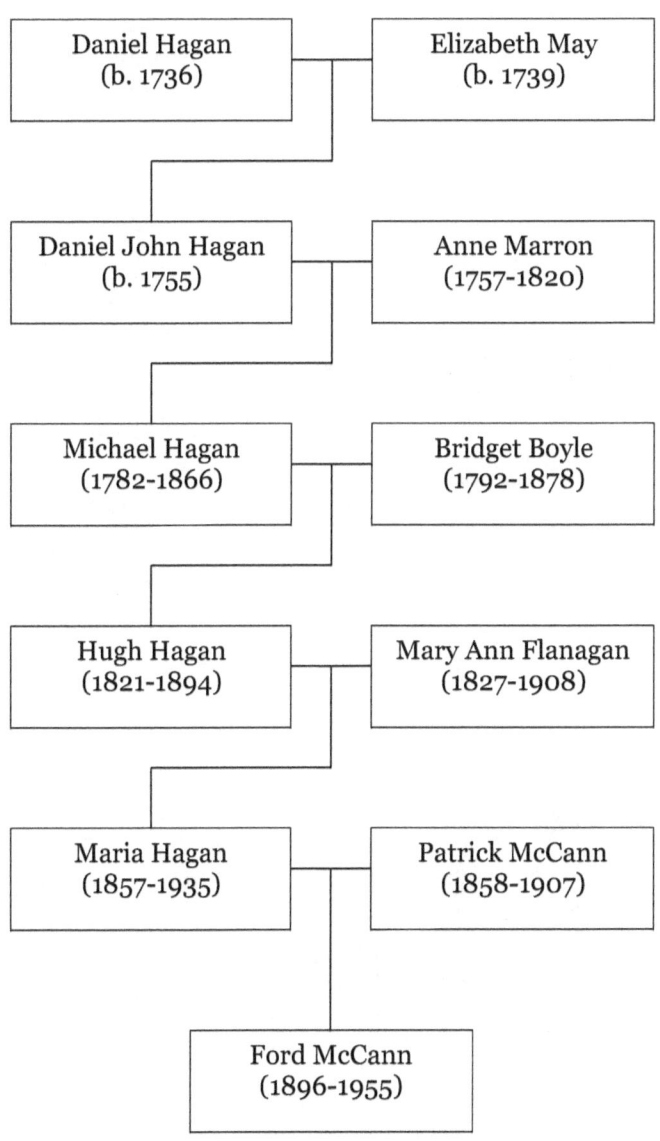

Endnotes

Chapter One

1. Killian Driscoll, *The Early Prehistory in the West of Ireland: Investigations into the Social Archaelogy of the Mesolithic West of Shannon, Ireland*. M.Litt. Thesis, Oct. 2006, National University of Ireland, Galway.

2. See R.J Edwards and A.J. Brooks, "The Island of Ireland: Drowning the Myth of an Irish Land-bridge?" in Davenport, J.J., Sleeman, D.P., Woodman, P.C. (eds.) *Mind the Gap: Postglacial Colonisation of Ireland. Special Supplement to The Irish Naturalists' Journal* (2008) pp. 19-34.

3. Driscoll, chapter 3.

4. Ibid.

5. Peter Berresford Ellis, *A Brief History of The Druids*. London: Constable & Robinson Ltd., 2002, p. 24.

6. T.F. O'Rahilly, *Early Irish History and Mythology* (Dublin: Dublin Institute for Advanced Studies, 1946).

7. If you're interested in learning more about the Picts, you might want to try Tim Clarkson, *The Picts: A History* (Edinburgh: Birlinn Limited, 2016).

8. O'Rahilly.

9. Thomas Cahill, *How the Irish Saved Civilization*. New York: Doubleday, 1995.

10. Alice Stopford Green, *Irish Nationality*. London: Williams and Norgate, 1911, p. 72.

11. Ibid, p. 72.

12. See Ellis, *A Brief History of the Druids*, for a fascinating exploration of the Druids and their influence.

13. Rev. Patrick Woulfe, *Sloinnte Gaedheal is Gall* (Irish Names and Surnames) (Dublin: M.H. Gill & Son, 1922), p. 15.

14. Ellis, *A Brief History of The Druids*, pp. 13-14.

15. The story of the Collas may be found in O'Rahilly and John O'Hart, *Irish Pedigrees*, Vol. 2, p. 575ff.

16. Cu Choicrich O'Clery, *The O'Clery Book of Genealogies*, Analecta Hibernica #18, Royal Irish Academy, Ms. 23-D-17.

Chapter Two

17. See Máire Ní Mhaonaigh, *Brian Boru: Ireland's Greatest King* (Stroud: Tempus, 2007) for his story.

18. If you're interested in this period, a standard history is *Ireland Under the Normans* by Goddard Henry Orpen, which was originally published by Oxford Press in two volumes in 1911 and two more in 1920. Clarendon Press reissued it in a single volume in 1968, but electronic copies of the Oxford volumes are available online for downloading from various websites at no cost.

19. William H. Hennessy, trans. *Annals of Ulster*, Vol. 1. Dublin: Alexander Thom & Co., 1887, p. 551.

20. John O'Hart, *Irish Pedigrees; or The Origin and Stem of the Irish Nation* (Second Series) (Dublin: M.H. Gill & Son, 1878), p. 239-40.

21. John O'Donovan, ed. and trans., *Annals of the Kingdom of Ireland by the Four Masters, from the Earliest Period to the Year 1171*. Dublin, 1849, M1155.8, p. 1115. This death is also recorded in the *Annals of Ulster*: "Amlaim Mac Canai (steward [lord] of Cenel-Aengusa) tower of the championship and activity of all Celen-Eogain, died" (Vol. 2, p. 129). Ard-Macha refers to the town of Armagh.

22. John O'Dubhagain, *The Topographical Poems of John O'Dubhagain and Giolla Na Naomh OHuidhrin*. Translated with notes by John O'Donovan. Dublin: The Irish Archaeological and Celtic Society, 1862, p. ix, n. 33.

23. *Annals of the Four Masters*, M.1212.7, p. 175. Recorded in the *Annals of Ulster* as occurring in 1213 (Vol. 2, p. 255).

24. *Annals of Ulster*, p. 261.

25. Emon O Doibhlin, "Ceart Ui Neill: A Discussion and Translation of the Document," *Seanchas Ardmhacha: Journal of the Armagh Diocesan Historical Society*, Vol. 5, No. 2 (1970), p. 324.

26. *Annals of Ulster*, Vol. 2, p. 159. O'Donovan then explains in his footnote: "This portion is omitted by the Four Masters. The offence is not stated in any authority accessible to me." For the vendetta, see the first item of 1170.

27. *Annals of Ulster*, Vol 2, p. 163. Ui-Caracain was a territory now known as Killyman, on the boundary of east Tyrone and west Armagh, just below the western tip of Lough Neagh.

28. *Annals of the Four Masters*, M1189.6, p. 86.

29. *Annals of Ulster*, 1266, Vol. 2, p. 341. O'Donovan notes that this event

more likely occurred in 1268. It would have been at Ard-Macha (Armagh).

30. *Leabhar na g-Ceart* (The Book of Rights), translated by John O'Donovan. Dublin: The Celtic Society, 1847, pp. 147-48, n. 7.

31. *Annals of Ulster*, 1260, p. 329.

32. Gilbride MacNamee, "Poem on the Battle of Dun," *Miscellany of the Celtic Society*, edited and translated by John O'Donovan. Dublin: The Celtic Society, 1849, p. 169.

33. Ibid.

34. George Hill, *An Historical Account of the Plantation of Ulster*, p. 259n.

Chapter Three

35. Richard Bagwell, *Ireland Under the Tudors*, Vol. 2. London: Longmans, Green and Co., 1885, pp. 2-4.

36. Bagwell, Vol. 2, pp. 33-34.

37. xi Elizabeth, Sess. 3, Cap. 1. From John T. Gilbert, ed., *A Contemporary History of Affairs in Ireland from 1641 to 1652* (Dublin: Irish Archaeological and Celtic Society, 1879), pp. 302-303.

38. Hiram Morgan, *Tyrone's Rebellion: The Outbreak of the Nine Years' War in Tudor Ireland* (Suffolk: The Boydell Press, 1999), p. 95.

39. Morgan, p. 96.

40. Herbert F. Hore, "Marshall Bagenal's Description of Ulster, Anno 1586," *Ulster Journal of Archaeology*, Vol. 2, 1854, p. 150.

41. Edmund Hogan, *The Description of Ireland and the state thereof as it is at this present In Anno 1598*. Dublin: M.H. Gill & Son, 1878, p. 20.

42. "Sir Arthur Chichester to Sir Robert Cecil, Carrickfergus, 21 Jul. 1601," *CSPI*, Nov. 1600-Jul. 1601: 448.

43. Eoin O'Neill, *O Estado Que Nunca Foi: Guerra e a Formação do Estado na Irlanda do Século XVI* (Ph.D. thesis, Instituto Universitario de Pesquisas do Rio de Janeiro, 2005), 613.

Chapter Four

44. C.W. Russell and John P. Prendergast, eds., *Calendar of the State Papers Relating to Ireland of the Reign of James I*, 1608-1610 (London: Longman & Company, 1874), lxxxi.

45. T.G.F. Paterson, ed. "County Armagh in 1622: a Plantation Survey," *Seanchas Ardmhacha: Journal of the Armagh Diocesan Historical Society*,

Vol. 4, No. 1 (1960/1961, 103-140), p. 104.

46. *Calendar*, lxxxv.

47. *Calendar*, October 14, 1608, 62.

48. *Calendar*, lxxxvi.

49. J.S. Brewer and William Bullen, eds., *Calendar of the Carew Manuscripts Preserved in the Archiepiscopal Library at Lambeth* (Nendeln/ Liechtenstein: Kraus Reprint, 1974), p. 88.

50. C.F. McGleenan, "The Medieval Parishes of Ballymore and Mullabrack," *Seanchas Ardmhacha: Journal of the Armagh Diocesan Historical Society*, vol 12, no.2, 1987, p. 14.

51. W. K. Sullivan, ed. *On the Manners and Customs of the Ancient Irish*, (London: Williams and Norgate, 1873), xcv n.

52. Sullivan, xciv.

53. Sullivan, xcv.

54. Rev. George Hill, *Plantation Papers: Containing a Summary Sketch of The Great Ulster Plantation in the Year 1610* (Belfast, reprinted from The Northern Whig, 1889), p. 38.

55. Sir James Chichester, "Certain Considerations Touching the Plantation of the Escheated Lands of Ulster," January 27, 1609, Russell and Pendergast, p. 356. Quoted by Hill, *Plantation Papers*, pp. 38-39.

56. Rev. George Hill, *An Historical Account of the Plantation in Ulster* (Belfast: McCaw, Stephenson & Orr, 1877), pp. 313-314.

57. Hill, *An Historical Account*, p. 569.

58. Hill, *An Historical Account*, pp. 313-314.

59. Edmund Hogan, *The Description of Ireland and The State Thereof as it is at this present in Anno 1598*. (Dublin: M.H. Gill & Son, 1878), p. 261.

60. O'Donovan, John, ed., *The Tribes of Ireland: A Satire, by Aengus O'Daly* (Dublin: John O'Daly, 1852), p. 24.

61. *Tribes of Ireland*, p. 63.

62. *Tribes of Ireland*, p. 63, footnote 5.

63. Rev. W. Reeves, "Irish Itinerary of Dr. Edmund MacCana," *Ulster Journal of Archaeology*, vol. 2 (Belfast: Archer and Sons, 1854), p. 44.

NOTES

64. Hill, *An Historical Account*, pp. 313-314.

65. TCD, *1641 Depositions Project*, online transcript January 1970. [http://1641.tcd.ie/deposition.php?depID<?php echo 836216r112?>] accessed Thursday 18 January 2018 01:50 PM.

66. Hill, *An Historical Account*, p. 348.

67. Eamon Darcy, *The Irish Rebellion of 1641 and the Wars of the Three Kingdoms* (Suffolk: Boydell & Brewer, Ltd., 2013), p. 52.

68. Examination of William Clarke, Killulta, Co. Antrim, 28 February 1653 [TCD MS 836, ff 177r-178v].

69. Deposition of Phillip Taylor, Portadown, 8 February 1642 [TCD MS 836, ff 7r-7v].

70. Examination of Valentine Blacker, n.p., n.d., [TCD MS 836, ff 242r-243v].

71. Deposition of Humphrey Stewartt, n.p., 3 May 1653 [TCD MS 837, ff 82r-82v].

72. Micheál Ó Siochrú and Mark S. Sweetnam, "The 1641 Depositions and Portadown Bridge." *Seanchas Ardmhacha: Journal of the Armagh Diocesan Historical Society*, vol 24, no. 1, 2012, pp. 72-103.

73. Deposition of Anthony Workeman, n.p., 28 February 1651 [TCD MS 836, ff 204r-205v].

74. Michael McCartan, "The Cromwellian High Courts of Justice in Ulster, 1653," *Seanchas Ardmhacha: Journal of the Armagh Diocesan Historical Society*, vol. 23, no. 1, 2010, p. 129.

75. Examination of William Brownelow, Armagh, 26 February 1652 [TCD MS 836, ff 202r-203v].

76. According to Kieran Clendinning in his self-published pamphlet *The Parish of Shankill: A Brief Ecclesiastical History*, 1983. This is a guy who understands the meaning of the word "brief."

77. Examination of Neece McConwell, Killvetagh Antrim [TCD MS 836, ff 256r-257v].

78. McCartan, p. 128.

79. Examination of Toole McRory McCann, n.p., 5 May 1653 [TCD MS 836, ff 240r-241v].

80. Examination of Nicholas Williams, n.p., 28 February 1653 [TCD MS 836, ff 204r].

Chapter Five

81. William Butler (1903), "Oliver Cromwell in Ireland". In O'Brien, R. Barry (ed.). *Studies in Irish History, 1649-1775*. Dublin: Browne and Nolan. p. 49. Viewed online at https://en.wikisource.org/wiki/ Studies_in_Irish_History,_1649-1775/Oliver_Cromwell_in_Ireland, accessed Oct. 28, 2021.

82. "August 1652: An Act for the Setling of Ireland," in *Acts and Ordinances of the Interregnum, 1642-1660*, eds. C H Firth and R S Rait (London, 1911), pp. 598-603.

83. Padraig Lenihan, *Consolidating Conquest, Ireland 1603–1727* (Abigdon: Routledge, 2008), p 135.

84. Micheál Ó Siochru, *God's Executioner: Oliver Cromwell and the Conquest of Ireland* (London: Faber and Faber, 2008), p. 232.

85. L. P. Murray, "The County Armagh Hearth Money Rolls, A.D. 1664." *Archivium Hibernicum*, vol. 8, 1941, pp. 121–202. JSTOR, www.jstor.org/stable/25485528. Accessed 16 Oct. 2020.

86. Murray, p. 121.

87. This location information was gleaned from the website placenamesni.org, the home of the Northern Ireland Place-Name Project that was conducted at Queen's University, Belfast. Its database holds more than 30,000 names, and it's an invaluable tool in sorting out the myriad variations of local place names. Although funding for the project has run out, the database was still available online as of January 1, 2023.

Chapter Six

88. Marriage Register for the Roman Catholic Congregation Assembling at Westport In the County of Leeds, Register of Marriages for 1853, Fr. John Foley, np.

89. Paterson, "Cromwellian Inquisition," pp. 244-45. I freely admit that I tried and failed to find out how these townlands were reassigned from Creggan to Killevy and then to Forkhill. I ran out of steam, and Internet hits, and surrendered to the forces of oblivion.

90. Kyla Madden, *Forkhill Protestants and Forkhill Catholics: 1787-1858*. (Montreal & Kingston: McGill-Queen's Press, 2005), p. 10.

91. Madden, *Forkhill Protestants*, p. 11.

NOTES

92. Madden, *Forkhill Protestants*, p. 12.

93. Madden, *Forkhill Protestants*, p. 44.

94. Madden, *Forkhill Protestants*, p. 12.

95. Madden, *Forkhill Protestants*, p. 67.

96. Cardinal Moran, *The Catholics of Ireland Under The Penal Laws In the Eighteenth Century* (London: Catholic Truth Society, 1899), p. 7. Moran noted that after the passage of this law, the courts were flooded with "idle and wicked vagrants" hoping to rip off Catholics of their land by informing on them about their profits. However, as a court official said in 1747, "It is no matter to the public in whose hands the estate is, provided it is not in the hands of a Papist" (p.8).

97. Robert Kee, *The Laurel and the Ivy: The Story of Charles Stewart Parnell and Irish Nationalism* (London: Hamish Hamilton, 1993), p.15

98. 7 Will III c. 4, IX.

99. Antonia McManus, *The Irish Hedge School and Its Books, 1695-1831* (Dublin: Four Courts Press, 2002), p. 16.

100. Donald Akenson, *The Irish Education Experiment: The National System of Education in the Nineteenth Century*, (Routledge, 2011), p. 53. See also McManus, above.

101. Madden, *Forkhill Protestants*, p. 65.

102. Madden, *Forkhill Protestants*, p. 29ff.

103. Madden, *Forkhill Protestants*, pp. 35-44.

CHAPTER SEVEN

104. "Trustees of Linen and Hempen Manufacturers, Premiums for growing flax," (Dublin, 1796). Found in Smyth, W.J., Whelan, K., Hughes, T.J. (1988) *Common ground: essays on the historical geography of Ireland presented to T. Jones Hughes*. Cork: Cork University, pp. 234-252.

105. Madden, *Forkhill Protestants*, p. 89.

106. Madden, pp. 90-93.

107. Tithe Applotment for the Parish of Forkhill, County Armagh. Public Record Office for Northern Ireland, Ref. FIN/5/A/143. Viewed at apps.proni.gov.uk/eCatNI_IE/BrowseSearchPage.aspx on Oct. 19, 2020.

108. Madden, *Forkhill Protestants*, p. 45.

109. Madden, *Forkhill Protestants*, pp. 44-45.

110. Madden, *Forkhill Protestants*, pp. 46-47.

111. Una Walsh and Kevin Murphy, eds., *Kick Any Stone: Townlands, People and Stories of Forkhill Parish: Includes 1821 Census.* Mullaghbawn: Mullaghbawn Community Association, 2003. Only a few copies of this book were printed, and I'm eternally grateful to Jane Cawley Murphy of Westport, Ontario, for the loan of her copy.

112. "Griffith's Valuation" refers to a government initiative conducted in the mid-1800s that consisted of a "general valuation of rateable property in Ireland." Conducted by Sir Richard Griffith, a civil engineer, this project unfolded in three stages, including: a survey of boundaries, between 1825 and 1837; a townland valuation, from 1829 to 1844, that assessed the values of land and buildings; and the general valuation, conducted from 1852 to 1864. It's the results of this third survey, referred to commonly as Griffith's valuation, that's of interest to us. The last book in his exhaustive general valuation was printed in December 1864, and it happened to be the results for Armagh—the final county to be completed in his ambitious survey. Given the date of this survey, and the fact that Arthur McCann and Anne Quinn emigrated in 1840 or 1841, these lists can't help us directly in our search for them in Ireland. However, maps made available online at askaboutireland.ie/griffith-valuation are very useful in documenting the locations of McCann properties 40 years after the 1821 census, and it gives us a chance to see who remained behind in Forkhill after Arthur McCann and Anne Quinn emigrated.

113. *Kick Any Stone*, pp. 182-183.

114. *Ring of Gullion: Towards a Management Strategy 2008-2013,* Belfast: Environment and Heritage Service, p.11.

115. V.B. Proudfoot, "The Economy of the Irish Rath," *Medieval Architecture*, 5:1, 1961, 94-122.

116. "Fairyism has been much connected with Danes in Ireland, in the traditions of the people; who considered the Danes to have erected the circular earthen ramparts or raths, called forts, and that the fairies were left there by the Danes to guard their treasures until their return to Ireland, which is expected to take place at some future time." John O'Hart, *Irish Pedigrees; or the Origin and Stem of the Irish Nation* (Second Series) (Dublin,: M.H. Gill & Son, 1878), p. 886.

117. William Anthony Smyth, *Sir Richard Griffith's Three Valuations*

NOTES

of Ireland 1826-1864. Ph.D Thesis, (Maynooth: National University of Ireland, 2008).

118. Reverend Diarmuid Mac Iomhair, "Urnai," Faughart Historical Properties Preservation Society. The webpage on which this article was found, which I viewed on June 22, 2005, no longer exists.

119. Ibid.

120. John P. Clarke, "Late Eighteenth Century Decorated Headstone at Urney Graveyard, Co. Louth," *The County Louth Archaeological Society*, Vol. XVI, No. 1 (1965) 1-4.

121. Photographs of Urney Church and Graveyard were accessed at the website geograph.ie and are reproduced according to the Creative Commons licence under which they are placed.

122. Mac Iomhair, "Urnai." Mac Iomhair was a very well known scholar in the 1940s and 1950s.

123. Ibid.

124. Ibid.

CHAPTER EIGHT

125. A very interesting description of what this migration would have been like can be found in *The Great Migration: The Atlantic Crossing by Sailingship 1770-1860* by Edwin C. Guillet (second edition, Toronto: University of Toronto Press, 1963). I've relied on this source for the next few pages.

126. For a remarkable description of a journey in an Irish "coffin ship" that ended at Grosse Île, see *Robert Whyte's 1847 Famine Ship Diary: The Journey of an Irish Coffin Ship*," edited by James J. Mangan (Mercier Press, 1994).

127. Another hazard would have been for the ship itself to run into trouble, such as the *Hannah*, an Irish brig that sailed from Warrenpoint bound for Quebec in April, 1849. Many of the passengers were bound for the Westport area; the ship struck ice and sank. Fortunately another ship, the *Nicaragua*, was nearby and picked up a number of survivors, many of whom completed their journey to settle in the Westport area. See *A Famine Link: The 'Hannah" South Armagh to Ontario* (Mullaghbane, Armagh: Mullaghbane Community Association, 2006).

128. Description of travel in Upper Canada in the 1840s based on information from *The Emigrant's Directory and Guide to Obtain Lands*

and Effect a Settlement in the Canadas by Francis A. Evans (Dublin: William Curry Jr., & Co., 1833), and also G.P. deT. Glazebrook, *A History of Transportation in Canada*, Vol. I (Ryerson Press, 1938; Toronto: McClelland and Stewart, 1964), p. 71 ff, and Peter Robinson's *Report on 1823 Emigration to the Bathurst District of Upper Canada*, which is found online at multiple locations that may be Googled.

129. Thaddeus William Henry Leavitt, *History of Leeds and Grenville* (Brockville: Recorder Press, 1879; Belleville: Mika Silk Screening Limited, 1972), p. 180.

130. Leavitt, p. 179.

131. David Roberts, *The Settlement of North Crosby 1806-1860,* Appendix I, North Crosby Reserve Settlement. (Opportunities for Youth Project. Unpublished typescript, 1972. Township archives, Westport Public Library.)

132. Leavitt, p. 21.

133. 1851 Census, Canada West, Leeds County, North Crosby Township, p. 78.

134. Ibid., p. 26.

135. 1851 Census, Canada West, Lanark County, North Burgess Township, Part 2, p. 40.

136. Robert Leslie Jones, *History of Agriculture in Ontario 1613-1880* (Toronto: University of Toronto Press, 1946), p. 67.

137. Strickland, Need, and Mrs. Jameson are all quoted by Robert Leslie Jones, *History of Agriculture*, pp. 70-71.

138. Susannah Moodie, *Roughing it in the Bush* (Toronto: McClelland and Stewart, 1962), pp. 68-69.

139. Edwin Guillet, *Pioneer Arts and Crafts* (Toronto: University of Toronto Press, 1963), pp. 7-10. The following descriptions of furniture are from the same source.

140. Kenneth Kelly, "The Impact of Nineteenth Century Agricultural Settlement on the Land," in J. David Wood, ed., *Perspectives on Landscape and Settlement in Nineteenth Century Ontario* (Toronto: McClelland and Stewart, 1975, 64-77), p. 67.

141. With fondness I acknowledge my former neighbour, the late Donald Morrison of Dalhousie, Quebec, for having taught me this piece of small-farm folklore.

142. Return of the Inhabitants of North Crosby 1848, and Other Statistical Information, obtained in pursuance of an Act, intituled, "An Act for taking the Census of this Province and obtaining Statistical Information therein," Library and Archives Canada (M-5909), pp. 57-59.

143. Peter Baskerville, "MacNAB, Sir ALLAN NAPIER," in *Dictionary of Canadian Biography*, vol. 9, University of Toronto/Université Laval, 2003–, accessed February 5, 2021, http://www.biographi.ca/en/bio/ allan_napier_9E.html.

144. See Robert Leslie Jones, p. 141.

Chapter Nine

145. O'Hart, *Irish Pedigrees*, Vol. I, p. 669 and p. 816.

146. *Kick Any Stone*, p. 216.

147. Pursuing the McArdle side of the family history was one particular rabbit hole I fell into years ago while working on a previous iteration of this "brief" history. I've made the executive decision to leave most of this material on the cutting room floor at this time for the sake of our collective sanity.

148. Parish records of St. John the Baptist Roman Catholic Church, Microfilm 1298996.

149. Instructions to enumerators on recording "unsound mind" from "Instructions to Officers Employed in the Taking of the First Census of Canada" (1871): "The heading 11 'unsound mind' is intended to include all those unfortunates who are plainly deprived of reason. As the enquiry on this head may be for many persons very painful, the enumerator, if he is acquainted with the family beforehand, must approach it with great delicacy, taking care, however, not to omit the entry of any such case. No attempt is made to distinguish between the various maladies affecting the intellect; as experience proves that the result of such enquiries made under such circumstances is perfectly worthless." (p. 14)

150. 1861 Census Canada West, Personal Census Enumeration District One, Township of North Crosby in the County of Leeds, Public Archives of Canada, microfilmed in 1955, p. 13.

151. Edgar McInnis, *Canada: A Political and Social History* (Toronto: Holt, Rinehart and Winston of Canada, 1969), p. 304.

152. Wisconsin Circuit Court (Pierce County), Wisconsin County Naturalization Records 1807-1992. Filmed by the Genealogical Society of

Utah, 1980, 2006. Many thanks to Philip Jones for supplying this image, and others related to the McArdles, to the author.

153. Pipestone County District Court Naturalization Records 1879-1954, FSC Call #101746142, "Declarations of Intention," Vol. A, 1879-1906, p. 92.

154. 1880 United States Census, Minnesota: Wabash (cont'd: E.D. 178, sheet 1-end), Wadena, Waseca, and Washington (part: beginning-E.D. 30, sheet 10) Counties (NARA series T9, Roll 636), pp. 466-67.

155. Francis's surname was another example of enumerators and other public officials struggling with an unfamiliar family name. Variously appearing in records as Couvion, Covoyoung, Covyia, and Coviong, it was no doubt, absent the constant mangling, supposed to be rendered "Couvillon," a well-known name in Quebec that was previously spelled in France as "Quevillon."

156. http://www.findagrave.com/memorial/181329285/isabella-coveyou. I know that Find a Grave is considered by many to be an unreliable source, and I agree, but I did manage to find primary sources and links on this website that weren't available elsewhere.

157. findagrave.com/memorial/181329207/francis-abraham-coveyou.

158. Information about the De Watteville Regiment was found in a transcription of the *Perth Courier* of June 6, 1924, provided by Christine Spencer at www.rootsweb.com/~onlanark/histdoc/Lest_We_Forget_4.htm. Land grant to Casper Speagle recorded in National Archives of Canada microfilm MG9 D8-27 Vol Reel C-4651 p. 7 line 176, transcribed by Christine Spencer and posted at rootsweb.com/~onlanark/Land_Property/landgrt8.htm.

159. Canada, Ontario Roman Catholic Church Records, 1760-1923. St. John's Church, Perth, p. 44. Ann died in 1833 and was interred in The Old Burying Grounds, Perth, Ontario.

160. Casper J. Speagle's involvement in Sacred Heart of Jesus Church found in "Sacred Heart of Jesus Church" at http://perthareachurches.ca/scheart_B.htm.

161. *Westport: Our Early History in Pictures from Settlement to Five Years after Incorporation* (Westport: Rideau District Musum, 2016), p. 203.

162. perthunionlibrary.ca/library-history/, viewed June 13, 2024.

163. Homestead Affidavit, Ashland, Wisconsin, October 9, 1893, Bayfield

Notes

County, Application No. 3473; Homestead Proof - Testimony of Claimant.

164. Peter Andersen and Hubert Houle, *Mariages Catholiques de La Region de Perth,* No. 84 (Ottawa: Le Centre de Genealogie S.C., 1986), p. 153. Mary is listed as Nancy Kierans in this transcription, but the parish register for St. Edwards Church records her as Mary Kierans, aligning with the 1821 Forkhill census.

165. Rev. Patrick Woulfe, *Sloinnte Gaedheal is Gall* (Irish Names and Surnames) (1923), libraryireland.com/names/oc/o-ciarain.php, viewed August 10, 2024.

166. Find a Grave, database and images (https://www.findagrave.com/memorial/70827807/michael-toale : accessed 12 October 2021), memorial page for Michael Toale (1825–27 Aug 1877), Find a Grave Memorial ID 70827807, citing Saint John's Catholic Cemetery, Independence, Buchanan County, Iowa, USA.

167. findagrave.com/memorial/52554898/peter-james-toale.

168. Yet another unsolved mystery!

169. Comparative statistics regarding Canada West wheat product obtained by dividing the total bushels produced in Canada West in 1851 by the total number of acres devoted to wheat, taken from Robert Leslie Jones, *History of Agriculture in Ontario 1613-1880*, p. 86.

170. Information about North Crosby rye producers obtained from the census of 1851, and the quotation regarding its use in distilleries is from Jones, p. 88.

171. Robert Leslie Jones, p. 86.

172. This information about John's farm production comes from the Agricultural portion of the 1851 census, also known as Schedule B.

173. The marriage between Sarah Coburn McCann and Stephen McElavey is found in Ontario Marriage Records, 1860, Ontario Archives Microfilm MS 248, p. 45. *Mitchell's Directory for 1865-66* lists Stephen McElavey as a mason located in Westport.

174. Find A Grave, https://www.findagrave.com/memorial/66128330/brenard-carberry, accessed January 13, 2023. Note that the misspelling is the correct URL.

175. Find A Grave, https://www.findagrave.com/memorial/114868284/bridget-henrietta-quin, accessed January 13, 2023.

176. As recorded in the 1901 census and also on his death certificate.

Chapter Ten

177. Guillet, *Pioneer Arts and Crafts*, p. 16.

178. Donald Akenson, *The Irish in Ontario: A Study in Rural History* (Montreal & Kingston: McGill-Queen's Press, 1984), p. 45.

179. *Perth Courier*, September 20, 1889.

180. Archives of Ontario; Toronto, Ontario, Canada; Collection: Ms935; Series: 61, 1891, record # 008359.

181. "St Patricks Cemetery – Minto ND – Worldwide Cemeteries on Waymark.com," waymarking.com/walymarks/wm9TQG_St_Patricks_Cemetery_Minto_ND, viewed April 22, 2024.

182. We know that Anne Kearns was illiterate from the 1871 census. It's important to note, as well, that her headstone was disturbed by vandals along with many others in St. Edward's cemetery some time before the 1980s, when I first visited the cemetery with my father. The custodian had placed a number of broken and uprooted headstones at the back of the lot, leaning up against the rail fence. I photographed the headstone as it was and transcribed the inscription. When I returned many years later, in May 2005, the priest of the day, Father Ed Keyes, had done a lot of work to restore many of the headstones, and I found Anne's marker back in place at her grave. The bottom portion of the stone ended up below the surface, but thankfully I'd recorded the inscription before it was lost to the ages.

Chapter Eleven

183. Margaret Anne's death notice was published in the *Perth Courier* on May 15, 1885. It was, transcribed by Christine Spencer and posted at www.rootsweb.com/~onlanark/NewspaperClippings/Spencer/PerthCourierTwentyTwo.htm, viewed on November 28, 2005. Infant Arthur McCann's death notice appeared in the *Perth Courier* on August 28, 1885, transcribed by Christine Spencer and posted on the same page as the previous item.

184. John's position as inspector of English classes is listed in *The Ottawa Directory 1888-89*, p. 591. His residence is listed on p. 367 of this publication. Information about his position with the Department of Defence was found at http://www.canadiana.org/ECO/PageView/46491/0026?id=0d 0668403547e90b, viewed August 4, 2005.

185. His Nepean Street address was listed in *The Ottawa Directory 1889-*

90, p. 330. In the *Directory of 1890-91*, p. 291, his address is 870 Maria Street, and in the *1899 Directory*, p. 310, it was 589 Gilmour Street.

[186.] Province of Ontario, Vital Statistics Act, Registration of Death, August 22, 1948, Division Registrar's Record No. 1221, 05-027856.

[187.] United States Census, 1930, Manhattan (Districts 0251-0500), New York, New York, United States; citing enumeration district (ED) ED 457, sheet 13A, line 4, family 344, NARA microfilm publication T626 (Washington D.C.: National Archives and Records Administration, 2002), roll 1557; FHL microfilm 2,341,292. FamilySearch, https://www.familysearch.org/ark:/61903/1:1:X42M-6PN, accessed 13 January 2023.

[188.] *London Gazette*, June 27, 1939, p. 4347.

[189.] Robert Berkow and Mark H. & Beers, eds., *The Merck Manual of Medical Information* (Home Edition) (New York, Pocket Books, 1997), pp. 885-91.

[190.] See Anonymous, St. Edward's Roman Catholic Cemetery, Ontario Genealogical Society, Kingston Branch, 1985, i.

[191.] Thomas J. McCann's address in Ottawa obtained from *The Ottawa City Directory, 1899*, p. 310. The listing includes the note "trav" for occupation. The 1901 census enumerates T.J. and his family in District 100 (Ottawa City), subdistrict St. George Ward, E-7, p. 15, lines 45 to 50.

[192.] *The Diary of Nell McCann* (Westport: The Rideau District Museum, nd), p. 46.

[193.] *Perth Courier*, Friday, May 17, 1940, Vol. CVI, No. 42, p. 10.

[194.] findagrave.com/memorial/27961392/william_h_leahy.

[195.] United States Census, 1910, Detroit City, Wayne County, Michigan, District 108, Eighth Ward, p. 13.

[196.] The children are listed in the *Census of Children Between the Ages of Eight and Fourteen Years, Municipality of Westport, Ontario*, original record found in the township archives of the Westport Public Library in 2005. Returns covered the period 1914 to 1917. Children of T.J. McCann of George Street were listed in each of these years, while the children of William E. McCann were listed for 1915 only.

[197.] Attestation papers for William E. McCann are found in the National Archives of Canada under MCCANN, WILLIAM, Regimental Numbers 1036060 and 2469803, Reference RG 150, Box 6615-21. They were found on the internet at www.collectionscanada.ca/archivianet/02010602_.html, viewed September 25, 2006.

198. See Major George Jager, CD, "Sinews of Steel: Canadian Railway Troops on the Western Front, 1914-1918," *The Canadian Army Journal*, Vol. 10, No. 3, Fall 2007, 65-79 for an interesting examination of the CRT.

199. David W. Klock, "Klock Connections, Part 5." klockconnections.com/Descendants%20of%20Christian%20and%20Barvalis%20Klock%20Nellis.%20Part%205.pdf, viewed May 10, 2024.

200. As stated on his 1918 draft registration card.

Chapter Twelve

201. Information listed in the funeral records book of N. Gray and Company, p. 538.

202. Anecdotal information found at freepages.rootsweb.com/~adrian/genealogy/FG0009.htm, viewed April 23, 2024.

203. Bridget Donnelly is referred to as "Biddy" in the 1851 census. She was five years old at the time.

204. Anecdotal information supplied to me by the late Kathy Flynn Simons, Bridget's great-granddaughter.

205. Gabriel Drouin, comp. Drouin Collection. Montreal, Institut Généalogique Drouin. Accessed online through Ancestry.ca. Quebec, Canada, Vital and Church Records (Drouin Collection), 1621-1968 [database online].

206. Commonwealth of Virginia—Certificate of Death, Medical Examiner's Certificate, 83 042989, filed January 17, 1984.

207. *Ottawa Journal*, September 3, 1974, p. 45, Col. 3.

208. The late Kathy Flynn Simons was an enthusiastic amateur genealogist who pursued her branch of the McCann family and provided me with much information, including photos of the daughters, the family photo, and other tidbits.

209. https://findagrave.com/memorial/156294602/jack-flynn, viewed May 17, 2024.

210. This information was contained in a newspaper clipping posted online at familysearch.org/tree/person/ memories/KD9J-YVM. As hard as I tried, I couldn't track down the source. I guess this is where the amateurs are

separated from the professionals, huh?

CHAPTER THIRTEEN

211. Neil A. Patterson, *History of the Township of North Crosby and Westport* (self-published; Westport, Ontario, 2006), p. 45.

212. Roubidoux, Léon A. *The Raftsmen of the Ottawa and St. Lawrence Rivers*. (Saint-Anne-De-Bellevue, QC, Shoreline Press, 2008), p. 110.

213. thegristmillplace.com/history/, viewed May 19, 2024.

214. *Perth Courier*, September 7, 1888, transcribed by Christine M. Spencer, found online at http://www.rootsweb.com/~onlanark/ NewspaperClippings/Spencer/PerthComingsAndGoings16.htm, posted November 4, 2003, viewed August 5, 2005.

215. *The Union Company's (of Ingersoll) Farmers and Business Directory*, Vol. IV (Ingersoll: The Union Publishing Company, 1891), p. 345; R.L. Polk, J.W. Weeks and A. Duffill, *Ontario Gazetteer and Business Directory, 1888-9* (Toronto: R.L. Polk & Co., 1988-9), p. 1154.

216. Patrick's newspaper obituary refers to his connection to the CMBA. Maria's newspaper obituary states: "She was one of the oldest members of the Westport sub-division of the Catholic Women's League."

CHAPTER FOURTEEN

217. ancestry.com/family-tree/person/tree/7288286/person/222464289748/ story.

218. Ireland, Catholic Parish Registers, 1655-1915, Armagh, Ardee, 1765-1799, ancestry.com/search/collections/61039, p. 113.

219. Ibid., p. 120.

220. Ibid., p. 134.

221. Ibid., p. 147.

222. Ibid., p. 167.

223. Ibid., p. 196.

224. Ibid., p. 215.

225. A fanciful account of this event is found online at https://www.familysearch.org/photos/artifacts/ 5826932?returnLabel=Patrick%20 Hagan%20(KLLF-F57)&returnUrl=https%3A%2F%2Ffamilysearch. org%2Ftree%2F%23view%3Dancestor%26person%3DKLLF-

F57%26section%3Dmemories. While not very believable, there is a record of a Patrick Hagan's transportation at nationalarchives.ie/article/penal-transportation-records-ireland-australia-1788-1868-2, which can be accessed through the link "Transportation Database." The record is found on p. 2244 of the resultant document, reference number CRF 1841 H 19. While we can't verify this is Michael Hagan's son, it seems reasonable to mention it as a possibility.

226. registers.nli.ie/registers/vtls000632581#page/86/mode/1up, Microfilm 05595/01, viewed June 1, 2024.

227. Library and Archives Canada, 1851 Census, Canada West, Leeds County, North Crosby Township, Agricultural Census, p. 79; data2collectionscanada.gc.ca/e/e095/e002356379.jpg, viewed June 1, 2024.

228. 1861 census, Township of North Crosby, p. 7.

229. The 1901 census lists his birthday as October 24, 1863, and his death certificate states he was only about a week away from his birthday when he died that September, but I'm inclined to go with the baptismal record from the St. Edward's church registry, which I've quoted here.

230. The last will and testament of Hugh Joseph Hagan was found online at ancestry.com/family-tree/person/tree/7288286/person/6086670289/gallery?galleryPage=1&tab=0, viewed June 8, 2024.

231. Neil A. Patterson also reproduces this photograph in his book *History of the Township of North Crosby and Westport*, p. 34. He gives the photo credit to Cecilia Merkley. In the caption, Jim is erroneously identified as his father Hugh. Not to be pedantic about the whole thing, but my grandmother knew Jim well, and if she said this was a photo of Jim, it's a photo of Jim.

232. Prevailing wisdom has it that the township was given its name by John Graves Simcoe, governor of Upper Canada, as a tribute to British M.P. John Polloxfen Bastard, a friend of his. It's a story, anyway.

233. For those who may not know about this dark chapter in the history of the Catholic church (which included myself), St. Francis Xavier had worked steadily in Japan beginning in 1552 to convert Japanese people to Christianity, to the point that by 1587 there were an estimated 200,000 Christians in that country. However, in 1597 the tide turned and persecution of Christians began, to the point that an estimated 1,200 were martyred altogether, including Jesuits, Dominicans, Franciscans, and lay Christians. See Louis Delplace, "Japanese Martyrs," *The Catholic Encyclopedia*, Vol. 9 (New York: Robert Appleton Company, 1910) www.newadvent.org/

cathen/09744a.html, viewed June 6, 2024.

234. See the 1871 census of North Crosby for the locations of their residences.

235. Information about the lockmasters at Narrows Lock was found in Ken Watson's online article "A History of the Rideau Lockstations: Narrows Lockstation," https://www.rideau-info.com/canal/history/locks/h35-narrows.html, viewed June 8, 2024.

236. Information about Tom Carty's hockey career was found in "Tom Carty Traded a Low-Paying Hockey Career for the Classroom," http://www.originalhockeyhalloffame.com/news-events/carty.html -->, viewed June 6, 2024, and hockeydb.com/ihdb/stats/pdisplay.php?pid=16235. I thank them for their permission to reproduce the action photo of Tom. It's so cool!

237. Maria's accident and subsequent death was reported in her obituary in the *Perth Courier*, March 1, 1935, p. 5.

Chapter Fifteen

238. John McParland's date of birth was listed on the 1901 census.

239. Monica's obituary was published in the Perth Courier, Friday, August 29, 1919, Vol LXXXVI, No. 4, column 1, p. 4.

240. St. John Chrysostom: OrthodoxWiki, "John Chrysostom," www.orthodoxwiki.org/John_Chrysostom, viewed August 4, 2006.

241. https://www.providence.ca/our-story/obituaries/sister-mary-chrysostom-mccann/, viewed June 12, 2024.

242. Ibid.

243. providence.ca/our-story/history/motherhouse/, viewed June 12, 2024.

244. *The Catholic Encyclopedia*, www.newadvent.org/cathen/05554b.htm, viewed August 4,2006.

245. https://providence.ca/our-story/obituaries/sister-mary-ethelreda-mccann/, viewed June 13, 2024.

246. Only six kilometres west of Dalhousie Mills, Ontario, where Lynn, Tim and I lived in the 1990s.

247. Archives of Ontario; Toronto, Ontario, Canada; Registrations of Deaths, 1936; Series 555, 022014, p. 407.

Chapter Sixteen

248. Edgar McInnis, *Canada: A Political and Social History* (Toronto: Holt, Rinehart and Winston, 1969), pp. 432-33.

249. "United States records," images, FamilySearch (https://www.familysearch.org/ark:/61903/3:1:3QS7-99D3-1S4J-3?view=explore : Jun 14, 2024), image 860 of 8244; United States. National Archives Trust Fund Board.

250. *Province of Ontario Gazetteer and Directory, 1910-1911* (Ingersoll: Union Publishing Company, 1910), p. 1331.

251. https://chineselaundry.wordpress.com/2020/12/19/what-chinese-laundry-names-really-mean/, viewed June 18, 2024.

252. Ibid.

253. Patterson, p. 80.

254. Anecdotal, related to me by my father Hugh.

255. Ford and Ida appear in the *Vernon's City of Peterborough Directory* for 1950 (p. 220) but not the previous year.

Chapter Seventeen

256. See "A Brief History of Michigan," legislature.mi.gov/documents/publications/manual/2001-2002/2001-mm-0003-0026-History.pdf, accessed June 22, 2024.

257. When Henry Allore's sister Mary Jane got married in 1897, the marriage record lists her place of birth as East China and her current residence as Marine City. So it's reasonable to assume the Allore farm might have been in East China specifically.

258. "England, Yorkshire, Parish Registers, 1538-2016," database, FamilySearch, https://www.familysearch.org/ark:/61903/1:166GH-BXK2:17, February 2022.

259. Her death notice appeared in the *Port Huron Times Herald* on June 17, 1941, p. 12.

260. Michigan Department of Community Health, Division of Vital Records and Health Statistics; Lansing, MI, USA; Michigan, Marriage Records, 1867-1952; Film: 39; Film Description: 1889 Kent-1889 St. Clair, p. 271.

NOTES

261. Library and Archives Canada, Canadian Expeditionary Force, CEF Personnel Files, 1914-1918, Accession 1992-93/166; Record Group 150, Box 124; ancestry.com/discoveryui-content/view/733859:61084, viewed July 4, 2024.

262. United States Selective Service System; World War I Selective Service System Draft Registration Cards, 1917-1918. Washington, D.C.: National Archives and Records Administration, M1509, ancestry.com/discoveryui-content/view/17894986:6482, viewed July 4, 2024.

263. The National Archives at St. Louis; St. Louis, Missouri; World War II Draft Cards (Fourth Registration) For the State of New York; Records of the Selective Service System; Record Group Number 147; Box 7; ancestry.com/discoveryui-content/view/16712596:1002, viewed July 4, 2024.

264. Pennsylvania, U.S., Marriages, 1852-1968; Affidavits, 1941 (no. 109) -1942 (no 367); ancestry.com/discoveryui-content/view/3571796:61381, viewed July 4, 2024. The form also tells us when Mabel "deserted" him.

265. *Manning's Cortland, Homer and McGraw* (New York) Directory (Schenectady, NY: H.A. Manning Company, 1960), p. 94.

266. U.S. Department of Veterans Affairs, BIRLS Death File, 1850-2010; ancestry.com/discoveryui-content/view/650605:2441, viewed July 4, 2024.

267. Michigan Births, 1867-1902, p. 72; familysearch.org/ark:/61903/3:1:S3HT-6QB7-9QY?i=486, viewed July 8, 2024.

268. Michigan, U.S., Death Records 1867-1952; ancestry.com/discoveryui-content/view/367843:60872, viewed July 8, 2024.

269. According to the 1911 census of Canada, Ontario District 90, Sub-District 3, Burgess Township, p. 15.

270. Canada, Ontario Marriages, 1896-1927, Marriage licenses and affidavits, 1914, no. 12667-13333, familysearch.org/ark:/61903/3:1:939K-YM51-F?i=1063, viewed July 5, 2024.

271. Canada, Ontario Births, 1869-1912; familysearch.org/ark:/61903/3:1:939J-DZH7-Qi-901, viewed July 8, 2024.

272. Information about P.J. McParland is a little confused. According to Murphy and Walsh, he was a native of Latbirget Townland in Forkhill Parish and was known as "Pat the Shop" when he returned to Ireland in the 1920s after the death of his wife, Margaret Stanley (*A Famine Link*, pp. 86, 88). On the other hand, the church record of his marriage states that he was the "son of Patrick McParland and Mary Quinn of

the parish of Lough Hill, County Armagh, Ireland." (Ontario, Canada, Roman Catholic Baptisms, Marriages, and Burials, 1760-1923, Baptism, Marriage, Burial, Confirmation, Perth, 1880-1910, p. 178; ancestry.com/imageviewer/collections/61505/images/FS_005070851_00097, viewed July 10, 2024.) Then again, another marriage register from St. John's church in Perth records his place of birth as "Lough Hill, Co. Antrim." (Various Church Records, Perth, 1842-89, 1896-99; ancestry.com/imageviewer/collections/61505/images/FS_005077542_00588, viewed July 10, 2024.) What to think? There's no Lough Hill in Armagh; the closest would be Loughgilly Parish. There is, however, a Loughhill Townland in Antrim, but it's not a parish. Pick your poison, I guess. At the end of the day, Mr. McParland is too minor a character in our *Brief History* to deserve any more time than this. Sorry, pal.

273. Abstract Index Books, ca. 1800-1959, Film #008637497, p. 75; familysearch.org/ark:/61903/3:1:3Q9M-C3H6-NSSM-R?i=45, viewed July 10, 2024. Also, Nell McCann made the following note of the transaction in her diary: "P.J. McParland sold his Hotel by Public Auction to Henry A & his house across the way to John Egan – lot up at Orange Hall to Ab – Warrenn [sic] May 2 Moved to Stanleyville to keep store at corner on May 18th in P. Donnelly Store" (*The Diary of Nell McCann*, p. 36).

274. https://villageofwestport.ca/part-seven-the-hotels-of-westport-part-three-d34/, viewed July 10, 2024.

275. The National Archives in Washington, D.C.; Manifests of Passengers Arriving At St. Albans, Vt. District Through Canadian Pacific and Atlantic Ports, 1895-1954; NAI: 4492490l Records of the Immigration and Naturalization Service, 1787-2004; Record Group Number 85; Series M1464; Roll 483. And Manifests of Alien and Citizen Arrivals At Hogansburng, Malone, Morristown, Nyando, Ogdensburg, Rooseveltown and Waddington, New York, July 1929-April 1956; NAI: 57229586; Records of the Immigration and Naturalization Service, 1787-2004; Record Group Number 85; Series M1482, Roll 002.

276. *Watertown, New York, City Directory, 1925* (Kimball's Directory Co., 1925), p. 252 (Henry), p. 517 (Gladys).

Chapter Eighteen

277. FamilySearch has two references, one as 1841 (familysearch.org/tree/person/sources/G3WG-WLN, viewed July 12, 2024), and the other as 1842 (familysearch.org/ark:/61903/1:1:6F5J-M359, viewed July 12, 2024). Neither is confirmed with a primary source.

278. Catholic Parish Records, Killeavy Lower, 1835-1860, p. 143; ancestry.com/discoveryui-content/view/6864366:61039, viewed July 12, 2024.

279. *Kick Any Stone*, p. 252.

280. This year of immigration is found in the 1901 census of North Crosby Township, p. 4, line 33.

281. *Kick Any Stone*, p. 267.

282. Murphy and Walsh, *A Famine Link: The "Hannah" South Armagh to Ontario*, pp. 42-45.

283. As recorded on his death certificate, Archives of Ontario, Toronto, Ontario, Canada, Registrations of Deaths, 1907; Series: 130, Lambton County, Division of Moore, No. 14.

284. From his obituary in the December 27, 1962 issue of the *Perth Courier*, Vol. 128, No. 24, Col. 7, p. 16.

285. Her brief death notice appeared in the February 8, 1968 issue of the *Perth Courier*, Vol. 134, No. 28, Col. 6, p. 5.

286. Michigan, U.S. Divorce Records, 1924-1947, Wayne Certificates 55,232-59,533; Michigan Department of Health, Bureau of Records and Statistics, Wayne County, Docket #231-095.

287. *Clare Sentinel*, July 31, 1974, p. 16.

288. *Manning's Cortland, Homer and McGraw* (New York) Directory, p. 94.

289. State of Tennessee, Department of Public Health, Division of Vital Statistics, Certificate of Death 53-02710.

290. 1950 U.S. Census, Watertown, Jefferson, New York State, Mercy Hospital, sheet 28, line 23.

291. Information about Kishor C. Mehta found at caee.utexas.edlu/alumni/academy-of-distinguished-alumni/176-mehta, viewed July 19, 2024.

292. Some information regarding Mary Ann Gaffney Mehta's life story was found in her obituary reproduced at findagrave.com/memorial/20160670/mary-ann-mehta, viewed July 19, 2024.

293. findagrave.com/memorial/239239398/j_richard-gaffney, viewed July 18, 2024.

294. Information found in a Tribute handout published by the *Watertown*

Daily Times on August 4, 1959.

CHAPTER NINETEEN

295. See Monica's obituary in the *Kingston Whig-Standard*, Tuesday, August 22, 1944, p. 13.

296. See "Monica McCann Instantly Killed in Car Accident," *Kingston Whig-Standard*, Monday, August 14, 1944, p. 2.

297. See Mary's obituary in the *Drumheller Mail*, Wednesday, April 18, 2001, p. 25.

298. Much of the following information about Wilf may be found in his military dossier on file at Library and Archives Canada, Genealogy / Military / Second World War Service Files – War Dead, 1939 to 1947; RG 24 Volume 26421; Item # 23065, Service # C52935; online at https://recherche-collection-search.bac-lac.gc.ca/eng/Home/Record?app=kia&IdNumber=23065&ecopy=44485_83024005549_0323-00044, viewed July 21, 2024.

299. Ibid.

300. Ibid.

301. "Operation Blockbuster," Canadian Battlefield Tours, canadianbattlefieldtours.ca/operation-blockbuster/, viewed July 22, 2024, and "The Battle for the Hochwald Gap," *Gagetown Gazette*, March 21, 2023; gagetowngazette.com/the-battle-for-the-hochwald-gap/, viewed July 22, 2024.

302. "Algonquin Regiment, War Diary, 7-10 March 1945," *Canada In the Second World War*, National Archives of Canada, RG-24, vol. 15001; junobeach.org/canada-in-wwii/articles/liberation-of-the-netherlands-and-capitulation-of-germany/algonquin-regiment-war-diary-7-10-march-1945/, viewed July 23, 2024.

303. Ibid.

304. Ibid.

305. The following description of the Algonquin Regiment's movements during the month of April 1945 is paraphrased from "War Diary of 1 BN. The Algonquin Regiment From 1 Apr 45 To 30 Apr 45," RG 24, vol. 15001, file serial # 1052 Algonquin Regt, April 1945; recherche-collection-search.bac-lac.gc.ca/eng/home/record?app=fonandcol&IdNumber=927683, viewed July 24, 2024.

NOTES

306. "War Diary," p. 1.

307. Ibid., p. 3.

308. Ibid., p. 9.

309. Document 54 in Wilf's official army file.

310. See Wilf's Service and Casualty Form (Part II), which is document 26 in his official army file. The notation for 28 Aug 45 reads: "Disemb UK & TOS from WTO on adm to 13 CGH UK."

311. Document 14 of Wilf's official army file.

312. Ibid., document 56.

313. A photocopy of this letter, held by the family, was provided to me by Anthea McCann.

314. Document 5 of Wilf's official army file.

315. Ibid., document 57.

316. Ibid., document 60.

317. Ian Elliott, "The Night The Who Rocked Kingston," *Kingston Whig-Standard*, www.thewho.org/ elliot.htm, viewed October 2, 2006.

318. Ibid.

319. Information about Veronica was anecdotal, passed to me by my father.

320. Again, information about Mike was anecdotal and passed to me by my father.

321. See https://globalnews.ca/video/10009268/kingston-man-selflessly-helps-the-homeless-on-a-daily-basis. Well done, Tony. We're all incredibly proud of you.

CHAPTER TWENTY

None, thankfully.

CHAPTER TWENTY-ONE

322. Rev. Patrick Woulfe, *Sloinnte Gaedheal is Gall*, libraryireland.com/names/oc/o-cadhla.php, viewed August 10, 2024

323. findagrave.com/memorial/197711749/michael_mccann, viewed August 10, 2024.

324. Ibid.

325. Canada, Ontario, Roman Catholic Church Records, 1760-1923, Film

#005077539, viewed on familysearch.org March 21, 2024.

326. Neil A. Patterson, p. 66.

327. Department of Agriculture, Dairy and Cold Storage Commissioner, "A List of the Cheese Factories, Creameries, and Condensed Milk Plants in Canada," Bulletin 31, Dairy and Cold Storage Series (Ottawa, 1911), p. 37.

328. Department of Agriculture, Dairy and Cold Storage Commissioner, "A List of the Cheese Factories, Creameries, Skimming Stations also Condensed Milk Manufacturers, City Milk Vendors and Ice Cream Manufacturers, Etc., in Canada," Bulletin 54, Dairy and Cold Storage Series (Ottawa, 1918), p. 12.

329. Department of Agriculture, Dairy and Cold Storage Commissioner, "List of the Cheese Factories and Creameries in Canada and Registered Numbers," Bulletin 109 (New Series) (Ottawa, 1928), p. 17.

330. Neil A. Patterson, pp. 66-67.

331. "The McCann family, of Leeds County, Ontario, from the Genealogy Page of John Blythe Dobson," http://cybrary.uwinnipeg.ca/people/Dobson/genealogy/ff/McCann.cfm. This page originally appeared 5 July 2006 and was last revised 13 August 2006. Viewed September 19, 2006. As I say, it has since been taken down by the author, John Blythe Dobson.

332. As indicated in the 1901 census return for the town of Perth for son John A. McCann.

333. See Hourigan's obituary in the *Smiths Falls Rideau Record*, March 27, 1902, transcribed and posted at www.old.kennytree.com/Irish/Family%20names/hourigan_how.htm, viewed August 14, 2024.

334. *Perth Courier*, November 8, 1889.

335. G. Pierre Normandin, ed. *The Canadian Parliamentary Guide 1951* (Ottawa, 1951), p. 221.

336. *The Diary of William Lyon Mackenzie King 1893-1950*, October 23, 1935, p. 4. Available online at "William Lyon Mackenzie King Diaries, 1893-1950 – Library and Archives Canada," at king.collectionscanada.ca/EN/Default.asp. Seriously considered for appointment as Minister of National Revenue: diary entry for Friday, June 28, 1940, p. 4.

337. H. Reginald Hardy, *Mackenzie King of Canada* (London: Oxford University Press, 1949), p. 310.

338. Ibid., diary entry for Monday, October 7, 1946, p. 2.

Select Bibliography

Akenson, Donald. *The Irish Education Experiment: The National System of Education in the Nineteenth Century*. London: Routledge and Kegan Paul and Toronto: University of Toronto Press, 1969.

Akenson, Donald. *The Irish in Ontario: A Study in Rural History.* Montreal and Kingston: McGill-Queen's Press, 1984.

Andersen, Peter and Hubert Houle,eds. *Mariages Catholiques de La Region de Perth*, No. 84. Ottawa: Le Centre de Genealogie S.C., 1986.

Anonymous, ed. *The Diary of Nell McCann*. Westport: The Rideau District Museum, nd.

Bagwell, Richard. *Ireland Under the Tudors*, Vol. 2. London: Longmans, Green and Co., 1885.

Berresford Ellis, Peter. *A Brief History of The Druids*. London: Constable & Robinson Ltd., 2002.

Brewer, J.S. and William Bullen, eds. *Calendar of the Carew Manuscripts Preserved in the Archiepiscopal Library at Lambeth.* Nendeln/Liechtenstein: Kraus Reprint, 1974.

Butler, William. "Oliver Cromwell in Ireland," *Studies in Irish History, 1649-1775.*, Edited by R. Barry O'Brien. Dublin: Browne and Nolan., 2018.

Cahill, Thomas. *How the Irish Saved Civilization*. New York: Doubleday, 1995.

Cardinal Moran, *The Catholics of Ireland Under The Penal Laws In the Eighteenth Century*. London: Catholic Truth Society, 1899.

Chichester, Sir James. "Certain Considerations Touching the Plantation of the Escheated Lands of Ulster," January 27, 1609. *Calendar of State Papers Relating to Ireland, of the Reign of James I, 1608-1610.* Edited by C.W. Russell and John P. Prendergast. London: Longman & Co., 1874.

Clarke, John P. "Late Eighteenth Century Decorated Headstone at Urney Graveyard, Co. Louth." *The County Louth Archaeological Society*, Vol. XVI, No. 1, 1965.

Darcy, Eamon. *The Irish Rebellion of 1641 and the Wars of the Three Kingdoms.* Suffolk: Boydell & Brewer, Ltd., 2013.

deT. Glazebrook, G.P. *A History of Transportation in Canada,* Vol. I. Ryerson Press, 1938; Toronto: McClelland and Stewart, 1964.

Driscoll, Killian. *The Early Prehistory in the West of Ireland: Investigations into the Social Archaeology of the Mesolithic West of Shannon, Ireland.* Galway: National University of Ireland, M.Litt. Thesis, Oct. 2006.

Evans, Francis A. *The Emigrant's Directory and Guide to Obtain Lands and Effect a Settlement in the Canadas.* Dublin: William Curry Jr., & Co., 1833.

Gilbert, John T., ed. *A Contemporary History of Affairs in Ireland from 1641 to 1652.* Dublin: Irish Archaeological and Celtic Society, 1879.

Guillet, Edwin C. *The Great Migration: The Atlantic Crossing by Sailing-ship 1770-1860* (Second Edition). Toronto: University of Toronto Press, 1963.

Guillet, Edwin. *Pioneer Arts and Crafts.* Toronto: University of Toronto Press, 1963.

Hardy, H. Reginald. *Mackenzie King of Canada.* London: Oxford University Press, 1949.

Hennessy, William H., trans. *Annals of Ulster.* Vol. 1. Dublin: Alexander Thom & Co., 1887.

Hill, Rev. George. *An Historical Account of the Plantation in Ulster.* Belfast: McCaw, Stephenson & Orr, 1877.

Hill, Rev. George. *Plantation Papers: Containing a Summary Sketch of The Great Ulster Plantation in the Year 1610.* Belfast: Reprinted from The Northern Whig, 1889.

Hogan, Edmund. *The Description of Ireland and the state thereof as it is at this present In Anno 1598.* Dublin: M.H. Gill & Son, 1878.

Hore, Herbert F. "Marshall Bagenal's Description of Ulster, Anno 1586." *Ulster Journal of Archaeology.* Vol. 2. Belfast: Queen's University, Belfast, 1854.

Jager, CD, Major George. "Sinews of Steel: Canadian Railway Troops on the Western Front, 1914-1918." *The Canadian Army Journal,* Vol. 10, No. 3, Fall 2007, 65-79.

Janeway, Christine. *Westport: Our Early History in Pictures from Settlement to Five Years after Incorporation.* Westport: Rideau District Museum, 2016.

Jones, Robert Leslie. *History of Agriculture in Ontario 1613-1880.* Toronto: University of Toronto Press, 1946.

Kee, Robert. *The Laurel and the Ivy: The Story of Charles Stewart Parnell and Irish Nationalism.* London: Hamish Hamilton, 1993.

Kelly, Kenneth. "The Impact of Nineteenth Century Agricultural Settlement on the Land." *Perspectives on Landscape and Settlement in Nineteenth Century Ontario,* J. David Wood, ed. Toronto: McClelland

Leavitt, Thaddeus William Henry. *History of Leeds and Grenville.* Brockville: Recorder Press, 1879; Belleville: Mika Silk Screening Limited, 1972.

Lenihan, Padraig. *Consolidating Conquest, Ireland 1603–1727.* Abigdon: Routledge, 2008.

Mac Iomhair, Reverend Diarmuid. "Urnai." *Faughart Historical Properties Preservation Society.* Dundalk: reprinted 1986.

MacNamee, Gilbride. "Poem on the Battle of Dun." *Miscellany of the Celtic Society.* Edited and Translated by John O'Donovan. Dublin: The Celtic Society, 1849.

Madden, Kyla. *Forkhill Protestants and Forkhill Catholics: 1787-1858.* Montreal & Kingston: McGill-Queen's Press, 2005.

Mangan, James J., ed. *Robert Whyte's 1847 Famine Ship Diary: The Journey of an Irish Coffin Ship.* Cork: Mercier Press, 1994.

McCartan, Michael. "The Cromwellian High Courts of Justice in Ulster, 1653." *Seanchas Ardmhacha: Journal of the Armagh Diocesan Historical Society,* Vol. 23, No. 1. Cambridge University Press, 2010.

McGleenan, C.F. "The Medieval Parishes of Ballymore and Mullabrack." *Seanchas Ardmhacha: Journal of the Armagh Diocesan Historical Society,* Vol 12, No.2. Cambridge University Press, 1987.

McInnis, Edgar. *Canada: A Political and Social History.* Toronto: Holt, Rinehart and Winston of Canada, 1969.

McManus, Antonia. *The Irish Hedge School and Its Books, 1695-1831.* Dublin: Four Courts Press, 2002.

Moodie, Susannah. *Roughing it in the Bush*. Toronto: McClelland and Stewart, 1962.

Morgan, Hiram. *Tyrone's Rebellion: The Outbreak of the Nine Years War in Tudor Ireland*. Suffolk: The Boydell Press, 1999.

Murphy, Kevin, and Una Walsh. *A Famine Link: The "Hannah" South Armagh to Ontario*. Shanroe, Mullaghbane, Co. Armagh: Mullaghbane Community Association, 2006.

Murray, L. P. "The County Armagh Hearth Money Rolls, A.D. 1664." *Archivium Hibernicum*, Vol. 8. Maynooth University, 1941.

Ní Mhaonaigh, Máire. *Brian Boru: Ireland's Greatest King*. Stroud: Tempus, 2007.

O Doibhlin, Emon. "Ceart Ui Neill: A Discussion and Translation of the Document," *Seanchas Ardmhacha: Journal of the Armagh Diocesan Historical Society*. Vol. 5, No. 2. Cambridge University Press, 1970.

Ó Siochrú, Micheál. *God's Executioner: Oliver Cromwell and the Conquest of Ireland*. London: Faber and Faber, 2008.

Ó Siochrú, Micheál, and Mark S. Sweetnam. "The 1641 Depositions and Portadown Bridge." *Seanchas Ardmhacha: Journal of the Armagh Diocesan Historical Society*, Vol. 24, No. 1. Cambridge University Press, 2012.

O'Clery, Cu Choicrich. *The O'Clery Book of Genealogies*, Analecta Hibernica #18, Royal Irish Academy Ms. 23-D-17.

O'Donovan, John, ed. and trans. *Annals of the Kingdom of Ireland by the Four Masters, from the Earliest Period to the Year 1171*. Dublin: 1849.

O'Donovan, John, ed. *The Tribes of Ireland: A Satire, by Aengus O'Daly*. Dublin: John O'Daly, 1852.

O'Donovan, John, trans. *Leabhar na g-Ceart* (The Book of Rights). Dublin: The Celtic Society, 1847.

O'Dubhagain, John. *The Topographical Poems of John O'Dubhagain and Giolla Na Naomh OHuidhrin*. Translated with notes by John O'Donovan. Dublin: The Irish Archaeological and Celtic Society, 1862.

O'Hart, John. *Irish Pedigrees; or The Origin and Stem of the Irish Nation* (Second Series). Dublin: M.H. Gill & Son, 1878.

O'Neill, Eoin. *O Estado Que Nunca Foi: Guerra e a Formação do Estado na Irlanda do Século XVI* . Ph.D. thesis, Instituto Universitario de Pesquisas do Rio de Janeiro, 2005.

O'Rahilly, T.F. *Early Irish History and Mythology.* Dublin: Dublin Institute for Advanced Studies, 1946.

Paterson , T.G.F., ed. "County Armagh in 1622: a Plantation Survey." *Seanchas Ardmhacha: Journal of the Armagh Diocesan Historical Society*, Vol. 4, No. 1. Cambridge University Press, 1960/1961, 103-140.

Patterson, Neil A. *History of the Township of North Crosby and Westport.* Westport: self-published, 2006.

Proudfoot, V.B. "The Economy of the Irish Rath." *Medieval Architecture*, 5:1, 1961, 94-122.

Reeves, Rev. W. "Irish Itinerary of Dr. Edmund MacCana." *Ulster Journal of Archaeology*, Vol. 2. Belfast: Archer and Sons, 1854.

Roberts, David. *The Settlement of North Crosby 1806-1860*. Appendix I, North Crosby Reserve Settlement. Westport: Opportunities for Youth Project. Unpublished typescript, 1972. Township archives, Westport Public Library.

Roubidoux, Léon A. *The Raftsmen of the Ottawa and St. Lawrence Rivers*. Saint-Anne-De-Bellevue, QC: Shoreline Press, 2008.

Russell, C.W. and John P. Prendergast, eds. *Calendar of the State Papers Relating to Ireland of the Reign of James I, 1608-1610*. London: Longman & Company, 1874.

Smyth, W.J., Whelan, K., and Hughes, T.J. *Common ground: essays on the historical geography of Ireland presented to T. Jones Hughes*. Cork: Cork University Press, 1988.

Smyth, William Anthony. *Sir Richard Griffith's Three Valuations of Ireland 1826-1864*. Ph.D. Thesis. Maynooth: National University of Ireland, 2008.

Stopford Green, Alice. *Irish Nationality*. London: Williams and Norgate, 1911.

Walsh, Una and Kevin Murphy, eds. *Kick Any Stone: Townlands, People and Stories of Forkhill Parish: Includes 1821 Census*. Mullaghbawn: Mullaghbawn Community Association, 2003.

Notes

Notes

Notes

Notes

Notes

Notes

Notes

INDEX

A

Aitchison
  Barry 309
  Douglas 309
  Edward 309
  Ethel, wife of Harry McCann 309
  John 309
  Suzanne 309
Algonquin Regiment, the 314, 315, 318
Allore
  Alexander, father of Henry 269, 271
  Alexander Jr., brother of Henry 271, 272
  Alphonsus, son of Henry
    1st marriage 293
    2nd marriage 294
    birth 293
    moves to Cortland Cty. 294
    moves to Syracuse 294
    works in shoe stores 294
  Beatrice Anastasia, daughter of Henry 293
  Edna, daughter of Henry
    birth 296
    immigrates to Watertown 285
    works at N.Y. Tel. Co. 296
  Genieve, sister of Henry 271, 272
  Gladys, daughter of Henry
    birth 295
    death 296
    immigrates to Watertown 285
    marries Honeybell 295
  Henry, father of Ida 295
    buys the Windsor Hotel 284
    death 285
    moves to Watertown 284
    returns to N. Burgess 285
    sells the hotel 284
    Windsor Hotel burns down 284
  Ida, wife of Ford McCann

    birth 293
    Joan, daughter of Alphonsus 294
    Mary Jane, sister of Henry 271
    Mary Lou, daughter of Alphonsus 294, 295
    Michael, father of Alexander 271
    Raymond A., nephew of Henry 273
    William, brother of Henry 271
    William Leo, son of Henry 294
        boarding with Alphonsus 295
Anglo-Normans, the 47
Annals of the Four Masters, the 31
Arghialla 31

B

Bach, Johann Sebastian 353
Bantle
    Debra, daughter of Mary McCann 311
    Philip, son of Mary McCann 311
    Sharon, daughter of Mary McCann 311
    Tony, husband of Mary McCann 310
Barber
    Jerry, husband of Linda McCann 335
    Kurtis, son of Linda McCann 335
    Melanie, daughter of Linda McCann 335
Bell, Robert the shoemaker 164
Bolton, Henry the shoemaker 164
Book of Ballymote, the 31
Book of Leinster, the 31
Borland, Homer 349
Bowman, Scotty 240
Boyd, Liona 354
Bream, Julian 353, 354
British Home Child 281
Brook
    Harry Sr., father of Janet 341
    Janet Irene, wife of Hugh McCann 341
Brown
    Catherine, daughter of Mike McCann 328
    Stephen, son of Mike McCann 328
Brownlow, William 71
Brushett

Diane, daughter of Anne McCann 324
James, husband of Anne McCann 324
Burgess
    Anne Violet, wife of W.E. McCann 201
Byrne
    Mary, 1st wife of Henry Allore 287, 288
    Michael, husband of Bridget Lee 288
    Thomas, brother of Mary 288
Byrnes
    Ann, daughter of Henry 143
    Henry 143

C

Cahill, Thomas 27
Cameron, F.A., the shoemaker 162
Carcassi Method, the 353
Carr
    Anne, daughter of Ellen McCann 331
    Dan, son of Ellen McCann 331
    Joanne, daughter of Ellen McCann 331
    Joe, 1st husband of Ellen McCann 331
    John, son of Ellen McCann 331
    Michael, son of Ellen McCann 331
    Paul, son of Ellen McCann 331
    Ron, son of Ellen McCann 331
    Rose Marie, daughter of Ellen McCann 331
    Terry, son of Ellen McCann 331
Carty
    Evaristus, son of Theresa Hagan 239
    Tom, son of Evaristus 239, 241
    William James, son of James 239
Catholic Women's League 242
Caulfield, Sir Toby 57
Celts, the
    Brehon Law 28
        Law of the Couple, the 28
    druids, the 28
    naming traditions 30
    origins 24
    religion 28, 29
    social organization 27

tuath, the 27
Census substitutes
   Flax Growers List 92
   Freeholders Lists 93
   Hearth Money Rolls, the 75
Chichester, Sir Arthur 55, 56, 57, 58, 61
Clanbrassil 46, 52, 54, 55, 59, 60, 62, 64, 67, 71, 72, 73
Clancann 45, 46, 53, 54, 59, 60, 65, 67
Clark-Flynn Candy Company 213
Coburn
   Sarah 173
Collas, the
   Colla da Chrioch 31
Connor, Matthew 139
Cormac Mac Art 28, 30
Cortland Corset Company 294
Covoyoung, William 141
Cromwell, Oliver 74, 75
Cruithins, the 25, 27

D

Davidson
   Charity, daughter of Margie McCann 333
   Hyrum, son of Margie McCann 333
   Joslyn, daughter of Margie McCann 333
   Ken, 2nd husband of Margie McCann 333
   Kevin, son of Margie McCann 333
de Visée, Robert 353
De Watteville Regiment 142, 143
Donnelly
   Bridget
      marries Michael J. 198
Douglass, George the shoemaker 163, 164
Down Survey, the 75
Duranceau, Noe 343, 345, 352

E

Eleven Years' War, the
   Dublin Castle 67
   Portadown Bridge 68
Ellis, Peter Berresford 24

Emain Macha 25, 31
Engli, Ambrose 352
Erainn, the 25

F

Flanagan
   Mary, mother of Maria Hagan 230
Flight of the Earls, the 54, 56
Flynn
   Jack, son of Anastasia Magdeline 213
   John James, husband of Anastasia Magdeline 211
   William Joseph 214
Forkhill Parish
   1821 census 97

G

Gaelic language. See Irish language
Gaels, the 26
Gaffney
   James J., father of Charles R. 297
Goidels, the. See Gaels
Green, Alice Stopford 27
Grosse Isle 115

H

Hagan
   Bridget, daughter of Hugh 230
   Hugh, father of Maria 230
      his farm 229
   Hugh Joseph, son of Hugh 337
   Maria, wife of Patrick McCann 201
      afraid of storms 242
      children 241
      death 243
      influence on her children 259
      marries 241
   Patrick, son of Hugh 230
Hill, George 45
Hogan, Richard D. 281
Honeybell
   George, husband of Gladys Allore 295, 296

James Henry, son of Gladys Allore 295
Mary Lou, daughter of Gladys Allore 295
Hutchins
    Clara, wife of Jack McCann 321

I

Invasions, a series of 24
Irish language 170

J

Jackson, Richard 88, 92
Johnston
    Bill, son of Rita McCann 326
    Bonnie, daughter of Rita McCann 326
    Howard, husband of Rita McCann 325
    Joe, son of Rita McCann 326

K

Kearns
    Anne 171
    Bernard 174
    Bridget 132
    Bridget, daughter of Owen 172
    Bridget, wife of Thomas McCoy 173, 291
        children 286
    Michael 138, 170, 173, 174, 175, 287
    Owen 132, 172, 173, 174, 175, 287, 291
    Patrick 175
    Peter 172
    Thomas 163
    William 174
Kelly, James the shoemaker 163
Kennedy
    Sharon, wife of Ollie McCann 333
Kenney, Edward the shoemaker 162
Ketcheson
    Debbie, daughter of Ethel McCann 330
    Ken, son of Ethel McCann 330
    Pete, 1st husband of Ethel McCann 330
    Sandra, daughter of Ethel McCann 330
    Tony, son of Ethel McCann 330

L

Laginians, the 25, 27
Lawrence, Grace 309
Lee
   Bridget, wife of Michael Byrne 288
Lochbiller
   Caroline, 2nd wife of A. Allore Sr. 273
   Joseph, father of Caroline 273
Lurgan, the Sacking of 71

M

Mackenzie King, Prime Minister William Lyon 373
MacNab, Allan 130
Madden, Kyla 88, 91, 97
McAllister, Alexander the shoemaker 164
McArdle
   Ann, daughter of John 137
   Catherine, daughter of John 137
   Catherine, daughter of Mary 141
McCabe
   Arthur 199
   Michael 198, 199
   Sarah
      death 201
   Sarah, wife of W.E. McCann 198
McCann
   Adella Louise, daughter of Patrick 241, 242
   Anastasia, daughter of Anne Kearns 163, 190
   Anastasia Magdeline, daughter of Bridget
      birth 211
      career in nursing 214
      death 215
      marries Flynn 211
   Anne, daughter of Ford 324
   Arthur
      Ballykeel 99
      Clarkhill 99
      formative years 88
      Freeholders' List 94
   Arthur F. 163

Brian, son of Charles 307
Bruce, son of Charles 307
Bryan McCarbery oge 65
Bryan McRory 64, 70
Carbery 57, 61, 62, 63, 65
Catherine, daughter of Pat 328
Charles, son of Ford 307
Christopher, son of Jack
   birth 322
   Bramble 322
   Chris McCann-Billy Pierce Trio 324
   McGill University professor of music 323
   meets The Who 323
   Rob Frayne/Chris McCann 323
Collowe 76
Connor 76
Cosmo Augustine, son of Patrick 241
Debbie, daughter of Jack 322
Donnell 62, 63, 65, 76
Edmond McCarbery 70
Ellen, daughter of Ford 331
Ethel, daughter of Ford 330
Ford, son of Patrick
   birth 173, 201, 241, 259
   death 343
   in Detroit 259
   musical talent 259
   schooling 259
   working at Alcan 339
Frances Agnes, daughter of Patrick 241, 259
Harry, son of Ford 309
Hugh McBrian 64, 65
Hugh, son of Ford
   American boaters 117
   an auto-didact 356
   birth 337
   death 362
   disability retirement 352
   injured at Nashua 347
   love of the guitar 353
   marries Janet Brook 342

INDEX

    moved to Snelgrove Road 357
    move to Dublin St. 348
    religious beliefs 358
    takes up the guitar 345
    worked at CGE 341
    worked at Nashua Paper 343
    worked at Peterborough Civic Hospital 350
    worked for Orrís Grocery Store 350
    worked for Peterborough Cardboard 351
    worked for Twin Cleaners 350
Jack, son of Ford 321
Jennifer, daughter of Jack 322
John A., son of Michael J. 163
Karen, daughter of Pat 328
Linda, daughter of Ford 335
Margaret Jewel, daughter of Anne Kearns 213
Margie, daughter of Ford 332
Mary, daughter of Arthur 136, 141
Mary, daughter of Ford 310
Mary, daughter of Michael J. 163, 173
Mary Veronica, daughter of Patrick 241, 242
    career in teaching 259
Matthew, son of Ollie McCann 334
Michael Clarence, son of W.E. 199, 200
Michael J.
    his shop 163
    moves into Westport 162
Michael, son of Ford 327
Monica Cecelia, daughter of Patrick 241
Monica, daughter of Ford 307
Monica, daughter of Patrick
    vocalist 242
Murtagh 76
Oliver, son of Ford 333, 357
Patrick McRory 64
Patrick, son of Ford 328
Patrick, son of Michael J. 163
    birth 217
Rita, daughter of Ford 325
Rorie McPatrick 64
Rory McPatrick 72

Sarah Cecelia, daughter of W.E. 199, 200
Sarah, daughter of Ollie McCann 334
Shawn, son of Pat 328
Tina, daughter of Ollie McCann 334
Toole McRory 64, 69, 71, 72, 73
Toole oge McToole 69
Veronica, daughter of Ford 326
Wilfred, son of Ford
   admitted to U.K. hospital 319
   assault on Beckhusen, Germany 317
   assigned to Algonquin Regiment 314
   at Almelo, Netherlands 317
   birth 311
   death 321
   first battle 316
   military training 313
   readmitted to Bramshott Hospital 320
   reports for enlistment 312
   transferred to convalescence facility 319
   wounded in action 318
William E., son of Michael J. 169
   birth 198
   church sexton 198
   marries Sarah M. 198
   military service 200
   moves to Ottawa 200
   remarries, A. Burgess 201
William Thomas, son of W.E. 199, 200
McCann, Edward
  son of Jack 322
McCann, Others
  Anne Fitzpatrick, wife of Patrick McCann 371, 376
  Dr. J.J. McCann 373
  James Parnell McCann. See Dr. J.J. McCann
  John A. McCann of Perth 372
  Mary Hourigan, wife of John of Perth 372, 373, 375
  Patrick McCann of S. Burgess 371, 376
  Samuel T. McCann
    Ardmore Cheese Factory 371
    birth 370
    Blairs Cheese Factory 370

INDEX

    Mountain View Cheese Factory 370
    Ontario Cheese Factory 371
    Salem Cheese Factory 371
    Westport Cheese Factory 371
  Thomas, son of Patrick and Anne 372
McCanns, Foley Mountain
  Andrew J., son of Andrew 364
  Andrew, son of Edward 364
  Andrew, son of Peter Jr. 364
  Andrew, son of Thomas 364
  Deming, son of James E. 365
  Edith Deming, wife of James E. McCann 365
  Edward, son of Peter Jr. 364
  Edward, son of Thomas 364
  George, son of Edward 364
  Hugh, son of Edward 364
  James Edward, son of Andrew 365
  James F., son of Michael 364
  James, son of Andrew 364
  James, son of Thomas 364
  John, son of Edward 364
  John S., son of Michael 364
  McCann, Peter, Jr. 363
  McCann, Peter, Sr. 363
  Michael, son of Peter, Jr. 364
  Michael, son of Thomas 364
  Patrick, son of Edward 364
  Peter, son of Andrew 364
  Peter, son of Edward 364
  Peter, son of Michael 364
  Peter, son of Thomas 364
  Thomas, son of Andrew 364
  Thomas, son of Edward 364
  Thomas, son of Peter, Jr. 364
  Thomas, son of Thomas 364
McCardle
  Ann, daughter of Mary 138
  Ann, daughter of Mary 139
  Bridget, daughter of Mary 138
  Catherine, daughter of Mary 138
  Isabella, daughter of Mary 138, 141

    John, son of Mary 139
    Mary Ann, daughter of Mary 138, 141
    Michael 137, 140
    Michael Jr., son of Mary 139
McCarroll
    Eleanor, daughter of Mary 139
McCoy
    Annie, mother of Ida Allore
        birth 286
        McCoys in the Windsor Hotel 283
    Ellen, sister of Annie McCoy 283, 292
    John B. 283
    Matthew, son of John 287, 288, 289, 291
    Matthew, son of Thomas 292
    Michael, husband of Martha O'Hare 288
    Thomas 132, 173, 289
    Thomas, father of Annie
        children 286
        marries Bridget Kearns 291
    Thomas, son of Thomas 292
McCoy Troy, Mary, daughter of Thomas and Bridget 283
McEathron
    Daniel, the shoemaker 162
    James, the shoemaker 162
    Stephen 162
McGraw Box Company 294
McIntosh, Harley, 2nd husband of Ethel McCann 330
McParland
    Patrick J., hotel man 283
McParland, Francis 241
Milan, Luis 353
Moodie, Susannah 133
Muirdeach Tirech 31
Murphy
    Alice, wife of Matthew McCoy 288, 289, 292
    Rose, wife of Peter McCann Jr. 363
Murphy, Patrick the shoemaker 164

N

New York Telephone Company 285, 296
Nine Years' War 54

INDEX

North Burgess Township 142

O

O'Brian, James 137
O'Brien, John, the shoemaker 163
O'Connor
    Phil, 2nd husband of Ellen McCann 332
O'Daly, Aengus 63
O'Hanlons, the (Ui Anluain) 62, 64
O'Hare
    Catherine, wife of Thomas Byrne 288
    Francis, father of the 3 sisters 286, 287
    Martha, wife of Michael McCoy 288
    Mary, mother of Mary Byrne 288
O'Neill
    Conn 49
    Matthew 49, 54
    Shane 49, 51
O'Neill
    Turlough Brasseil 52
O'Rahilly, T.F. 25
Operation Blockbuster 315, 316
Orange Order 162
Orpheus Music Store, the 345, 346

P

Pale, the 47, 49
Parkening, Christopher 353
Parkerís Cleaners 342
Peterborough Cardboard 330, 351, 352
Picts, the. See Pretani
Presti, Ida, and Alexander Lagoya 353
Pretani, the 25

Q

Quinn
    Ann 15, 99, 135, 163
    Ann, wife of Owen Kearns 172, 173, 292
    Bernard 132
    Owen 132
    Peter 132

Quinn Kearns, Ann 132

R

Rawlinson
    Charles, husband of Margaret Jewel 213
Rideau District Museum 365
Rights of O'Neill, the (Ceart Ui Neill) 28
Robinson, Peter 115
Roncalli, Lodovico 355
Ryan, James 173, 176, 259

S

Sanz, Gaspar 353
Segovia, AndrÈs 345, 353
Shoemaker's trade, the 161
Simons
    Kathleen Flynn 213
Singleton, Dr. A.B. 170
Sisters of Providence of St. Vincent de Paul 242, 321, 330
Smith, Jennie, mother of Janet Brook 341
Smith, John the shoemaker 161, 162
Smiths Falls 335
Smythe, Elizabeth, mother of the 3 sisters 286
Sor, Fernando 353
Speagle
    Adella, daughter of Catherine 143
    Anna R., daughter of Catherine 143
    Casper 142
    Casper J. 143
    Elizabeth, daughter of Casper 143
    Elizabeth, daughter of Catherine 143
    Isabel, daughter of Catherine 143
    James 142, 143, 198
    James Jr, son of Catherine 143
    John, son of Catherine 143
    Laura, daughter of Catherine 143
    Mary Ann, daughter of Catherine 143
    Michael J. 143
Spiegle
    Johann 143
Stanley, Michael 283

Stanleyville 143, 213, 281, 283, 295
Stanleyville 294
Stanleyville, Lanark County 132, 293
Stephens
   Holly Ann, daughter of Margie McCann 332
   Len, 1st husband of Margie McCann 332
Stephenson
   Edward, father of Mary Jane 271
   Mary Jane, mother of Henry Allore 269, 271, 273
St. Laurent, Prime Minister Louis 375
Strohm, Elaine, wife of Mike McCann 328

T

Tatay, Vincente 346
Thornton, Esther 357
Toole
   Michael 139, 173
Townsend, Geoffrey 345, 346, 347
Troy
   Daniel 283, 292
   Josephine, daughter of Mary 281, 283
   Mary, sister of Annie McCoy 283
Troy, Daniel, son of Frank 292
Troy, Frank 292
Troy, Frank, son of Daniel and Mary 292
Troy, Josephine 292
Troy, Mary, daughter of Daniel and Mary 292

U

Ulaidh, the 25, 26, 31
Upthegrove
   Gold Ardela, 1st wife of Alph. Allore 293

W

Ward, James 289, 291
Wardrobe Hotel 283
Whelan, Walter 281
Whyte, David 352
Wilson, Anthea, wife of Pat McCann 328
Windsor House Hotel 281, 284, 293, 295, 296

www.ingramcontent.com/pod-product-compliance
Lightning Source LLC
Chambersburg PA
CBHW022007300426
44117CB00005B/64